MW01346972

The Tutorverse

MAKING THE UNIVERSE BRIGHTER, ONE STUDENT AT A TIME

HSPT Reading Comprehension, Verbal, and Language: 1,700+ Practice Questions

HSPT Reading Comprehension, Verbal, and Language: 1,700 Practice Questions

March 2024

Published in the United States of America by:

The Tutorverse, LLC

222 Broadway, 19th Floor

New York, NY 10038

Web: www.thetutorverse.com

Email: hello@thetutorverse.com

For information about buying this title in bulk or to place a special order, please contact us at hello@thetutorverse.com.

ISBN-13: 978-1-7321677-8-0

ISBN-10: 1-7321677-8-8

Available in Print & eBook Formats
visit thetutorverse.com/books

The Tutorverse
THE
SAT
1,500+
PRACTICE QUESTIONS
MORE QUESTIONS
THAN 10 FULL-LENGTH EXAMS

The Tutorverse
2025 EDITION
HIGH SCHOOL PLACEMENT TEST
HSPT
MATHEMATICS
& QUANTITATIVE REASONING
1,300+ PRACTICE QUESTIONS

The Tutorverse
NEW YORK CITY
SHSAT
UPDATED 2024 SHSAT
FEATURING NEW
POETRY AND MATH QUESTIONS!
1,200+
PRACTICE QUESTIONS
MORE QUESTIONS FOR THE
NYC SPECIALIZED HIGH SCHOOLS ADMISSIONS TEST
THAN 10 FULL-LENGTH EXAMS

The Tutorverse
2025 EDITION
LOWER LEVEL
ISEE
1000+
PRACTICE QUESTIONS
MORE LOWER LEVEL ISEE QUESTIONS
THAN 8 FULL-LENGTH EXAMS

The Tutorverse
2025 EDITION
MIDDLE LEVEL
ISEE
1000+
PRACTICE QUESTIONS
MORE MIDDLE LEVEL ISEE QUESTIONS
THAN 6 FULL-LENGTH EXAMS

The Tutorverse
2025 EDITION
UPPER LEVEL
ISEE
1500+
PRACTICE QUESTIONS
MORE UPPER LEVEL ISEE QUESTIONS
THAN 10 FULL-LENGTH EXAMS

The Tutorverse
2025 EDITION
ELEMENTARY LEVEL
SSAT
1000+
4
PRACTICE QUESTIONS
ORGANIZED BY TOPIC AND QUESTION TYPE
TEST-ALIGNED FORMATTING AND PRESENTATION
MORE PRACTICE QUESTIONS
THAN 10 REAL TESTS

The Tutorverse
2025 EDITION
MIDDLE LEVEL
SSAT
1000+
2
PRACTICE QUESTIONS
ORGANIZED BY TOPIC AND QUESTION TYPE
TEST-ALIGNED FORMATTING AND PRESENTATION
MORE PRACTICE QUESTIONS
THAN 6 REAL TESTS

The Tutorverse
2025 EDITION
UPPER LEVEL
SSAT
1500+
3
PRACTICE QUESTIONS
ORGANIZED BY TOPIC AND QUESTION TYPE
TEST-ALIGNED FORMATTING AND PRESENTATION
MORE PRACTICE QUESTIONS
THAN 10 REAL TESTS

View or Download Answer Explanations
at thetutorverse.com/books

Table of Contents

HSPT Reading Comprehension, Verbal, and Language: 1,700+ Practice Questions

Welcome

Dear Students, Parents, and Educators,

We believe that the key to scoring well on the High School Placement Test (HSPT) is practice—lots of practice. While test-taking tips and tricks can be helpful, we believe a solid foundation of core learning and subject-matter proficiency is the bedrock on which high-performance relies.

That's why this workbook contains over 1,700 practice math questions. We've painstakingly identified core concepts and crafted questions of varying difficulty to help prepare students for the exam. Our questions help to build confidence, test mastery, and introduce new concepts, skills, and knowledge to students.

The HSPT is a speed test. Testing students on nearly 300 questions in about 2 hours and 30 minutes, the HSPT asks students to complete about two problems per minute—a heavy lift for many 8th graders, for many of whom this is their first experience with this kind of test. Because students can only take the HSPT once, it's of vital importance that they go into the testing site as prepared for what they're going to see as possible. That preparation comes in many forms: developing content knowledge, test understanding, and the self-confidence that comes from thorough study.

The test may be intimidating, but with practice students can confidently master its tricks. Taking the time to go through the material, some of which is beyond what students cover in average grade-level courses, is essential. This is what our workbook offers.

Test preparation is a long, arduous journey, with plenty of challenges ahead for parents and students alike. Though the process might be at times discouraging, we are here to support you every step of the way.

This workbook helps students to identify skills and concepts requiring further development. It also provides ample practice for many of the subject areas on the HSPT. Whether you use this workbook for independent study or with a professional tutor or teacher, we believe that the practice you will receive will benefit you both on the HSPT and far beyond.

Best wishes, good luck, and welcome to The Tutorverse!

Regards,

The Team at The Tutorverse

How to Use This Book

Overview

The purpose of this workbook is to provide students, parents, and educators with practice math materials for the HSPT. Though this workbook includes information regarding the test's structure and content, our primary goal is to provide students with copious practice materials that reinforce their learning and introduce them to new words, concepts, and skills as necessary.

Organization

This workbook is organized into five main sections. Each section is designed to accomplish different objectives. These sections and objectives are as follows:

- Diagnostic Test
  This section is designed to help students identify topics requiring the most practice. Though not the full length of a real HSPT test (as the diagnostic only features English language arts questions), students can use this diagnostic to familiarize themselves with the speed at which the test moves and to build their stamina and endurance for the full-length practice tests at the end of the book. This first test should be used as a gauge to estimate the amount of additional practice needed on each topic, and not as an estimate of how the student will perform on the actual test.

- Verbal Skills
  Verbal Skills is the first of three practice sections in this workbook. This section provides practice for the verbal classification, synonym, antonym, analogy, and logic questions that appear in this first part of the test.

- Reading Comprehension
  This section is the second of three practice sections in this workbook, and includes many passages and questions that assess skills tested on the HSPT. The Reading Comprehension section is further divided into three types of passages: expository, narrative, and persuasive. Vocabulary questions round out the section, as they round out the Reading Comprehension section on the actual exam as well.

- Language Skills
  The final practice section of this workbook, Language Skills provides practice in punctuation and capitalization, correct English usage, spelling, and composition.

- Practice Test 1 and 2
  These practice tests help to familiarize students with the format, organization, and time allotments on the HSPT. The length of these tests mirrors that of the real test. These tests should be taken once students have completed the diagnostic tests and spent sufficient time answering the appropriate questions in the practice sections.

At the beginning of each of the above listed sections are detailed instructions. Students should carefully review these instructions, as they contain important information about the actual exam and how best to practice.

Strategy

Every student has different strengths and abilities. We don't think there is any one strategy that will help every student ace the exam. Instead, we believe there are core principles to keep in mind when preparing for the HSPT. These principles are interrelated and cyclical in nature.

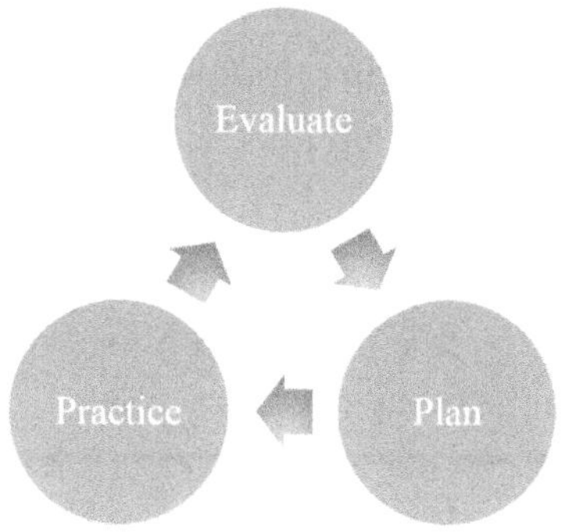
Evaluate
Plan
Practice

- Evaluate
  A critical step in developing a solid study plan is to have a clear idea of how to spend your time. What subjects are more difficult for you? Which types of questions do you frequently answer incorrectly? Why? These and many other questions should be answered before developing any study plan. The diagnostic test is just one way to help you evaluate your abilities.

- Plan
  Once you've taken stock of your strengths and abilities, focus on actions. How much time do you have before the test? How many areas do you need to work on during that time, and which areas do you need to work on? How many questions (and of which type) do you need to do each day, or each week? The answers to these and other questions will help you determine your study and practice plan.

- Practice
  Once you settle on a plan, try to stick with it as much as you can. To study successfully requires discipline, commitment, and focus. Try turning off your phone, TV, tablet, or other distractions. Not only will you learn more effectively when you're focused, but you may find that you finish your work more quickly, as well.

- Reevaluate
  Because learning and studying is an ongoing process, it is important to take stock of your improvements along the way. This will help you see how you are progressing and allow you to make adjustments to your plan. The practice test at the end of this workbook is designed to help you gauge your progress.

Help

Preparing for a standardized test such as the HSPT can be difficult and trying. In addition to challenging material, preparing for a standardized test can often feel like an extra responsibility on top of students' already busy lives. For these reasons, it's important to recognize when students need extra help.

Because not all schools cover the same material at the same level, some students may find material in this workbook to be difficult or entirely new. This is normal and to-be-expected, as certain material included in this workbook may not yet have been taught to some students.

We encourage you to reach out to trusted educators to help you prepare for the HSPT. Strong tutors, teachers, mentors, and consultants can help you with many aspects of your preparation—from evaluating your needs, to creating an effective plan, to helping you make the most of your practice, reaching out for help when you need it is always a smart move.

Diagnostic Practice Test

Overview

The first step in an effective study plan is to know your strengths and areas for improvement.

This diagnostic test assesses your mastery of certain skills and concepts that you may see on the actual exam. The main difference between the diagnostic and practice tests and the actual test is that the diagnostic tests are scored differently from how the actual exam is scored. On the actual exam, your score will be determined by how well you did compared to other students in your grade. On the diagnostic and practice tests, however, we will score every question in order to gauge your mastery over skills and concepts. In addition to this, the diagnostic test only concerns material **covered in this book**, meaning only material in the verbal skills, reading comprehension, and language skills sections.

This diagnostic test should *not* be used as a gauge of how you will score on the test.

Format

The format of the diagnostic test is similar to that of the actual test. The number of questions included in each section mirror those of the actual test, *even though the actual test includes questions that will not be scored*. This is done by design, in order to help familiarize you with the actual length of each section of the test.

The diagnostic includes the following sections:

Diagnostic Test Section	Questions	Time Limit
Verbal Skills	60	16 minutes
Reading Comprehension	62	25 minutes
Language Skills	60	25 minutes
Total	**182**	**1 hr. 6 min.**

Generally, 2 brief breaks are given between sections of the test; however, the timing and duration of the breaks are determined by the individual school that is administering the exam. For the purpose of this diagnostic test, you can choose to take only one break to reflect the abbreviated time or to take a shorter break between each section.

Answering

Use the answer sheet provided on the next several pages to record your answers. You may wish to tear this page out of the workbook.

Diagnostic Practice Test 1

Diagnostic Test Answer Sheet

[Carefully tear or cut out this page.]

Section 1: Verbal Skills

1 ⒶⒷⒸⒹ	14 ⒶⒷⒸⒹ	27 ⒶⒷⒸ	40 ⒶⒷⒸⒹ	53 ⒶⒷⒸⒹ
2 ⒶⒷⒸⒹ	15 ⒶⒷⒸⒹ	28 ⒶⒷⒸⒹ	41 ⒶⒷⒸⒹ	54 ⒶⒷⒸⒹ
3 ⒶⒷⒸⒹ	16 ⒶⒷⒸⒹ	29 ⒶⒷⒸⒹ	42 ⒶⒷⒸ	55 ⒶⒷⒸ
4 ⒶⒷⒸⒹ	17 ⒶⒷⒸⒹ	30 ⒶⒷⒸⒹ	43 ⒶⒷⒸⒹ	56 ⒶⒷⒸⒹ
5 ⒶⒷⒸⒹ	18 ⒶⒷⒸⒹ	31 ⒶⒷⒸ	44 ⒶⒷⒸⒹ	57 ⒶⒷⒸ
6 ⒶⒷⒸ	19 ⒶⒷⒸⒹ	32 ⒶⒷⒸⒹ	45 ⒶⒷⒸⒹ	58 ⒶⒷⒸⒹ
7 ⒶⒷⒸⒹ	20 ⒶⒷⒸⒹ	33 ⒶⒷⒸⒹ	46 ⒶⒷⒸⒹ	59 ⒶⒷⒸⒹ
8 ⒶⒷⒸⒹ	21 ⒶⒷⒸ	34 ⒶⒷⒸⒹ	47 ⒶⒷⒸⒹ	60 ⒶⒷⒸⒹ
9 ⒶⒷⒸⒹ	22 ⒶⒷⒸⒹ	35 ⒶⒷⒸⒹ	48 ⒶⒷⒸⒹ	
10 ⒶⒷⒸⒹ	23 ⒶⒷⒸⒹ	36 ⒶⒷⒸⒹ	49 ⒶⒷⒸⒹ	
11 ⒶⒷⒸⒹ	24 ⒶⒷⒸⒹ	37 ⒶⒷⒸⒹ	50 ⒶⒷⒸⒹ	
12 ⒶⒷⒸⒹ	25 ⒶⒷⒸⒹ	38 ⒶⒷⒸⒹ	51 ⒶⒷⒸⒹ	
13 ⒶⒷⒸ	26 ⒶⒷⒸⒹ	39 ⒶⒷⒸ	52 ⒶⒷⒸ	

Section 2: Reading

61 ⒶⒷⒸⒹ	74 ⒶⒷⒸⒹ	87 ⒶⒷⒸⒹ	100 ⒶⒷⒸⒹ	113 ⒶⒷⒸⒹ
62 ⒶⒷⒸⒹ	75 ⒶⒷⒸⒹ	88 ⒶⒷⒸⒹ	101 ⒶⒷⒸⒹ	114 ⒶⒷⒸⒹ
63 ⒶⒷⒸⒹ	76 ⒶⒷⒸⒹ	89 ⒶⒷⒸⒹ	102 ⒶⒷⒸⒹ	115 ⒶⒷⒸⒹ
64 ⒶⒷⒸⒹ	77 ⒶⒷⒸⒹ	90 ⒶⒷⒸⒹ	103 ⒶⒷⒸⒹ	116 ⒶⒷⒸⒹ
65 ⒶⒷⒸⒹ	78 ⒶⒷⒸⒹ	91 ⒶⒷⒸⒹ	104 ⒶⒷⒸⒹ	117 ⒶⒷⒸⒹ
66 ⒶⒷⒸⒹ	79 ⒶⒷⒸⒹ	92 ⒶⒷⒸⒹ	105 ⒶⒷⒸⒹ	118 ⒶⒷⒸⒹ
67 ⒶⒷⒸⒹ	80 ⒶⒷⒸⒹ	93 ⒶⒷⒸⒹ	106 ⒶⒷⒸⒹ	119 ⒶⒷⒸⒹ
68 ⒶⒷⒸⒹ	81 ⒶⒷⒸⒹ	94 ⒶⒷⒸⒹ	107 ⒶⒷⒸⒹ	120 ⒶⒷⒸⒹ
69 ⒶⒷⒸⒹ	82 ⒶⒷⒸⒹ	95 ⒶⒷⒸⒹ	108 ⒶⒷⒸⒹ	121 ⒶⒷⒸⒹ
70 ⒶⒷⒸⒹ	83 ⒶⒷⒸⒹ	96 ⒶⒷⒸⒹ	109 ⒶⒷⒸⒹ	122 ⒶⒷⒸⒹ
71 ⒶⒷⒸⒹ	84 ⒶⒷⒸⒹ	97 ⒶⒷⒸⒹ	110 ⒶⒷⒸⒹ	
72 ⒶⒷⒸⒹ	85 ⒶⒷⒸⒹ	98 ⒶⒷⒸⒹ	111 ⒶⒷⒸⒹ	
73 ⒶⒷⒸⒹ	86 ⒶⒷⒸⒹ	99 ⒶⒷⒸⒹ	112 ⒶⒷⒸⒹ	

Section 3: Language Skills

123 ⒶⒷⒸⒹ	127 ⒶⒷⒸⒹ	131 ⒶⒷⒸⒹ	135 ⒶⒷⒸⒹ	139 ⒶⒷⒸⒹ
124 ⒶⒷⒸⒹ	128 ⒶⒷⒸⒹ	132 ⒶⒷⒸⒹ	136 ⒶⒷⒸⒹ	140 ⒶⒷⒸⒹ
125 ⒶⒷⒸⒹ	129 ⒶⒷⒸⒹ	133 ⒶⒷⒸⒹ	137 ⒶⒷⒸⒹ	141 ⒶⒷⒸⒹ
126 ⒶⒷⒸⒹ	130 ⒶⒷⒸⒹ	134 ⒶⒷⒸⒹ	138 ⒶⒷⒸⒹ	142 ⒶⒷⒸⒹ

(Section 3: Language Skills continued on reverse)

143 ⒶⒷⒸⒹ	151 ⒶⒷⒸⒹ	159 ⒶⒷⒸⒹ	167 ⒶⒷⒸⒹ	175 ⒶⒷⒸⒹ
144 ⒶⒷⒸⒹ	152 ⒶⒷⒸⒹ	160 ⒶⒷⒸⒹ	168 ⒶⒷⒸⒹ	176 ⒶⒷⒸⒹ
145 ⒶⒷⒸⒹ	153 ⒶⒷⒸⒹ	161 ⒶⒷⒸⒹ	169 ⒶⒷⒸⒹ	177 ⒶⒷⒸⒹ
146 ⒶⒷⒸⒹ	154 ⒶⒷⒸⒹ	162 ⒶⒷⒸⒹ	170 ⒶⒷⒸⒹ	178 ⒶⒷⒸⒹ
147 ⒶⒷⒸⒹ	155 ⒶⒷⒸⒹ	163 ⒶⒷⒸⒹ	171 ⒶⒷⒸⒹ	179 ⒶⒷⒸⒹ
148 ⒶⒷⒸⒹ	156 ⒶⒷⒸⒹ	164 ⒶⒷⒸⒹ	172 ⒶⒷⒸⒹ	180 ⒶⒷⒸⒹ
149 ⒶⒷⒸⒹ	157 ⒶⒷⒸⒹ	165 ⒶⒷⒸⒹ	173 ⒶⒷⒸⒹ	181 ⒶⒷⒸⒹ
150 ⒶⒷⒸⒹ	158 ⒶⒷⒸⒹ	166 ⒶⒷⒸⒹ	174 ⒶⒷⒸⒹ	182 ⒶⒷⒸⒹ

Verbal Skills

Questions 1-60, 16 Minutes

1. Devour most nearly means
   (A) construct
   (B) consume
   (C) cook
   (D) create

2. Please means the opposite of
   (A) change
   (B) distort
   (C) find
   (D) upset

3. Which word does *not* belong with the others?
   (A) aggressive
   (B) agreeable
   (C) amicable
   (D) friendly

4. Lawyer is to profession as couch is to
   (A) chair
   (B) comfort
   (C) furniture
   (D) judge

5. Uproar most nearly means
   (A) savagery
   (B) turmoil
   (C) violence
   (D) wildness

6. All chinchillas are soft. Some chinchillas are pets. All pets are soft. If the first two statements are true, then the third is
   (A) True
   (B) False
   (C) Uncertain

7. Which word does *not* belong with the others?
   (A) cow
   (B) horse
   (C) monkey
   (D) pig

8. Teacher is to principal as employee is to
   (A) assistant
   (B) boss
   (C) peer
   (D) secretary

9. Endure most nearly means
   (A) endanger
   (B) escape
   (C) save
   (D) survive

10. Delicate most nearly means
    (A) dainty
    (B) fancy
    (C) radiant
    (D) valuable

11. Actor is to play as writer is to
    (A) book
    (B) model
    (C) pretend
    (D) professional

12. Ashamed means the opposite of
    (A) awesome
    (B) beloved
    (C) brave
    (D) proud

13. All rabbits have fur. Some people have rabbits as pets. All pets have fur. If the first two statements are true, then the third is
    (A) True
    (B) False
    (C) Uncertain

14. Which word does *not* belong with the others?
   (A) blouse
   (B) clothing
   (C) overalls
   (D) suit

15. Chase is to catch as work is to
   (A) company
   (B) earn
   (C) fail
   (D) relax

16. Which word does *not* belong with the others?
   (A) sand
   (B) snow
   (C) sun
   (D) waves

17. Hurricane is to storm as apple is to
   (A) fruit
   (B) orange
   (C) rain
   (D) tree

18. Expedite means the opposite of
   (A) delay
   (B) fulfill
   (C) generalize
   (D) spite

19. Which word does *not* belong with the others?
   (A) actor
   (B) chemist
   (C) musician
   (D) painter

20. Student is to school as prisoner is to
   (A) freedom
   (B) jail
   (C) police
   (D) punishment

21. Harry is left-handed. Some people believe left-handed people are more creative. Harry is a creative person. If the first two statements are true, then the third is
   (A) True
   (B) False
   (C) Uncertain

22. Which word does *not* belong with the others?
   (A) cat
   (B) dog
   (C) hamster
   (D) pet

23. Annihilate is to destroy as antagonize is to
   (A) bother
   (B) rebuild
   (C) strategize
   (D) suffer

24. Defend most nearly means
   (A) assist
   (B) compete
   (C) guard
   (D) help

25. Which word does *not* belong with the others?
   (A) hurricane
   (B) rain
   (C) thunder
   (D) wind

26. Quell most nearly means
   (A) ask
   (B) burn
   (C) ignite
   (D) smother

27. Alicia has more pencils than Eric. Eric has more pencils than Jack and Rashid. Alicia has more pencils than Rashid. If the first two statements are true, then the third is
   (A) True
   (B) False
   (C) Uncertain

28. Which word does *not* belong with the others?
    (A) café
    (B) diner
    (C) restaurant
    (D) store

29. Arrogant means the opposite of
    (A) aggressive
    (B) forward
    (C) malevolent
    (D) unpretentious

30. Ponder is to reflect as nurture is to
    (A) consider
    (B) children
    (C) ignore
    (D) nourish

31. Some clothing is made with cotton. Clothing made with cotton is very soft. Some clothing is very soft. If the first two statements are true, then the third is
    (A) True
    (B) False
    (C) Uncertain

32. Cotton is to wool as oak is to
    (A) fabric
    (B) pine
    (C) tree
    (D) wood

33. Which word does *not* belong with the others?
    (A) season
    (B) spring
    (C) summer
    (D) winter

34. Prevent means the opposite of
    (A) enable
    (B) halt
    (C) prevail
    (D) stop

35. Compose most nearly means
    (A) compare
    (B) craft
    (C) perform
    (D) stand

36. Serene most nearly means
    (A) complete
    (B) natural
    (C) placid
    (D) secret

37. Wealthy means the opposite of
    (A) confident
    (B) derelict
    (C) fancy
    (D) opulent

38. Which word does *not* belong with the others?
    (A) playground
    (B) seesaw
    (C) slide
    (D) swings

39. Mirabel is Jonah's friend. Bruno is Jonah's friend. Mirabel is Bruno's friend. If the first two statements are true, then the third is
    (A) True
    (B) False
    (C) Uncertain

40. Optimistic means the opposite of
    (A) cheery
    (B) cynical
    (C) hopeful
    (D) mystic

41. Which word does *not* belong with the others?
    (A) clarinet
    (B) instrument
    (C) saxophone
    (D) trumpet

42. All quadrilaterals have four sides. A square is a quadrilateral. All squares have four sides. If the first two statements are true, then the third is
    (A) True
    (B) False
    (C) Uncertain

43. Confident means the opposite of
    (A) assured
    (B) composed
    (C) insecure
    (D) personable

44. Compassion most nearly means
    (A) assistance
    (B) comparison
    (C) cruelty
    (D) kindness

45. Which word does *not* belong with the others?
    (A) explanation
    (B) purpose
    (C) question
    (D) reason

46. Illusion most nearly means
    (A) drawing
    (B) fantasy
    (C) reality
    (D) sickness

47. Which word does *not* belong with the others?
    (A) blinds
    (B) curtains
    (C) shades
    (D) window

48. Constrict most nearly means
    (A) expand
    (B) grow
    (C) lecture
    (D) shrink

49. Careful is to cautious as reckless is to
    (A) careless
    (B) dangerous
    (C) irresponsible
    (D) thoughtful

50. Which word does *not* belong with the others?
    (A) comedy
    (B) drama
    (C) film
    (D) horror

51. Linger most nearly means
    (A) dawdle
    (B) forget
    (C) hurry
    (D) leave

52. Frank plays soccer. Some soccer players are very fast. Frank is very fast. If the first two statements are true, then the third is
    (A) True
    (B) False
    (C) Uncertain

53. Destroy most nearly means
    (A) guard
    (B) defend
    (C) annihilate
    (D) damage

54. Which word does *not* belong with the others?
    (A) agenda
    (B) event
    (C) plan
    (D) schedule

55. All cheetahs are fast. All cheetahs are mammals. All mammals are fast. If the first two statements are true, then the third is
    (A) True
    (B) False
    (C) Uncertain

56. Which word does *not* belong with the others?
    (A) succinct
    (B) brief
    (C) concise
    (D) lengthy

57. Some people have freckles. Some people have red hair. People who have freckles also always have red hair. If the first two statements are true, then the third is
    (A) True
    (B) False
    (C) Uncertain

58. Derision means the opposite of
    (A) contempt
    (B) disdain
    (C) praise
    (D) vision

59. Challenging most nearly means
    (A) hard
    (B) simple
    (C) special
    (D) unique

60. Congregation most nearly means
    (A) complication
    (B) corporation
    (C) dispute
    (D) gathering

Reading

Questions 61-122, 25 Minutes

The "humanities" refers to the study of human society and culture. Subjects like literature, history, art, philosophy, and law all fall under the humanities umbrella. For centuries, the study of the humanities has been considered an essential part of a well-rounded education. However, in the last few decades, there has been a general shift away from the study of the humanities in schools. There are two reasons for this drop: first, a general concern about America's ability to compete in a global economy, and second, a lack of adequate funding for public and private schools.

Near the end of the 1990s, a report released by the US National Academies of Science, Engineering, and Medicine (NASEM) showed that American students were not achieving in science, technology, engineering, or math (STEM) at the same rate as students in other nations. This lack of achievement suggested that, in the future, not enough people in the U.S. would have the education and training required to work important STEM-related jobs. People with STEM training are helpful in solving global problems, and are good for the economy. After the release of this report, legislators passed laws to address the poor performance of U.S. students in STEM fields, quickly making STEM education the focus for most schools across the nation, which decreased the attention students and schools were able to pay to the humanities.

In addition to the new focus on STEM education, shrinking budgets have forced many schools to make difficult decisions; to find money to pay for updated computers, science lab renovations, or robotics equipment, many schools reduced the size of their art, music, and drama programs. Many humanities programs were eliminated altogether. Students who may previously have been interested in creative writing, foreign language, or the performing arts are now choosing to enroll in programs like math, science, and engineering instead.

Concern about the economy and a lack of school funding have taken the spotlight off the humanities in schools. However, in the last few years, some people have begun to call for a return of the humanities to education, with many advocates suggesting that, without the humanities, students will struggle to learn the creativity and reasoning skills required even for jobs in STEM. Only time will tell whether the decrease in the study of the humanities was warranted or if it resulted in a negative change for our education system.

61. This passage is mostly about
    (A) the importance of STEM education.
    (B) the decline in the study of the humanities.
    (C) the challenges schools face in paying for educational programs.
    (D) US economic problems.

62. According to the passage, which of the following are examples of subjects in the humanities?
    (A) Computer science and robotics
    (B) Drama and medicine
    (C) Music and history
    (D) Engineering and law

63. Based on the passage, which of the following can be inferred about a "well-rounded education?"
    (A) It is too expensive for most schools to fund.
    (B) It is no longer recommended for 21st century students.
    (C) It is a fairly new concept.
    (D) It is an equal balance of both STEM and humanities studies.

64. As it is used in the passage, the word "adequate" most nearly means
    (A) enough.
    (B) excessive.
    (C) superfluous.
    (D) tremendous.

65. According to the passage, all of the following is true about the NASEM report EXCEPT that it
    (A) suggested too few students might go on to work in STEM fields.
    (B) led to an increase in STEM education.
    (C) recommended greater funding for the arts.
    (D) revealed weaknesses in American students' knowledge compared to other countries.

66. Which of the following can be inferred from the passage?
    (A) Students will be more successful studying math or science than language arts.
    (B) The shifted focus from humanities to STEM is not guaranteed to be beneficial for society.
    (C) Humanities programs cost more to run than STEM programs.
    (D) Professions in the humanities are not necessary for a thriving economy.

67. The rationale for an increase in STEM education was based on
    (A) a high US unemployment rate.
    (B) concern about the future of the US economy.
    (C) a lack of girls studying STEM.
    (D) pressure that parents were putting on lawmakers.

68. What can be inferred from the idea that "legislators from both political parties passed laws" supporting increased funding for STEM education?
    (A) It was a popular idea among many different types of people.
    (B) There was heated debate before the laws were passed.
    (C) Only politicians were in favor of increased STEM education.
    (D) The laws finally made STEM programs legal throughout the US.

69. As it is used in the passage, the word "warranted" most nearly means
    (A) acceptable.
    (B) corrected.
    (C) foolish.
    (D) justified.

70. What would be the most appropriate title for this passage?
    (A) Where Have the Humanities Gone?
    (B) STEM: A Bright Idea
    (C) The Broken US Education System
    (D) The Well-Rounded Student

Bugs, bugs, bugs. Bugs make up over 80% of all species on Earth! There are over one million already-identified species of insects populating the planet, and some scientists estimate that there are as many as 10 million species yet to be identified. Of the millions of types of insects, one family stands out from the others—the praying mantis. This insect not only has a unique look and name, but also some remarkable features that set it apart from the hordes of other insects.

The praying mantis received its name because of its large and folded front legs extending away from its body, making it look like it's praying. However, it's hardly a <u>pacifist</u>; in reality, the mantis is a fierce predator. It makes quick work not only of other crawly bugs like beetles and caterpillars, but also pollinators like bees, butterflies, and hummingbirds. Occasionally, the mantis can even be found munching on small reptiles like frogs and lizards.

In order to catch prey often larger than itself, the mantis has developed some unusual characteristics beneficial for hunting. The mantis is extremely <u>agile</u> and can leap up to twice its body length in the blink of an eye, pouncing on an unsuspecting snack. In addition to its quick movements, the mantis has outstanding vision and is the only invertebrate who can see in 3-D like us. This, along with having the rare ability to turn its head, makes the mantis an especially successful hunter.

While the mantis seems like a ruthless killer, it also has its own share of predators. Birds, bats, and larger lizards all love to dine on the mantis, when they can catch one. The mantis has some clever defenses. For instance, when it hears a bat coming, it can rapidly leap out of the bat's flight path and land on the ground. The bat, who is blind and relies on echolocation to find food, can't find the mantis. It is left confused while the mantis escapes to safety.

The praying mantis, with its rare qualities and unusual appearance, has fascinated people for centuries. Whether you admire it for its beauty and unusual traits or find it harmful to much-needed pollinators, there's no doubt the praying mantis is an impressive creature.

71. This passage is mostly about
    (A) the predatory nature of the mantis.
    (B) how the mantis acquired its name.
    (C) a unique family of insects.
    (D) predators of the mantis.

72. According to the passage, which of the following is true?
    (A) A praying mantis can go many days without eating a meal.
    (B) The praying mantis's name is due to its appearance.
    (C) The mantis praying mantis makes up 80% of the insects on Earth.
    (D) The praying mantis can escape from predators by interfering with their senses of smell.

73. It can be inferred from the passage that pollinators
    (A) have a beneficial effect on the world.
    (B) are top predators of the mantis.
    (C) work with the mantis to catch prey.
    (D) are an extinct species.

74. As it is used in the passage, the word "<u>pacifist</u>" most nearly means
    (A) aggressive.
    (B) hostile.
    (C) obedient.
    (D) peaceful.

75. According to the passage, the mantis is unusual for its
    (A) range in size.
    (B) 3-D vision.
    (C) sensitive hearing.
    (D) solitary nature.

76. Which of the following can be inferred from the passage?
    (A) Most insects cannot turn their heads.
    (B) Mantises eat their prey alive.
    (C) Mantises play a vital role in crop production.
    (D) A hummingbird is a type of insect.

77. Which of the following are both predator and prey of the mantis?
    (A) Frogs and bats
    (B) Birds and frogs
    (C) Bats and frogs
    (D) Lizards and birds

78. Based on the passage, which of the following can be inferred about the mantis?
    (A) They only eat invertebrates.
    (B) Not much is known about this rare insect.
    (C) They are challenging prey for their predators to hunt.
    (D) They are elusive and rarely seen in the wild.

79. As it is used in the passage, the word "agile" most nearly means
    (A) deliberate.
    (B) quick.
    (C) resourceful.
    (D) secretive.

80. What would be the most appropriate title for the passage?
    (A) Praying Mantis: Zen Master
    (B) Praying Mantis: A Gardener's Best Friend
    (C) A Most Unusual Insect
    (D) Predatory Habits of Insects

Close your eyes and imagine an animal with the brown, furry body of a beaver and the webbed feet and bill of a duck. Though the image sounds like something out of a fantasy, it actually describes a unique and very real animal: the platypus. George Shaw, the first person to scientifically describe the animal, named it *platypus anatinus*, which means "flat-footed duck." Little did he know, however, that the name he chose was already in use, describing a type of beetle. After a few more changes, the animal became scientifically known as *ornithorhynchus anatinus*. Still, the common name "platypus" had already stuck, and the animal is still called that to this day.

The first thing people usually notice about the platypus is its unusual appearance. It is an animal known for its odd combination of features. It is so unique looking that early observers thought it was a <u>hoax</u>, rather than a real creature—some researchers even thought the platypus's bill was sewn on with thread! Early scientists had difficulty classifying the platypus because it had characteristics of mammals, birds, and reptiles all at once. They settled on classifying the platypus as a monotreme, a special kind of mammal that lays eggs. Just like other mammals, though, after they're born, baby platypuses depend on their mother.

Nicknamed "duckbill," the platypus is an aquatic mammal that only lives in creeks and rivers in Australia. Platypuses are energetic little critters that who spend most of their day in the water searching for food. As carnivores, they <u>scrounge</u> through the bottoms of rivers for small insects and other critters. They also eat frogs or fish from the surface of the water. Platypuses are solitary animals, usually living alone rather than in groups. Platypuses live and lay their eggs in burrows they dig into the edge of streams. Their sleek bodies, webbed feet, and large tails make them excellent swimmers. Though a very unusual creature, the platypus is an example of an animal perfectly adapted to its environment.

81. This passage is mostly about
    (A) unique characteristics of a specific mammal.
    (B) how to protect the endangered platypus.
    (C) how platypuses have evolved over the years.
    (D) the complicated origins of the platypus's name.

82. What would be the most appropriate title for this passage?
    (A) Australian Mammals
    (B) Mammals, Birds, and Reptiles
    (C) One Bizarre Mammal
    (D) The Discovery of the Platypus

83. According to the passage, which of the following is true?
    (A) Platypuses build dams like beavers.
    (B) Platypuses are classified as reptiles because they lay eggs.
    (C) Platypuses are found in Australia and South America.
    (D) The platypus's scientific name has changed over time.

84. According to the facts of the passage, platypuses
    (A) live in dense woody forests.
    (B) are unusually aggressive animals.
    (C) are lazy and sleep most of the day.
    (D) spend most of their days looking for food.

85. The author would most likely agree with which of the following statements?
   (A) Platypuses are hazardous to their environment.
   (B) Platypuses have many lessons to teach humanity.
   (C) Platypuses are interesting creatures worthy of study.
   (D) Platypuses exist only in folklore.

86. Which of the following can be inferred from the passage?
   (A) Platypuses are not found in the wild outside of Australia.
   (B) Platypuses are likely to soon go extinct.
   (C) Platypuses are the fastest swimmers in Australia.
   (D) Platypuses are probably related to ducks.

87. As it is used in the passage, the word "hoax" most nearly means
   (A) game.
   (B) prank.
   (C) study.
   (D) truth.

88. As it is used in the passage, the word "scrounge" most nearly means
   (A) forage.
   (B) glide.
   (C) sleep.
   (D) swim.

89. According to the facts of this passage, platypuses
   (A) are neither mammals nor reptiles.
   (B) are a special type of mammal called a monotreme.
   (C) leave their young to survive on their own.
   (D) have no major differences from other mammals.

90. You would probably find this passage in
   (A) a diary.
   (B) a newspaper.
   (C) a college newsletter.
   (D) a brochure from a zoo.

Audrey was in a foul mood. She was short with her mom at breakfast. She sat alone on the bus ride to school. And when her best friend, Lila, bounced up to her locker with a smile and a bright "Hey!" Audrey merely responded with a scowl.

"Oh right, I forgot, you're going on that Biology trip today," said Lila sympathetically. "Cheer up! Maybe it won't be as bad as you think!"

"Are you kidding? You know what they do to those animals! Do I need to remind you—" The bell rang for homeroom.

"I'll catch up with you after school," Lila said, turning to walk down the hall. "I can't be late to class or I'll get another demerit. You can tell me all about the trip after you get back!"

Audrey sat alone again on the bus ride to Hub City Zoo. She felt like one of those poor animals, trapped and alone, a captive taken out of her comfort zone. She didn't have any friends in Biology. When she protested about the trip in class two weeks ago, everyone stared at her like she had sprouted ten eyes. Mr. Green even seemed annoyed; he said that zoos were much kinder than she realized. But she couldn't help herself! She was an animal lover and had done her research; zoos were prisons! People brought their uncaring kids to the zoo to mock animals stolen from their natural habitats and to watch majestic creatures put on <u>degrading</u> performances forced onto them by the heartless and cruel zookeepers.

Once they arrived at the zoo, determined not to enjoy any part of the field trip, Audrey lagged behind the group and <u>sulked</u> her way through the guided tour. She tried her best to not look at the animals in their enclosures, surely alone and unloved. She knew if she looked, her heart would break. After about an hour, Mr. Green appeared beside her. "Audrey, I think you'll enjoy the next part of the zoo."

Audrey rolled her eyes. "I doubt it."

"Just you wait," he said, smiling from ear to ear.

When Audrey returned to school that afternoon, she was a changed person. She thanked Mr. Green when she got off the bus and raced to find Lila, who was waiting by her locker when Audrey ran up.

"Lila! You'll never guess," Audrey said between pauses to catch her breath, "Zoos are wonderful!"

"What?" said Lila. This could not be the Audrey who had talked to her earlier in the day.

At first, I thought it was awful! But then we met an ape named Kiko who the zoo rescued from poachers! He found his soulmate (named Juana) at the zoo, and they had four of the cutest babies together! They let us hold the youngest, Hana. The zookeeper said he's never seen Hana bond with anyone so quick as she bonded with me—I even got to bottle feed her! Then right before we left, Kiko and Juana started holding hands and sitting under a tree to take a nap together. It was beautiful! And that's not even the end!"

Audrey could barely catch her breath as she excitedly told Lila about her day at the zoo. One thing was certain—she'd be back to visit soon.

91. This story is mostly about
   (A) a young activist's hatred of zoos.
   (B) the importance of having sympathetic friends.
   (C) the challenges of science classes.
   (D) one girl's change of heart.

92. As it is used in the passage, the word "<u>degrading</u>" most nearly means
   (A) cute.
   (B) decaying.
   (C) humiliating.
   (D) perishing.

93. The author would most likely agree with which of the following statements?
   (A) Teachers don't care about their students.
   (B) There's always room to change your mind.
   (C) Nothing good ever comes from questioning the status quo.
   (D) Zoos are cruel and inhumane.

94. It can be inferred from the story that Lila
   (A) has received demerits before.
   (B) is going on the same field trip another day.
   (C) does not care about animals.
   (D) has not known Audrey for very long.

95. Audrey dislikes zoos for all of the following reasons EXCEPT that
   (A) she had a bad childhood experience at one.
   (B) they exploit their animals.
   (C) the visitors are uncaring.
   (D) the animals are taken from their habitats.

96. Based on the information in the passage, it can be inferred that
   (A) nobody else at the school cares about animals.
   (B) Mr. Green disagreed with Audrey's initial opinions on zoos.
   (C) Audrey only recently began caring about animals.
   (D) Audrey is Mr. Green's favorite student.

97. According to the passage, when she came back to school, Audrey
   (A) was different than she was when she left for the field trip.
   (B) told Lila about the cruel treatment of the apes at the zoo.
   (C) asked Mr. Green to never take her on a field trip to the zoo again.
   (D) decided to become a biologist.

98. As it is used in the passage, the word "<u>sulked</u>" most nearly means
   (A) complained.
   (B) pouted.
   (C) protested.
   (D) stumbled.

99. Based on the passage, Audrey can be described as
   (A) closed-minded and disrespectful.
   (B) anti-social and selfish.
   (C) passionate and caring.
   (D) intelligent and indifferent.

100. What would be the most appropriate title for the story?
   (A) The Surprising Field Trip
   (B) Bio Class Disaster
   (C) Zoos and Audrey: Perfect Together
   (D) Mr. Green's Least Favorite Student

Vocabulary

101. To <u>resist</u> change
    (A) benefit
    (B) deliberate
    (C) send
    (D) withstand

102. A <u>pathetic</u> excuse
    (A) amazing
    (B) mended
    (C) pitiful
    (D) special

103. An <u>aggressive</u> warrior
    (A) lazy
    (B) nubile
    (C) precious
    (D) violent

104. A <u>surplus</u> of supplies
    (A) addition
    (B) appetite
    (C) excess
    (D) volition

105. A <u>horde</u> of people
    (A) crowd
    (B) dabble
    (C) minimum
    (D) verification

106. To <u>comprehend</u> an idea
    (A) impel
    (B) jest
    (C) specialize
    (D) understand

107. To <u>vanquish</u> an enemy
    (A) appreciate
    (B) defeat
    (C) love
    (D) validate

108. An <u>invincible</u> hero
    (A) helpless
    (B) pathetic
    (C) timid
    (D) unflinching

109. A <u>ravenous</u> diner
    (A) creative
    (B) lonely
    (C) hungry
    (D) violent

110. The <u>disruptive</u> neighbors
    (A) active
    (B) disorganized
    (C) rowdy
    (D) silly

111. A <u>monotonous</u> lecture
    (A) boring
    (B) fabulous
    (C) promotional
    (D) unintelligent

112. To <u>demonstrate</u> a task
    (A) decorate
    (B) destroy
    (C) miss
    (D) show

113. An <u>abrupt</u> ending
    (A) introductory
    (B) slow
    (C) sudden
    (D) vibrant

114. A <u>disastrous</u> failure
    (A) brave
    (B) catastrophic
    (C) impressive
    (D) successful

115. A <u>scholarly</u> professor
(A) bold
(B) confident
(C) intellectual
(D) serious

116. An <u>insightful</u> observation
(A) aspirational
(B) creational
(C) effervescent
(D) perceptive

117. My comfortable <u>abode</u>
(A) creation
(B) home
(C) insight
(D) load

118. She <u>cherished</u> her friends
(A) appreciated
(B) caused
(C) forgot
(D) haunted

119. To <u>mitigate</u> one's fear
(A) absolve
(B) believe
(C) lessen
(D) operate

120. A <u>talented</u> musician
(A) beneficial
(B) delectable
(C) forgettable
(D) skilled

121. A <u>capable</u> leader
(A) audible
(B) effective
(C) homey
(D) jesting

122. The legislator's <u>debatable</u> suggestion
(A) able
(B) disputed
(C) elegant
(D) lovable

Language Skills

Questions 123-182, 25 Minutes

For questions 123-162, choose the sentence that contains an error in punctuation, capitalization, or usage. If there is no error, select choice (D).

123. (A) The game was real difficult.
 (B) Their children were too polite.
 (C) Her dog was adorable.
 (D) No mistake.

124. (A) Her eye's were green.
 (B) His dream's coming true.
 (C) Dolphins are mammals; sharks are not mammals.
 (D) No mistake.

125. (A) The capital of Mexico is Mexico city.
 (B) Her first car was a Ford Mustang.
 (C) The first of April is a silly holiday.
 (D) No mistake.

126. (A) The news anchor had a charming demeanor.
 (B) Trina had a persian cat as a pet.
 (C) The Ancient Greeks worshiped many gods.
 (D) No mistake.

127. (A) Canada and Mexico are part of north America.
 (B) Madagascar is an island country in Africa.
 (C) The giraffes were an incredible sight on the safari.
 (D) No mistake.

128. (A) She needs to get to class quickly.
 (B) Her phone is broken and useless.
 (C) He plays the saxophone very poor.
 (D) No mistake.

129. (A) Too inflexible for gymnastics.
 (B) Their car was too slow.
 (C) She cheated on the test.
 (D) No mistake.

130. (A) They were tired; they were going to bed.
 (B) Only Maria, Luisa, and Cara were left.
 (C) "Is he here?" asked the teacher.
 (D) No mistake.

131. (A) When she moved to the left, she felt her shoe slip.
 (B) He looks at her and exclaimed, "What a wonderful idea!"
 (C) Being a part of the wedding was the best present she could have been given.
 (D) No mistake.

132. (A) Jasmine submitted her project for review.
 (B) They accidentally parked their car in the wrong spot.
 (C) I am hoping my report card isn't in the mailbox.
 (D) No mistake.

133. (A) Ireland had never seen a drought.
 (B) The fields were never used for recess.
 (C) They won't hardly make it to the show.
 (D) No mistake.

134. (A) She didn't need an umbrella for the storm.
 (B) He couldn't imagine a world without her.
 (C) She wasn't ready to take the test.
 (D) No mistake.

135. (A) Nobodys car had enough gas.
(B) She ate a burger; he ate a salad.
(C) "Are you home?" asked Aliah.
(D) No mistake.

136. (A) The storm's power overwhelmed them.
(B) "Oh wow!" exclaimed Missy.
(C) They verified the information was correct.
(D) No mistake.

137. (A) The dentist told her she needs to floss after brushing.
(B) Whenever her son gets sick, she provided his coach with a doctor's note.
(C) Yesterday, Kate accidentally left her phone in her locker.
(D) No mistake.

138. (A) Thomas couldn't believe he had failed his math test.
(B) The students decided to major in English studies.
(C) In fifth grade, Nadia decided her favorite subject was Science.
(D) No mistake.

139. (A) Jeremy's answer's were all correct.
(B) The first, second, and third dates all work.
(C) He's planning a surprise party.
(D) No mistake.

140. (A) She would never refuse a favor.
(B) They had received hardly none of their pay.
(C) Both of her ankles finally gave out.
(D) No mistake.

141. (A) His campaign was more impressive than hers.
(B) She was more smarter than her mother.
(C) His car was the shiniest in the lot.
(D) No mistake.

142. (A) Too challenging a feat to complete.
(B) Her headache was distracting.
(C) The siren wouldn't stop blaring.
(D) No mistake.

143. (A) Her eyes were bluer than her sister's.
(B) She was the cutest pig in the pen.
(C) The plane was higher than the helicopter.
(D) No mistake.

144. (A) Jenna was the best player on the lacrosse team.
(B) The Clippers are a basketball team in Los Angeles.
(C) The students struggled to learn how to conjugate verbs in french.
(D) No mistake.

145. (A) After work, she planned to drive to her sister's house.
(B) There's no way they can escape.
(C) It's no surprise he failed the test.
(D) No mistake.

146. (A) Katy was the singer who got all the solos.
(B) Mr. Henderson was the teacher which gave lots of exams.
(C) Nicky immediately regretted her mistake.
(D) No mistake.

147. (A) Aliyah celebrated her acceptance into the University of Michigan.
(B) The admissions building was located in the center of campus.
(C) Luis can't believe he's going to be in College in a month.
(D) No mistake.

148. (A) The cat wasnt sure if its whiskers were clean.
(B) The theater's policy was strict.
(C) The dogs' paws were all filthy.
(D) No mistake.

149. (A) Luisa carried home every book and every assignment.
(B) Marie was worried about her son succeeding and found him a tutor.
(C) Bruno walked to the corner, got on the bus, and riding home.
(D) No mistake.

150. (A) He'll never make a decision.
(B) The artist, a painter, was featured in the exhibition.
(C) I wonder, thought Jess, if he'll change his mind.
(D) No mistake.

151. (A) They thought the test was more harder than the last one.
(B) She is more capable than her sister.
(C) Her nails were prettier than his.
(D) No mistake.

152. (A) It wasn't theirs.
(B) "Hooray" shouted Chris.
(C) They lost the dog's collar.
(D) No mistake.

153. (A) One of her cats loves to gaze out the window.
(B) Fifty dollars are not enough money to buy a drum set.
(C) The thunder scared her in the middle of the night.
(D) No mistake.

154. (A) Her hats were always flying away.
(B) Moved all the way to Denver.
(C) Mirabel loved dancing.
(D) No mistake.

155. (A) Her Mom and Dad couldn't believe she failed.
(B) Amy's grandfather left her the house.
(C) Jessica's favorite flowers were peonies.
(D) No mistake.

156. (A) The cats in the house watches the bird.
(B) Every window in the house was open.
(C) The students are working together to create a presentation.
(D) No mistake.

157. (A) Do you know what will be covered on tomorrow's test!
(B) Will it ever be finished?
(C) "I'm so sad," cried Elijah.
(D) No mistake.

158. (A) Leah is always forgetting her laptop at home.
(B) The entire class helped clean up the cafeteria after school.
(C) The teacher, counselor, or principal are proctoring the standardized test.
(D) No mistake.

159. (A) A popular destination in Oregon is Crater Lake.
(B) The only genre of music that Gregory would listen to was Jazz.
(C) The first day of spring brings many people joy.
(D) No mistake.

160. (A) Alyssa sent Ben letters every week, yet they only responded once.
(B) He had promised to give the baseball team his bat.
(C) She wouldn't let go of her mistakes.
(D) No mistake.

161. (A) Marina forgot to wash her dirty dishes.
(B) Mark always cooked his family dinner.
(C) Andre brought a pie because he knew his friends would think they were delicious.
(D) No mistake.

162. (A) The shape of Florida is unique.
(B) Her favorite city was London, England.
(C) She planned to move to Australia.
(D) No mistake.

Spelling

For questions 163-172, choose the sentence that contains an error in spelling. If there is no error, select choice (D).

163. (A) Our neighborhood has many parks.
(B) Please call me tomorrow to give me your answer.
(C) Let's schedule our meeting for Sunday.
(D) No mistake.

164. (A) Thomas is taller then his uncle.
(B) Can penguins fly?
(C) Lay the baby in the crib carefully.
(D) No mistake.

165. (A) James was on his way to school.
(B) Paul was ready to merry his fiancé.
(C) Marcy's favorite movie was still in theaters.
(D) No mistake.

166. (A) The cat chased the mouse around the house.
(B) The only bennefit of working in the office was the free coffee.
(C) It was difficult to change his sister's mind.
(D) No mistake.

167. (A) He was known for being very independent.
(B) Growing up, we had a pool at our house.
(C) He told me to swim acrost the pool and back
(D) No mistake.

168. (A) He hoped to acheive his goals.
(B) Betty had tricked me.
(C) She felt so relieved.
(D) No mistake.

169. (A) Her mother was always too busy.
(B) The cat was mean and agressive.
(C) She ran a successful business.
(D) No mistake.

170. (A) It was a beautiful day for a picnic.
(B) Although she was hungry, she couldn't eat.
(C) Both of his cousins were boared.
(D) No mistake.

171. (A) She was apparently too scared to watch the movie.
(B) He was too bussy to exercise every day.
(C) They didn't believe he was lying.
(D) No mistake.

172. (A) They went to the cemetary to leave flowers.
(B) Her worst memory happened on that corner.
(C) Her sister was really starting to irritate her.
(D) No mistake.

Composition

173. Which of the following best fits under the topic "How to Train Your Dog"?

(A) Dogs come in many shapes and sizes.
(B) Patience is important when teaching a dog a new command.
(C) Some dogs enjoy playing fetch while some do not.
(D) A dog park is a great place to play with your dog.

174. Choose the group of words that best completes the sentence.

The choir sounded their best when they ________________.

(A) were daily rehearsing
(B) rehearsed daily
(C) daily rehearsed
(D) rehearsing daily

175. Choose the word that best completes the sentence.

Christine knew the cereal was on the shelf ________ the snacks in her grandma's pantry.

(A) about
(B) allow
(C) above
(D) around

176. Which choice most clearly expresses the intended meaning?

(A) Swimming all afternoon, the towel dried me off.
(B) After swimming all afternoon, I dried off with a towel.
(C) The towel dried me off after swimming all afternoon.
(D) none of these

177. Choose the word or phrase that best completes the sentence.

The dog was dirty from playing outside; ________ his owner gave him a bath.

(A) because,
(B) therefore,
(C) in other words,
(D) none of these

178. Choose the group of words that best completes the sentence.

Before laying down a new rug, ________________________.

(A) vacuuming the floor was what Linda did.
(B) vacuum the floor was first for Linda.
(C) Linda first vacuumed the floor.
(D) the ground was vacuumed, Linda ensured.

179. Which choice most clearly expresses the intended meaning?

(A) The flowers were arranged by the florist beautifully.
(B) The flowers arranged by the florist were beautiful.
(C) The florist's flowers, when arranged, were beautiful.
(D) The florist arranged the flowers beautifully.

180. Which sentence does *not* belong in the paragraph?

(1) The students were looking forward to winter break. (2) Many students talked to each other about their plans for the holidays. (3) Four students forgot to turn in their homework. (4) The countdown to break had begun!

(A) Sentence 1
(B) Sentence 2
(C) Sentence 3
(D) Sentence 4

181. Choose the word that best completes the sentence.

Garrett ____________ removed the hot baking pan from the oven.

(A) jokingly
(B) casually
(C) carefully
(D) nonchalantly

182. Which topic is best for a one-paragraph passage?

(A) Climate Change
(B) How to Build a House
(C) Astrology
(D) How to Make a Grilled Cheese

Scoring the Diagnostic Practice Test

Using your answer sheet and referring to the answer key at the back of the book, calculate the percentage of questions you answered correctly in each section by taking the number of questions you answered correctly in that section and dividing it by the number of questions in that section. Multiply this number by 100 to determine your percentage score. The higher the percentage, the stronger your performance in that section. The lower the percentage, the more time you should spend practicing that section.

Note that the actual test will not evaluate your score based on percentage correct or incorrect. Instead, it will evaluate your performance relative to all other students in your grade who took the test.

Record your results here:

Section	**Questions Correct**	**Total Questions**	**Percent Questions Correct**
Verbal Skills	____	60	____%
Reading Comprehension	____	62	____%
Language	____	60	____%

Carefully consider the results from your diagnostic test when coming up with your study plan. Remember that, depending on the curriculum at your school, there may be material on this test that you have not yet been taught. If this is the case, and you would like to improve your score beyond what is expected of your grade, consider outside help from an adult—such as a tutor or teacher—who can help you learn more about the topics that are new to you.

Answer Key

The keys are organized by section, and each question has an answer associated with it. Remember: there are detailed answer explanations available online at www.thetutorverse.com/books. Be sure to obtain permission before going online.

Verbal Skills

On the Actual Test

In the Verbal Skills section of the HSPT, you will encounter five types of questions:

- Verbal Classifications
- Synonyms
- Antonyms
- Verbal Analogies
- Logic

All of these questions are designed to test your vocabulary and reasoning skills.

On the actual HSPT exam, there will be 60 questions in the Verbal Skills section, which you will have 16 minutes to complete.

In This Practice Book

The practice questions in this section of the workbook *are not* structured like an actual HSPT exam. Instead, these sections contain many exams' worth of materials to help you practice. This will allow you to drill for each type of question you will find on the Verbal Skills section.

There may be additional instructions and recommendations at the beginning of each section, which you should review before starting.

Remember: there are detailed answer explanations available online at www.thetutorverse.com/books. Be sure to obtain permission before going online.

Verbal Classifications

Overview

The verbal classification questions present four words and ask that you pick the word that does not fit with the others. This tests your word knowledge and your ability to think logically. Consider relationships between words to find the one that does not fit. Think creatively and look at the four words from different perspectives.

Here are some examples of types of relationships you might encounter:

- Whole and parts of that whole
- Leader to group
- Types of animals or plants
- Category and examples from that category
- Profession to tool
- And many others!

We recommend that you practice at least 15-20 questions per week in preparing for the exam.

Tutorverse Tips!

You may find some of the words in this section to be challenging. Don't be surprised if you need to look them up in a dictionary!

Verbal Classifications Exercises

1. Which word does *not* belong with the others?
   (A) bird
   (B) crow
   (C) owl
   (D) robin

2. Which word does *not* belong with the others?
   (A) diamond
   (B) jewel
   (C) ruby
   (D) sapphire

3. Which word does *not* belong with the others?
   (A) expression
   (B) frown
   (C) grimace
   (D) smile

4. Which word does *not* belong with the others?
   (A) aunt
   (B) brother
   (C) family
   (D) grandfather

5. Which word does *not* belong with the others?
   (A) dolphin
   (B) seagull
   (C) shark
   (D) whale

6. Which word does *not* belong with the others?
   (A) crafts
   (B) knitting
   (C) pottery
   (D) sewing

7. Which word does *not* belong with the others?
   (A) burglar
   (B) criminal
   (C) robber
   (D) thief

8. Which word does *not* belong with the others?
   (A) lake
   (B) ocean
   (C) river
   (D) valley

9. Which word does *not* belong with the others?
   (A) meteor
   (B) planet
   (C) star
   (D) universe

10. Which word does *not* belong with the others?
    (A) concert
    (B) performance
    (C) show
    (D) theater

11. Which word does *not* belong with the others?
    (A) education
    (B) instructor
    (C) mentor
    (D) teacher

12. Which word does *not* belong with the others?
    (A) cheese
    (B) granola
    (C) milk
    (D) yogurt

13. Which word does *not* belong with the others?
    (A) journey
    (B) train
    (C) trek
    (D) trip

14. Which word does *not* belong with the others?
    (A) grow
    (B) improve
    (C) progress
    (D) stall

15. Which word does *not* belong with the others?
    (A) buy
    (B) earn
    (C) purchase
    (D) spend

16. Which word does *not* belong with the others?
    (A) alter
    (B) build
    (C) change
    (D) revise

17. Which word does *not* belong with the others?
    (A) drive
    (B) highway
    (C) route
    (D) street

18. Which word does *not* belong with the others?
    (A) bloom
    (B) daisy
    (C) rose
    (D) tulip

19. Which word does *not* belong with the others?
    (A) accident
    (B) injury
    (C) scar
    (D) wound

20. Which word does *not* belong with the others?
    (A) bike
    (B) car
    (C) scooter
    (D) skates

21. Which word does *not* belong with the others?
    (A) custom
    (B) feast
    (C) ritual
    (D) tradition

22. Which word does *not* belong with the others?
    (A) beak
    (B) bird
    (C) claw
    (D) wing

23. Which word does *not* belong with the others?
    (A) create
    (B) eliminate
    (C) generate
    (D) produce

24. Which word does *not* belong with the others?
    (A) artsy
    (B) creative
    (C) painter
    (D) talented

25. Which word does *not* belong with the others?
    (A) band
    (B) bass
    (C) drums
    (D) guitar

26. Which word does *not* belong with the others?
    (A) envelope
    (B) letter
    (C) mail
    (D) stamp

27. Which word does *not* belong with the others?
    (A) cherry
    (B) fudge
    (C) nuts
    (D) sundae

28. Which word does *not* belong with the others?
    (A) book
    (B) cover
    (C) page
    (D) spine

29. Which word does *not* belong with the others?
    (A) award
    (B) bronze
    (C) gold
    (D) silver

30. Which word does *not* belong with the others?
    (A) animal
    (B) fish
    (C) mammal
    (D) reptile

31. Which word does *not* belong with the others?
 (A) actor
 (B) director
 (C) film
 (D) writer

32. Which word does *not* belong with the others?
 (A) child
 (B) family
 (C) kid
 (D) offspring

33. Which word does *not* belong with the others?
 (A) flowers
 (B) food
 (C) guests
 (D) wedding

34. Which word does *not* belong with the others?
 (A) angry
 (B) scream
 (C) shout
 (D) yell

35. Which word does *not* belong with the others?
 (A) bold
 (B) brave
 (C) considerate
 (D) courageous

36. Which word does *not* belong with the others?
 (A) adhesive
 (B) clingy
 (C) magnetic
 (D) materials

37. Which word does *not* belong with the others?
 (A) mate
 (B) parent
 (C) partner
 (D) spouse

38. Which word does *not* belong with the others?
 (A) grapes
 (B) olives
 (C) peaches
 (D) raspberries

39. Which word does *not* belong with the others?
 (A) dancing
 (B) exercise
 (C) jogging
 (D) skating

40. Which word does *not* belong with the others?
 (A) break
 (B) damage
 (C) fracture
 (D) repair

41. Which word does *not* belong with the others?
 (A) labor
 (B) leisure
 (C) relaxation
 (D) rest

42. Which word does *not* belong with the others?
 (A) ambition
 (B) aspiration
 (C) career
 (D) determination

43. Which word does *not* belong with the others?
 (A) comfort
 (B) depression
 (C) melancholy
 (D) sorrow

44. Which word does *not* belong with the others?
 (A) memory
 (B) recall
 (C) recollect
 (D) remember

45. Which word does *not* belong with the others?
 (A) creepy
 (B) eerie
 (C) terrifying
 (D) weird

46. Which word does *not* belong with the others?
 (A) forgiving
 (B) lenient
 (C) merciful
 (D) strict

47. Which word does *not* belong with the others?
 (A) earn
 (B) gain
 (C) goods
 (D) obtain

48. Which word does *not* belong with the others?
 (A) building
 (B) church
 (C) library
 (D) museum

49. Which word does *not* belong with the others?
 (A) charismatic
 (B) cruel
 (C) hilarious
 (D) personality

50. Which word does *not* belong with the others?
 (A) floral
 (B) fruity
 (C) scent
 (D) smoky

51. Which word does *not* belong with the others?
 (A) ant
 (B) beetle
 (C) insect
 (D) wasp

52. Which word does *not* belong with the others?
    (A) chamomile
    (B) earl grey
    (C) matcha
    (D) tea

53. Which word does *not* belong with the others?
    (A) almond
    (B) milk
    (C) oat
    (D) soy

54. Which word does *not* belong with the others?
    (A) ethereal
    (B) ghost
    (C) spooky
    (D) terrifying

55. Which word does *not* belong with the others?
    (A) herb
    (B) oregano
    (C) parsley
    (D) sage

56. Which word does *not* belong with the others?
    (A) brownie
    (B) dessert
    (C) pie
    (D) sorbet

57. Which word does *not* belong with the others?
    (A) driveway
    (B) garage
    (C) house
    (D) shed

58. Which word does *not* belong with the others?
    (A) loaf
    (B) rye
    (C) sourdough
    (D) wheat

59. Which word does *not* belong with the others?
    (A) shower
    (B) stove
    (C) toilet
    (D) tub

60. Which word does *not* belong with the others?
    (A) centaur
    (B) dolphin
    (C) mermaid
    (D) unicorn

61. Which word does *not* belong with the others?
    (A) conclusion
    (B) introduction
    (C) letter
    (D) signature

62. Which word does *not* belong with the others?
    (A) cheetah
    (B) cougar
    (C) giraffe
    (D) leopard

63. Which word does *not* belong with the others?
    (A) bed
    (B) dresser
    (C) oven
    (D) rug

64. Which word does *not* belong with the others?
    (A) gloves
    (B) hat
    (C) sandals
    (D) scarf

65. Which word does *not* belong with the others?
    (A) government
    (B) legislator
    (C) president
    (D) senator

66. Which word does *not* belong with the others?
    (A) critical
    (B) important
    (C) significant
    (D) trivial

67. Which word does *not* belong with the others?
    (A) conquer
    (B) fail
    (C) lose
    (D) struggle

68. Which word does *not* belong with the others?
    (A) change
    (B) continue
    (C) maintain
    (D) preserve

69. Which word does *not* belong with the others?
    (A) conditioner
    (B) floss
    (C) shampoo
    (D) soap

70. Which word does *not* belong with the others?
    (A) paprika
    (B) pepper
    (C) salt
    (D) sugar

71. Which word does *not* belong with the others?
    (A) dirt
    (B) grass
    (C) mulch
    (D) park

72. Which word does *not* belong with the others?
    (A) annoy
    (B) assist
    (C) bother
    (D) irritate

73. Which word does *not* belong with the others?
(A) bush
(B) garden
(C) hose
(D) tulip

74. Which word does *not* belong with the others?
(A) mouse
(B) rat
(C) rodent
(D) squirrel

75. Which word does *not* belong with the others?
(A) equation
(B) figure
(C) math
(D) symbol

76. Which word does *not* belong with the others?
(A) cough
(B) fever
(C) headache
(D) sickness

77. Which word does *not* belong with the others?
(A) lightning
(B) rain
(C) storm
(D) thunder

78. Which word does *not* belong with the others?
(A) barge
(B) canoe
(C) goose
(D) raft

79. Which word does *not* belong with the others?
(A) gums
(B) nostril
(C) teeth
(D) tongue

80. Which word does *not* belong with the others?
(A) copy
(B) imitation
(C) original
(D) replica

81. Which word does *not* belong with the others?
(A) apple
(B) cereal
(C) granola
(D) oatmeal

82. Which word does *not* belong with the others?
(A) companion
(B) friend
(C) partner
(D) rival

Synonyms

Overview

The questions in the synonym section test your word knowledge and ability to associate related words. You will be given a word and asked to pick the word in the answer choices that most nearly means the word given.

You may find many of the words in this section to be challenging. Don't be surprised if you need to look up many of the words that you encounter in this section! The purpose of this section is to introduce you to new words. We encourage you to make a list of words that give you trouble, whether they appear in questions or answer choices. Write down the definition of each word as well as a sentence using the word. You might also want to consider writing down positive or negative associations, any root words that can help you remember the word, or any words that are commonly encountered with that word.

We recommend that you practice at least 15-20 questions per week in preparing for the exam.

Tutorverse Tips!

As you read the question word, think of a word that you might use instead of the question word. Then check the answers to see if there is a similar word to your choice offered.

Sometimes, words can have more than one meaning. Don't let this confuse you! Look at the answer choices to make an educated guess as to which meaning is being used in the question. Then, use your reasoning skills to select the word that most nearly means the same as the given word.

Synonyms Exercises

1. Punish most nearly means
   (A) banish
   (B) discipline
   (C) instruct
   (D) lock

2. Urgently most nearly means
   (A) crucially
   (B) forcefully
   (C) slowly
   (D) terribly

3. Pierce most nearly means
   (A) mend
   (B) perfect
   (C) puncture
   (D) scare

4. Grandiose most nearly means
   (A) disgusting
   (B) humble
   (C) magnificent
   (D) obsessive

5. Ferocity most nearly means
   (A) audacity
   (B) excitement
   (C) kindness
   (D) violence

6. Record most nearly means
   (A) mock
   (B) note
   (C) remind
   (D) steal

7. Revise most nearly means
   (A) change
   (B) mimic
   (C) observe
   (D) return

A

8. Accumulate most nearly means
   (A) delay
   (B) gather
   (C) spread
   (D) waste

9. Elaborate most nearly means
   (A) detailed
   (B) ecstatic
   (C) expensive
   (D) simple

10. Peculiar most nearly means
(A) atypical
(B) familiar
(C) mysterious
(D) terrifying

11. Apprehensive most nearly means
(A) ambitious
(B) cautious
(C) oblivious
(D) pensive

12. Rebellious most nearly means
(A) dangerous
(B) defiant
(C) devoted
(D) impressive

13. Evoke most nearly means
(A) anger
(B) evolve
(C) ignore
(D) inspire

14. Eccentric most nearly means
(A) average
(B) ordinary
(C) quirky
(D) unnecessary

15. Meek most nearly means
(A) arrogant
(B) incapable
(C) modest
(D) showy

C

16. Contempt most nearly means
(A) comfort
(B) desire
(C) respect
(D) scorn

D

17. Slovenly most nearly means
(A) desperate
(B) groomed
(C) stylish
(D) unkempt

18. Consolation most nearly means
(A) reassurance
(B) rejection
(C) respect
(D) reward

19. Defy most nearly means
(A) amaze
(B) disobey
(C) explain
(D) mystify

20. Subtly most nearly means
(A) blatantly
(B) crookedly
(C) obviously
(D) sneakily

21. Benign most nearly means
(A) dangerous
(B) harmless
(C) noxious
(D) uninteresting

B

22. Orator most nearly means
(A) athlete
(B) creator
(C) lecturer
(D) manager

23. Disparity most nearly means
(A) adversity
(B) difference
(C) hardship
(D) identity

B

24. Affinity most nearly means
(A) aversion
(B) charisma
(C) disposition
(D) kindness

25. Forfeit most nearly means
(A) feign
(B) permit
(C) retain
(D) waive

D

26. Stamina most nearly means
(A) disease
(B) endurance
(C) experiment
(D) nutrition

27. Hindrance most nearly means
(A) deterrent
(B) guidance
(C) secret
(D) stimulant

A

28. Trepidation most nearly means
(A) delight
(B) dread
(C) excitement
(D) intimidation

B

29. Solace most nearly means
(A) chance
(B) comfort
(C) depression
(D) silence

B

30. Acuity most nearly means
(A) creativity
(B) flexibility
(C) intelligence
(D) sharpness

C

31. Marvel most nearly means
(A) challenge
(B) clash
(C) sensation
(D) vision

D

32. Rampage most nearly means
(A) celebration
(B) expedition
(C) journey
(D) uproar

33. Guile most nearly means
(A) craftiness
(B) disguise
(C) dismissal
(D) rejection

A

34. Avarice most nearly means
(A) change
(B) flight
(C) greed
(D) growth

35. Blunder most nearly means
(A) argument
(B) blessing
(C) mistake
(D) storm

36. Resolution most nearly means
(A) conclusion
(B) conflict
(C) confrontation
(D) creation

37. Minimize most nearly means
(A) build
(B) customize
(C) diminish
(D) increase

38. Wrangle most nearly means
(A) impress
(B) quarrel
(C) recur
(D) validate

39. Memoir most nearly means
(A) artist
(B) author
(C) biography
(D) novel

40. Rebuke most nearly means
(A) reflect
(B) reject
(C) remind
(D) reprimand

41. Theory most nearly means
(A) experiment
(B) hypothesis
(C) proof
(D) science

42. Novice most nearly means
(A) amateur
(B) expert
(C) genius
(D) specialist

43. Surmise most nearly means
(A) discover
(B) guess
(C) prove
(D) surface

44. Abrasion most nearly means
(A) abnormality
(B) bruise
(C) defense
(D) invasion

45. Arduous most nearly means
(A) demanding
(B) fervent
(C) luscious
(D) practical

46. Rescind most nearly means
(A) cancel
(B) complete
(C) forget
(D) initiate

47. Docile most nearly means
(A) dire
(B) impossible
(C) submissive
(D) worthwhile

48. Integrity most nearly means
(A) beauty
(B) honesty
(C) jealousy
(D) patience

49. Apathy most nearly means
(A) assistance
(B) emotion
(C) generosity
(D) insensitivity

50. Gruesome most nearly means
(A) adorable
(B) ghastly
(C) makeshift
(D) wholesome

51. Imperative most nearly means
(A) direction
(B) opinion
(C) possibility
(D) tension

52. Tirade most nearly means
(A) celebration
(B) defeat
(C) praise
(D) rant

53. Obscure most nearly means
(A) clear
(B) murky
(C) obvious
(D) pure

54. Citadel most nearly means
(A) challenge
(B) excursion
(C) fortress
(D) game

55. Tawdry most nearly means
(A) childish
(B) funny
(C) gaudy
(D) stylish

56. Qualm most nearly means
(A) ease
(B) peace
(C) serenity
(D) uncertainty

57. Servile most nearly means
(A) confident
(B) sheepish
(C) simple
(D) unintelligent

58. Oblique most nearly means
(A) flexible
(B) indirect
(C) mysterious
(D) strong

59. Churlish most nearly means
(A) amusing
(B) entertaining
(C) impolite
(D) orderly

60. Stoic most nearly means
(A) composed
(B) expensive
(C) lonely
(D) stealthy

61. Pallid most nearly means
(A) bright
(B) chewy
(C) pale
(D) sharp

62. Dexterous most nearly means
(A) awkward
(B) complex
(C) limber
(D) pleasant

63. Effigy most nearly means
(A) companion
(B) history
(C) statue
(D) story

64. Myriad most nearly means
(A) famous
(B) haunting
(C) unique
(D) various

65. Amplify most nearly means
(A) aid
(B) enlarge
(C) hide
(D) mend

66. Adjust most nearly means
(A) adapt
(B) arrange
(C) schedule
(D) show

67. Alien most nearly means
(A) distant
(B) scary
(C) secret
(D) unfamiliar

68. Deceive most nearly means
(A) debunk
(B) fool
(C) please
(D) reveal

69. Assert most nearly means
(A) assign
(B) complain
(C) dismiss
(D) profess

70. Capture most nearly means
(A) chase
(B) lead
(C) obtain
(D) pursue

71. Plausible most nearly means
(A) believable
(B) comfortable
(C) honorable
(D) unlikely

72. Precise most nearly means
(A) accurate
(B) brief
(C) plain
(D) powerful

73. Concept most nearly means
(A) difficulty
(B) idea
(C) mystery
(D) object

74. Hefty most nearly means
(A) adhesive
(B) massive
(C) tiny
(D) tricky

75. Misguided most nearly means
(A) appreciated
(B) arranged
(C) forgotten
(D) misled

76. Authority most nearly means
(A) adult
(B) criminal
(C) expert
(D) novice

77. Spontaneous most nearly means
(A) amusing
(B) original
(C) sudden
(D) wrong

Antonyms

Overview

Like the synonym questions, the antonym questions test your word knowledge. However, here you are given four choices and asked to select the choice that most nearly means the *opposite* of the given word.

As with the synonym section, you may find many of the words in the antonym section to be challenging. Don't be surprised if you need to look up many of the words that you encounter in this section! The purpose of this section is to introduce you to new words. We encourage you to make a list of words that give you trouble, whether they appear in questions or answer choices. Write down the definition of each word as well as a sentence using the word. You might also want to consider writing down positive or negative associations, any root words that can help you remember the word, or any words that are commonly encountered with that word.

We recommend that you practice at least 15-20 questions per week in preparing for the exam.

Tutorverse Tips!

As you read the question words, think of a word that you might use instead of the question word. Then, think of a word that is opposite that word. Then check the answers to see if there is a similar word to your choice offered.

Sometimes, words can have more than one meaning. Don't let this confuse you! Look at the answer choices to make an educated guess as to which meaning is being used in the question. Then, use your reasoning skills to select the word that most nearly means the opposite of the given word.

Antonyms Exercises

1. Arduous means the opposite of
   (A) basic
   (B) challenging
   (C) easy
   (D) impossible

2. Evaluate means the opposite of
   (A) assess
   (B) build
   (C) complicate
   (D) dismiss

3. Condemn means the opposite of
   (A) correct
   (B) dismiss
   (C) honor
   (D) sleuth

4. Independent means the opposite of
   (A) capable
   (B) lonely
   (C) needy
   (D) serious

5. Greedy means the opposite of
   (A) dreary
   (B) generous
   (C) mean
   (D) selfish

6. Feud means the opposite of
   (A) cooperate
   (B) disagree
   (C) fear
   (D) vie

7. Stupendous means the opposite of
   (A) astonishing
   (B) miraculous
   (C) ordinary
   (D) wonderful

8. Shriek means the opposite of
   (A) exclaim
   (B) deceive
   (C) scream
   (D) whisper

9. Courageous means the opposite of
   (A) brave
   (B) heroic
   (C) mediocre
   (D) timid

10. Vivid means the opposite of
(A) bright
(B) dim
(C) simple
(D) valid

11. Admire means the opposite of
(A) commend
(B) despise
(C) relish
(D) advise

12. Ambition means the opposite of
(A) aspiration
(B) determination
(C) indifference
(D) nutrition

13. Disgruntled means the opposite of
(A) abrasive
(B) composed
(C) irritable
(D) pleasure

14. Dire means the opposite of
(A) foreboding
(B) comforting
(C) intense
(D) serious

15. Avid means the opposite of
(A) apathetic
(B) eager
(C) infectious
(D) restless

16. Vibrant means the opposite of
(A) dull
(B) invisible
(C) radiant
(D) tense

17. Flourish means the opposite of
(A) aspire
(B) feel
(C) grow
(D) wilt

18. Brazen means the opposite of
(A) bubbly
(B) insane
(C) meek
(D) shameless

19. Lucrative means the opposite of
(A) banal
(B) gainful
(C) ridiculous
(D) unprofitable

20. Sublime means the opposite of
(A) delicious
(B) impressive
(C) surprising
(D) unremarkable

21. Traitorous means the opposite of
(A) contentious
(B) disastrous
(C) loyal
(D) political

22. Rebel means the opposite of
(A) adhere
(B) dare
(C) dread
(D) revolt

23. Encroach means the opposite of
(A) approach
(B) disgust
(C) neglect
(D) retreat

24. Seize means the opposite of
(A) capture
(B) hold
(C) release
(D) verify

25. Ensure means the opposite of
(A) assure
(B) guarantee
(C) secure
(D) undermine

26. Deceive means the opposite of
(A) bamboozle
(B) relieve
(C) trick
(D) unveil

27. Appropriate means the opposite of
(A) acceptable
(B) deserved
(C) improper
(D) tolerable

28. Pompous means the opposite of
(A) cavalier
(B) conscious
(C) sheepish
(D) unrelated

29. Reckless means the opposite of
(A) cautious
(B) destructive
(C) hapless
(D) jealous

30. Sovereign means the opposite of
(A) ally
(B) follower
(C) monarch
(D) ruler

31. Compel means the opposite of
(A) agree
(B) dissuade
(C) insist
(D) perpetuate

32. Incompetent means the opposite of
    (A) capable
    (B) careless
    (C) familiar
    (D) restless

33. Eligible means the opposite of
    (A) able
    (B) disqualified
    (C) expert
    (D) playful

34. Resolve means the opposite of
    (A) conclude
    (B) disrupt
    (C) need
    (D) tolerate

35. Tentative means the opposite of
    (A) bold
    (B) helpful
    (C) hesitant
    (D) nervous

36. Mitigate means the opposite of
    (A) alleviate
    (B) exacerbate
    (C) merge
    (D) soothe

37. Toxic means the opposite of
    (A) elegant
    (B) harmful
    (C) safe
    (D) substance

38. Derogatory means the opposite of
    (A) complimentary
    (B) critical
    (C) forgetful
    (D) scathing

39. Copious means the opposite of
    (A) extravagant
    (B) lavish
    (C) meager
    (D) poisonous

40. Dawdle means the opposite of
    (A) delay
    (B) hurry
    (C) laugh
    (D) mope

41. Acknowledge means the opposite of
    (A) admit
    (B) learn
    (C) negate
    (D) pledge

42. Conclusive means the opposite of
    (A) controversial
    (B) definitive
    (C) explosive
    (D) indecisive

43. Confront means the opposite of
    (A) approach
    (B) dodge
    (C) frustrate
    (D) meet

44. Gleaming means the opposite of
    (A) brilliant
    (B) frightening
    (C) gloomy
    (D) jovial

45. Hurtle means the opposite of
    (A) assist
    (B) crawl
    (C) jet
    (D) speed

46. Vain means the opposite of
    (A) conceited
    (B) dire
    (C) humble
    (D) jealous

47. Dissent means the opposite of
    (A) accord
    (B) conflict
    (C) disagreement
    (D) disappointment

Verbal Analogies

Overview

This section tests your ability to see relationships between words and concepts.

You will need to define a relationship between two words, and then apply that relationship to a new set of words.

Some examples of types of relationships are:

- Part to whole (e.g., *page* to *book*)
- Cause and effect (e.g., *study* to *pass*)
- Antonym (e.g., *intact* to *broken*)
- Synonym (e.g., *cat* to *feline*)
- Degree (e.g., *stream* to *river*)
- Function (*conductor* to *train*)
- Characteristic (e.g., *shiny* to *metal*)
- Purpose (e.g., *blanket* to *cover*)

We recommend that you practice at least 15-20 questions per week in preparing for the exam.

Tutorverse Tips!

Consider the "direction" of the relationship. For example, *stove* to *heat* shows a different relationship than *heat* to *stove*. A stove *produces* heat, but heat *is produced by* a stove. Avoid answers that show a similar relationship to the first two words, but in the wrong direction.

Verbal Analogies Exercises

1. Soldier is to army as musician is to
   (A) artist
   (B) instrument
   (C) orchestra
   (D) war

2. Prior is to previous as initial is to
   (A) final
   (B) first
   (C) order
   (D) time

3. Dance is to music as watch is to
   (A) artistic
   (B) movie
   (C) observe
   (D) sing

4. Supervisor is to employees as lifeguard is to
   (A) pool
   (B) summer
   (C) swimmers
   (D) whistle

5. Ignorance is to knowledge as freedom is to
   (A) equality
   (B) imprisonment
   (C) laws
   (D) right

6. Aggressive is to violence as kind is to
   (A) compassion
   (B) cruel
   (C) nice
   (D) trait

7. Page is to book as tree is to
   (A) birds
   (B) forest
   (C) grass
   (D) plant

8. Drizzle is to pour as giggle is to
   (A) cry
   (B) funny
   (C) guffaw
   (D) reaction

9. Feud is to quarrel as collaboration is to
   (A) cooperation
   (B) friends
   (C) group
   (D) relationship

10. Stick is to drum as bow is to
    (A) finale
    (B) music
    (C) show
    (D) violin

11. Plank is to floor as brick is to
    (A) build
    (B) stone
    (C) wall
    (D) wood

12. Sauce is to pasta as syrup is to
    (A) ingredient
    (B) pancakes
    (C) sweet
    (D) topping

13. Spoon is to stir as knife is to
    (A) cook
    (B) serve
    (C) slice
    (D) utensil

14. Country is to citizen as club is to
    (A) activity
    (B) hobby
    (C) member
    (D) school

15. Chorus is to symphony as singer is to
    (A) instrument
    (B) musician
    (C) performance
    (D) group

16. Clerk is to store as officer is to
    (A) museum
    (B) precinct
    (C) school
    (D) theater

17. Chew is to gum as mold is to
    (A) candy
    (B) clay
    (C) fabric
    (D) paint

18. Pigeon is to bird as cheetah is to
    (A) deer
    (B) feline
    (C) pet
    (D) sparrow

19. Leaf is to branch as tomato is to
    (A) broccoli
    (B) tree
    (C) vine
    (D) worm

20. Toast is to bread as boil is to
    (A) chop
    (B) dinner
    (C) pasta
    (D) pot

21. Dream is to future as remember is to
    (A) family
    (B) memory
    (C) past
    (D) present

22. Fish is to pond as panther is to
    (A) claws
    (B) jungle
    (C) leopard
    (D) movie

23. Instruction is to classroom as exercise is to
    (A) basketball
    (B) coach
    (C) gym
    (D) practice

24. Dye is to hair as blush is to
    (A) cheeks
    (B) color
    (C) make-up
    (D) rose

25. Singer is to choir as guitarist is to
    (A) band
    (B) instrument
    (C) musician
    (D) song

26. Flour is to baking as oil is to
    (A) chef
    (B) frying
    (C) painting
    (D) stove

27. Scales is to snake as fur is to
    (A) brush
    (B) cat
    (C) fish
    (D) soft

28. Stream is to show as play is to
    (A) actor
    (B) music
    (C) part
    (D) speaker

29. Antennae is to butterfly as antlers is to
    (A) animal
    (B) attack
    (C) deer
    (D) head

30. Peach is to fruit as broccoli is to
    (A) dinner
    (B) salad
    (C) steam
    (D) vegetable

31. Moss is to tree as vine is to
    (A) fence
    (B) grapes
    (C) leaves
    (D) plant

32. Sand is to beach as grass is to
(A) grow
(B) meadow
(C) mow
(D) pond

33. Hat is to head as gloves is to
(A) cold
(B) hands
(C) scarf
(D) winter

34. Crayon is to box as paint is to
(A) artist
(B) can
(C) painter
(D) wall

35. Traffic is to highway as crowd is to
(A) busy
(B) concert
(C) people
(D) road

36. Easy is to simple as difficult is to
(A) challenge
(B) complete
(C) demanding
(D) task

37. Scissors is to barber as hammer is to
(A) build
(B) carpenter
(C) nail
(D) tools

38. Polite is to rude as friendly is to
(A) cold
(B) cordial
(C) kind
(D) personality

39. Crane is to construction as needle is to
(A) doctor
(B) medicine
(C) sewing
(D) sharp

40. Moustache is to lip as eyebrow is to
(A) beard
(B) eye
(C) face
(D) hair

41. Hoof is to horse as paw is to
(A) claws
(B) dog
(C) foot
(D) shoe

42. Scar is to skin as dent is to
(A) blemish
(B) crash
(C) harm
(D) metal

43. Fleas is to fur as lice is to
(A) bug
(B) dog
(C) germs
(D) hair

44. Seeds is to watermelon as pit is to
(A) ditch
(B) fruit
(C) juice
(D) plum

45. Dentist is to teeth as optometrist is to
(A) eyes
(B) health
(C) medicine
(D) office

46. Wool is to sweater as denim is to
(A) clothing
(B) fabric
(C) jeans
(D) material

47. Scientist is to lab as photographer is to
(A) artist
(B) camera
(C) professional
(D) studio

48. Map is to treasure as code is to
(A) destination
(B) gold
(C) message
(D) money

49. Sleep is to bed as sit is to
(A) chair
(B) eat
(C) table
(D) walk

50. Reasonable is to irrational as compassionate is to
(A) heartless
(B) kind
(C) logical
(D) unfair

51. Sauce is to pasta as dressing is to
(A) cooking
(B) dinner
(C) ravioli
(D) salad

52. Shame is to pride as greed is to
(A) arrogance
(B) generosity
(C) money
(D) steal

Logic

Overview

Logic questions are the most unique type of question in the Verbal Skills section.

Here, you are given two statements and asked to determine if a third statement is true, false or uncertain based on the first two statements.

These questions have only three possible answers:

- A—when the third statement is true
- B—when the third statement is false
- C—when you cannot determine the truth of the third statement based on the first two

Tutorverse Tips!

Consider making a simple diagram of the situation to better understand relationships! Mapping it out can help.

Logic Exercises

1. Gavin is stronger than Will. Will is stronger than George. Gavin is stronger than George. If the first two statements are true, then the third is
   (A) True
   (B) False
   (C) Uncertain

2. Jeremy is allergic to chocolate. A mocha is a drink that contains chocolate. Jeremy cannot drink mochas. If the first two statements are true, then the third is
   (A) True
   (B) False
   (C) Uncertain

3. All snakes have scales. Some snakes are pets. Some pets have scales. If the first two statements are true, then the third is
   (A) True
   (B) False
   (C) Uncertain

4. Some music is sad. Some music contains violin. All violin players are sad. If the first two statements are true, then the third is
   (A) True
   (B) False
   (C) Uncertain

5. Some candles have floral scents. Some people like putting candles in their bathrooms. Some people like their bathrooms to have a floral scent. If the first two statements are true, then the third is
   (A) True
   (B) False
   (C) Uncertain

6. Succulents don't need much water to survive. Aloe vera is a type of succulent. Aloe vera does not need a lot of water to survive. If the first two statements are true, then the third is
   (A) True
   (B) False
   (C) Uncertain

7. Kade plays the trumpet. The trumpet is a brass instrument. Kade can play all brass instruments. If the first two statements are true, then the third is
   (A) True
   (B) False
   (C) Uncertain

8. Mark is doing well in his calculus class. Mark only does well in subjects he enjoys. Mark enjoys doing calculus. If the first two statements are true, then the third is
   (A) True
   (B) False
   (C) Uncertain

9. The desert is a very dry habitat. Cacti need very little water to survive. Cacti can survive in the desert. If the first two statements are true, then the third is
   (A) True
   (B) False
   (C) Uncertain

10. Dumbo has bigger ears than Winnie. Winnie has bigger ears than Poe. Dumbo has bigger ears than Poe. If the first two statements are true, then the third is
    (A) True
    (B) False
    (C) Uncertain

11. Rose has a pet cat. Rose's friend Josh is allergic to cats. Josh hates Rose. If the first two statements are true, then the third is
    (A) True
    (B) False
    (C) Uncertain

12. Beth is afraid of ghosts. Some novels contain stories about ghosts. Beth does not read any novels. If the first two statements are true, then the third is
    (A) True
    (B) False
    (C) Uncertain

13. Ariana has more money than Maureen. Maureen has more money than Alex. Alex has less money than Ariana. If the first two statements are true, then the third is
    (A) True
    (B) False
    (C) Uncertain

14. Some birds live in cages. Some birds are pets. All pets live in cages. If the first two statements are true, then the third is
    (A) True
    (B) False
    (C) Uncertain

15. Cliff diving is an extreme sport. Some extreme sports are dangerous. Cliff diving is a dangerous sport. If the first two statements are true, then the third is
    (A) True
    (B) False
    (C) Uncertain

16. The green car is faster than the silver car. The red car is faster than the silver car. The red car is faster than the green car. If the first two statements are true, then the third is
    (A) True
    (B) False
    (C) Uncertain

17. Riding the train is a form of transportation. Some forms of transportation are good for the environment. Riding the train is good for the environment. If the first two statements are true, then the third is
    (A) True
    (B) False
    (C) Uncertain

18. Ballet is a form of dance. Ballet is very challenging. All dance forms are challenging. If the first two statements are true, then the third is
    (A) True
    (B) False
    (C) Uncertain

19. Moths have antennae. Moths are a type of insect. All insects have antennae. If the first two statements are true, then the third is
(A) True
(B) False
(C) Uncertain

20. Jake has more shoes than Krystal. Leon has more shoes than Krystal. Jake has more shoes than Leon. If the first two statements are true, then the third is
(A) True
(B) False
(C) Uncertain

21. Sharks are fish. Fish cannot survive outside of water. Sharks cannot survive outside of water. If the first two statements are true, then the third is
(A) True
(B) False
(C) Uncertain

22. Ross is a scientist who studies dinosaur fossils. Paleontologists are scientists who study dinosaur fossils. Ross is a paleontologist. If the first two statements are true, then the third is
(A) True
(B) False
(C) Uncertain

23. Rome is a city in Italy. Italy is a country in Europe. Rome is in Europe. If the first two statements are true, then the third is
(A) True
(B) False
(C) Uncertain

24. Some boots are expensive. Boots are a type of shoe. All shoes are expensive. If the first two statements are true, then the third is
(A) True
(B) False
(C) Uncertain

25. Bats are mammals. Bats are nocturnal. All mammals are nocturnal. If the first two statements are true, then the third is
(A) True
(B) False
(C) Uncertain

26. Joseph loves art. Museums contain a lot of art. Joseph likes going to museums. If the first two statements are true, then the third is
(A) True
(B) False
(C) Uncertain

27. Moss grows on trees. Barnacles grow on docks. Moss and barnacles are part of the same species. If the first two statements are true, then the third is
(A) True
(B) False
(C) Uncertain

28. Bulls have hooves. Donkeys have hooves. Donkeys are a type of bull. If the first two statements are true, then the third is
(A) True
(B) False
(C) Uncertain

29. Mexico is in North America. Canada is in North America. Mexico is in Canada. If the first two statements are true, then the third is
(A) True
(B) False
(C) Uncertain

30. Eric is in a band. Some bands have guitar players. Eric is a guitar player. If the first two statements are true, then the third is
(A) True
(B) False
(C) Uncertain

31. Pleasantville is a small town. Some small towns are boring. Pleasantville is a boring town. If the first two statements are true, then the third is
(A) True
(B) False
(C) Uncertain

32. Jade dislikes action movies. Archie likes action movies. Jade dislikes Archie. If the first two statements are true, then the third is
   (A) True
   (B) False
   (C) Uncertain

33. Cherries are a type of fruit. Some fruit have pits. Cherries have pits. If the first two statements are true, then the third is
   (A) True
   (B) False
   (C) Uncertain

34. Riding a bike is a form of transportation. Some forms of transportation are bad for the environment. Riding a bike is bad for the environment. If the first two statements are true, then the third is
   (A) True
   (B) False
   (C) Uncertain

35. Seth is a movie director. Some movie directors make a lot of money. Seth makes a lot of money. If the first two statements are true, then the third is
   (A) True
   (B) False
   (C) Uncertain

36. Sarah hates the flavor of peppermint. Some toothpastes are peppermint flavored. Sarah hates all toothpastes. If the first two statements are true, then the third is
   (A) True
   (B) False
   (C) Uncertain

37. Some college students study a lot. Some college students get good grades. All students who study a lot get good grades. If the first two statements are true, then the third is
   (A) True
   (B) False
   (C) Uncertain

38. Michelle has longer hair than Nim. Naomi has longer hair than Nim. Naomi has longer hair than Michelle. If the first two statements are true, then the third is
   (A) True
   (B) False
   (C) Uncertain

39. Dinosaurs are extinct. A triceratops is a type of dinosaur. Triceratops is extinct. If the first two statements are true, then the third is
   (A) True
   (B) False
   (C) Uncertain

40. Adrienne hates tomatoes. Salads often contain tomatoes. Adrienne never eats salads. If the first two statements are true, then the third is
   (A) True
   (B) False
   (C) Uncertain

41. Turtles have shells. Turtles' shells protect them from harm. Turtles are frequently in danger. If the first two statements are true, then the third is
   (A) True
   (B) False
   (C) Uncertain

42. Owls are nocturnal. Nocturnal animals sleep during the day. Owls sleep during the day. If the first two statements are true, then the third is
   (A) True
   (B) False
   (C) Uncertain

43. Robert loves showers. Showers help people stay clean. Robert is often clean. If the first two statements are true, then the third is
   (A) True
   (B) False
   (C) Uncertain

44. Cranberries are sour. Myrtle hates sour foods. Myrtle hates cranberries. If the first two statements are true, then the third is
   (A) True
   (B) False
   (C) Uncertain

45. All horses have hooves. Some horses are pets. All pets have hooves. If the first two statements are true, then the third is
    (A) True
    (B) False
    (C) Uncertain

46. Monarch butterflies migrate over long distances. Monarch butterflies are a type of insect. All insects migrate long distances. If the first two statements are true, then the third is
    (A) True
    (B) False
    (C) Uncertain

47. Hiking is strenuous. Hiking is fun. All strenuous activities are fun. If the first two statements are true, then the third is
    (A) True
    (B) False
    (C) Uncertain

48. Some lipstick is expensive. Some lipstick is red. All red lipstick is expensive. If the first two statements are true, then the third is
    (A) True
    (B) False
    (C) Uncertain

49. Writing in pen cannot be erased. Maggie likes to be able to erase her writing. Maggie dislikes using pens. If the first two statements are true, then the third is
    (A) True
    (B) False
    (C) Uncertain

50. All flowers have petals. Some petals are pink. All flowers are pink. If the first two statements are true, then the third is
    (A) True
    (B) False
    (C) Uncertain

51. Ron hates hot weather. Texas has very hot summers. Ron does not want to live in Texas. If the first two statements are true, then the third is
    (A) True
    (B) False
    (C) Uncertain

52. Kevin hates horror movies. Some horror movies feature zombies. Kevin hates zombies. If the first two statements are true, then the third is
    (A) True
    (B) False
    (C) Uncertain

Reading

On the Actual Test

In the Reading section of the HSPT, there are two parts:

- Reading Comprehension
  - four passages, each with 10 questions
  - topics including science, history, art, and literature
  - questions testing main idea, inference, details, and style, among others
- Vocabulary
  - 22 questions requiring students to utilize context clues to choose the best definition of a given word as used in the passage

You will have 25 minutes to complete the 40 reading comprehension questions and 22 vocabulary questions in this section.

In This Practice Book

The practice questions in this section of the workbook contain many exams' worth of materials to help you practice. This will allow you to drill for each type of question you will find on the Reading section.

Reading Comprehension

Overview

This section is broken down into the types of reading comprehension passages that you will practice in this section:

- Expository—an objective explanation or discussion of a topic
- Narrative—relates a story
- Persuasive—aims to convince the reader of a point of view

How to Use This Section

As determined by your study plan, including the results of your diagnostic tests, we encourage you to focus on the topics that are most challenging to you. This section will give you exposure to the different types of questions that are presented in reading comprehension, and give you the practice to finding the path to the correct answer. If you find that you are challenged by this area and need additional help, remember to reach out to a trusted educator. Don't get discouraged! Take the materials to a teacher or tutor if you need additional enrichment in any given topic.

Tutorverse Tips!

Remember to annotate and write down the main ideas as you read! Notations can help you remember key ideas and relationships. Pay attention to details in the answer choices that make an answer incorrect. Eliminating incorrect choices is a great way to reveal the correct answer!

Reading Comprehension Exercises

Expository

Expository Passage #1

Photography is one of the most popular art forms today. Nearly anything—from people to places to everyday objects—can be the subject of a photographer's work. However, the artistic community did not always consider photography a form of art. Early photographers had to advocate for their work to be taken seriously. One of those early photographers was a man by the name of Ansel Adams. Adams was an American photographer born in San Francisco, California on February 20, 1902. Though he was born in the city, from his youth, Adams loved nature. As a child, he could often be found hiking and wandering through nature. As an adult, he became famous for his black and white photographs of landscapes of the American West.

Throughout his childhood, Adams had studied music. He taught himself to read sheet music and play the piano. At first, Adams intended to follow a career in music. He only dabbled in photography as a hobby. It was not until 1927, at the age of 25, that he published his first set of photographs. Ultimately, he gave up music to focus on photography. Adams continued to take photos and soon began to receive recognition from other artists for his photographs' distinct visual style. Adams had an intense energy and passion for his work. He would often work more than eighteen hours per day for weeks at a time. He did not take vacations or days to rest. In fact, he worked so hard that he would often become ill due to overworking and would have to spend several days in bed.

As his career progressed, Adams supported the photography community in many ways. In 1940, he helped found the world's first museum department of photography at the Museum of Modern Art in New York City. This was a significant achievement that marked photography as a finally respected form of artistic expression. In 1946, Adams established the first academic photography department at the California School of Fine Arts in San Francisco. This was the first college to teach professional photography as a fine art. In 1980, Adams was awarded the Presidential Medal of Freedom. The president of the United States gives this award to people who have made significant contributions to society. Though Ansel Adams died on April 22, 1984, he left behind a powerful legacy in the artistic community.

1. This passage is mostly about
   (A) famous art museums.
   (B) different types of photography.
   (C) how to start a career in photography.
   (D) a famous photographer.

2. What would be the most appropriate title for this passage?
   (A) How to Become a Photographer
   (B) Black and White Photography
   (C) The Best Photography Schools in America
   (D) The Man Behind the Camera

3. According to the passage, Ansel Adams
   (A) loved nature even as a child.
   (B) preferred to work in the spring.
   (C) only spent time in nature when he was working.
   (D) loved nature because he was born in the country.

4. According to the facts in the passage,
   (A) Adams tried but was unable to play the piano.
   (B) Adams' mother taught him to play the piano.
   (C) Adams was mostly self-educated in regards to music.
   (D) Adams enjoyed listening to music but never played any instruments.

5. Based on the details in the passage, Ansel Adams
   (A) never became a published photographer.
   (B) published his first set of photographs in 1940.
   (C) published his first set of photographs at the age of 25.
   (D) did not have his photographs published until after his death.

6. The author would most likely agree with which of the following statements?
   (A) Photography is not a real art form.
   (B) Photography has no influence on the world.
   (C) Photographs should only be displayed in art museums.
   (D) Photography should be as respected just as much as other art forms.

7. You would probably find this passage in
   (A) a brochure.
   (B) a personal journal.
   (C) an art magazine.
   (D) a college admissions pamphlet.

8. Which of the following can be inferred from the passage?
   (A) Photography is competitive.
   (B) Ansel Adams was not very successful.
   (C) Photographers have an easy job.
   (D) Ansel Adams was dedicated to his work.

9. As it is used in the passage, the word "<u>intense</u>" most nearly means
   (A) absent.
   (B) extreme.
   (C) frightening.
   (D) lazy.

10. As it is used in the passage, the word "<u>found</u>" most nearly means
    (A) establish.
    (B) discover.
    (C) lose.
    (D) forget

Expository Passage #2

When many people see a bald eagle, they recognize it as a symbol of the United States of America. These large animals have been the national bird of the United States since 1782. That's almost as long as the United States has been a country!

Bald eagles are one of the largest birds in North America. With an immense wingspan of six to eight feet, they make other large birds seem small. Adult bald eagles have white heads and tails, but dark brown bodies and wings. Their razor-sharp talons and beak are a distinctive yellow color. Before bald eagles are fully grown, they are dark brown all over. Their heads and tails do not turn white until adulthood, which happens at around five years of age. The average lifespan of a bald eagle is between 15 and 50 years in captivity and 15 and 30 years in the wild.

Bald eagles soar high in the sky with their wings flat like a board. While flying, they use their excellent eyesight to search for prey, such as fish and small mammals. Bald eagles can see a fish in water from up to a mile away! They swoop down from the air to catch their prey with their talons before flying away to feast.

Bald eagles often live near water, such as lakes, rivers, marshes, or coastlines. They build nests high up in trees. This is where they raise their young. Bald eagles live in pairs consisting of one male and one female. They can be told apart by their size. Female bald eagles are slightly larger than males. The two parents take turns looking after their babies. Some pairs return to the same nest year after year, while others move and build new nests in different locations.

Unfortunately, bald eagles nearly went extinct because of hunting and pollution. However, in 1940 congress passed the Bald Eagle Protection Act which helped protect eagles by outlawing the hunting and trade of the symbolically important bird. Following subsequent bans on the use of certain chemicals, bald eagles have made a tremendous comeback and, as of 2007, are no longer considered endangered or threatened.

1. What would be the most appropriate title for this passage?
   (A) National Birds
   (B) Endangered Animals
   (C) All About Birds
   (D) America's National Bird

2. This passage is mostly
   (A) an overview of bald eagles.
   (B) a list of physical traits of bald eagles.
   (C) about how the turkey vulture was nearly America's national bird.
   (D) about how the bald eagle was chosen as the national bird of the United States.

3. The author states that bald eagles
   (A) were never endangered.
   (B) are still critically endangered.
   (C) were nearly driven to extinction because of the effects of humans
   (D) have decreased in population and no longer need any protection.

4. Based on the details given in the passage, bald eagles
   (A) hunt in large groups.
   (B) are scavengers and do not hunt.
   (C) use their keen vision to search for prey.
   (D) have poor eyesight and rely on their hearing to find their prey.

5. According to the facts in the passage, bald eagles
   (A) always return to the same nest each year.
   (B) are solitary and live alone.
   (C) live with their families forever.
   (D) are larger than many other birds in the country.

6. Based on the passage, which of the following is true?
   (A) Bald eagles live longer in the wild.
   (B) Bald eagle parents take care of their young.
   (C) Bald eagle babies are white all over.
   (D) Bald eagles only eat fish.

7. It can be inferred from the passage that bald eagles
   (A) are great hunters.
   (B) are slow flyers.
   (C) have difficulty hunting.
   (D) spend a lot of time sleeping.

8. The author would most likely agree with which of the following statements?
   (A) Bald eagles should be protected by humans.
   (B) Bald eagles are not a very recognizable bird.
   (C) It would not matter of bald eagles went extinct.
   (D) The United States should have a different national bird.

9. As it is used in the passage, the word "<u>immense</u>" most nearly means
   (A) capable.
   (B) huge.
   (C) invisible.
   (D) sharp.

10. As it is used in the passage, the word "<u>subsequent</u>" most nearly means
   (A) later.
   (B) previous.
   (C) first.
   (D) last.

Expository Passage #3

You may have heard of the Great Lakes, a group of five freshwater lakes in the northern United States and southern Canada. However, you may not know that the Great Lakes can be incredibly dangerous. Over the years, rough storms that form on these lakes have caused many terrible accidents, including the especially disastrous shipwreck of the SS *Edmund Fitzgerald* on one of the Greak Lakes, Lake Superior, in 1975.

During the early to mid-20th century, the Great Lakes were commonly used for shipping. Large freighters carried materials from one region to another. The *Fitzgerald* was first launched in 1958. The ship measured 729 feet long and weighed over 13,600 tons, making it the largest ship on the Great Lakes in its time. As an "Iron Boat," the *Fitzgerald* carried iron ore and other metals across the Great Lakes. On the day the *Fitzgerald* sank, it was carrying 26,116 tons of iron ore pellets—enough material to build 7,500 cars.

On November 10, 1975, a dangerous storm raged across Lake Superior. Powerful, high waves crashed over the *Fitzgerald*, damaging the ship, and causing it to fill with water. The storm that sank the *Fitzgerald* has since been categorized as one of the worst storms in Great Lakes history. The captain of the *Fitzgerald* radioed to nearby ships for help, but radio contact was soon lost.

The sinking of the *Fitzgerald* shocked the nation because of the ship's reputation as a well-built and powerful vessel. In fact, it was the largest ship to sail the Great Lakes for many years, even receiving the title "The Queen of the Great Lakes" for its length. At the time of the sinking, the wreck of the *Fitzgerald*, in which all 29 crew members lost their lives was the deadliest disaster on the Great Lakes in over 11 years.

In 1995, divers recovered a 200-pound bell from the wreck of the *Fitzgerald* on an underwater expedition. The bell is now on display at the Great Lakes Shipwreck Museum to honor the crewmembers who lost their lives in the wreck. The wreck of the SS *Edmund Fitzgerald* remains one of the most notable shipwrecks to ever occur on the Great Lakes.

1. What would be the most appropriate title for this passage?
   (A) Famous Shipwrecks
   (B) The Great Lakes
   (C) Lake Superior
   (D) The SS *Edmund Fitzgerald*

2. This passage is mostly about
   (A) Lake Superior.
   (B) shipwrecks on the Great Lakes.
   (C) the families of those who died on a sinking ship.
   (D) the history of a ship and its famous sinking.

3. According to the facts in the passage, the SS *Edmund Fitzgerald*
   (A) was used to carry cars.
   (B) was a passenger boat.
   (C) was used to carry metal.
   (D) was only used for shipping in emergencies.

4. According to the passage, which of the following is true?
   (A) No one knows where the SS *Edmund Fitzgerald* ultimately sank.
   (B) An important item was recovered from the SS *Edmund Fitzgerald.*
   (C) The SS *Edmund Fitzgerald* was made of iron ore pellets.
   (D) Large portions of the ship were recovered and are on display near Lake Superior.

5. Based on the details in the passage, the SS *Edmund Fitzgerald*
   (A) was thought likely to sink.
   (B) was named after the ship's first captain.
   (C) was so large that it was given a special title.
   (D) was named after a famous car designer.

6. The author would most likely agree with which of the following statements?
   (A) Shipwrecks are not interesting.
   (B) The SS *Edmund Fitzgerald* was a small ship.
   (C) The SS *Edmund Fitzgerald* has a fascinating history.
   (D) The sinking of the SS *Edmund Fitzgerald* was to be expected.

7. You would probably find this passage in
   (A) a diary.
   (B) a history magazine.
   (C) a school newspaper.
   (D) a hospital brochure.

8. Which of the following can be inferred from the passage?
   (A) The captain of the SS *Edmund Fitzgerald* knew the ship was in trouble.
   (B) It is dangerous and illegal to sail on any of the Great Lakes.
   (C) The Great Lakes are great for recreational activities.
   (D) Lake Superior is the most dangerous of the Great Lakes.

9. As it is used in the passage, the word "freighters" most nearly means
   (A) crewmembers.
   (B) packages.
   (C) ships.
   (D) tourists.

10. As it is used in the passage, the word "expedition" most nearly means
   (A) duty.
   (B) journey.
   (C) guide.
   (D) traveler.

Expository Passage #4

Though thoughts of venomous animals often conjure images of land creatures like snakes and scorpions, some of the world's most venomous animals actually live in the ocean. One of the most dangerous among them is a group of five fish species known as stonefish. Found in the Indian and Pacific Oceans, stonefish are the most venomous fish in the world. Though they are mostly known for their venom, stonefish also have other unusual characteristics that make them some of the most unique fish in the sea.

Stonefish get their name from their appearance. They have crusty brown or gray skin with bright patches of yellow, red, or orange. Stonefish typically live in shallow waters near rocky or coral reefs, where they burrow into the sand, covering themselves completely. Well-camouflaged to their environment, they blend into the sand to hide from predators and prey alike.

Stonefish have several predators, such as stingrays and large sharks. They are also predators themselves, mainly feeding on shrimp and small fish. Since stonefish are slow swimmers, they hide and ambush their prey. This is where their camouflage comes in handy. Stonefish blend into the sand and wait for prey to swim right up to them. When it attacks, a stonefish swallows its prey in less than a second!

The stonefish has thirteen spines in the fin on its back. Each of these spines contains venom. When a stonefish feels threatened, it sticks its spines in the air as a warning. Stonefish are most dangerous to humans when hidden in the sand in shallow waters. Swimmers may not be aware that a dangerous stonefish lurks in the sand. If a person steps on a stonefish, the fish's spines release poisonous venom, which can cause severe pain, paralysis, and even heart failure. The stonefish poses great danger both to its prey and unsuspecting humans. It is the stonefish's powerful venom and unique camouflaging abilities that make it such a formidable and unique sea creature.

1. What would be the most appropriate title for this passage?
   (A) Animals of the Coral Reefs
   (B) Predators of the Stonefish
   (C) Venomous Sea Creatures
   (D) A Hidden and Dangerous Sea Creature

2. This passage is mostly about
   (A) how stonefish are critically endangered.
   (B) the most venomous animals in the world.
   (C) the traits that make a specific fish unique and dangerous.
   (D) how stonefish live and reproduce.

3. Based on the details of the passage, stonefish are
   (A) not dangerous to humans.
   (B) the most venomous type of fish.
   (C) only venomous when disturbed.
   (D) territorial and aggressive even when not bothered.

4. According to the facts in the passage, stonefish
   (A) hunt mainly creatures like small fish and shrimp.
   (B) are herbivores that mostly eat seaweed and stingrays.
   (C) are scavengers who eat scraps from the ocean floor.
   (D) swim to chase down their prey.

5. According to the passage, which of the following is true?
   (A) There are no natural predators of stonefish.
   (B) Stonefish live in large groups called schools.
   (C) Stonefish have never been studied by scientists.
   (D) Other marine animals hunt stonefish.

6. Which of the following can be inferred from the passage?
   (A) A stonefish sting can be deadly if not treated.
   (B) A stonefish sting is only as bad as a ant sting.
   (C) Stonefish stings are deadly to other fish but not to humans.
   (D) Rinsing with soap and water is adequate to clean a stonefish sting.

7. It can be inferred from the passage that stonefish
   (A) are well adapted to their environment.
   (B) struggle to survive in their environment.
   (C) are likely to become extinct soon.
   (D) are not good hunters since they are not fast and cannot swim.

8. The author would most likely agree with which of the following statements?
   (A) Stonefish are not afraid of humans.
   (B) It is unlikely for a person to be harmed after a stonefish sting.
   (C) Humans should use caution when wading in shallow ocean waters.
   (D) Humans should not worry about encountering a stonefish since they only live in deep waters.

9. As it is used in the passage, the word "<u>burrow</u>" most nearly means
   (A) avoid.
   (B) bury.
   (C) home.
   (D) slide.

10. As it is used in the passage, the word "<u>formidable</u>" most nearly means
   (A) brave.
   (B) honest.
   (C) intimidating.
   (D) trustworthy.

Expository Passage #5

Andy Warhol is an American artist best known for his involvement in the Pop Art movement. Born in Pittsburgh, Pennsylvania on August 6, 1928, Warhol grew up in poverty and had few luxuries during his childhood. His father was a construction worker and his mother was an embroiderer and artist. At age eight, Warhol was diagnosed with Sydenham's chorea, which is a disorder that affects the nervous system. The symptoms of the disorder caused Warhol to be bedbound. While he was confined to bed, Warhol's mother taught him to draw These humble beginning became the starting point for Warhol eventually becoming a prolific artist.

After he graduated from high school, Warhol studied commercial art at the Carnegie Institute of Technology. Following college, Warhol moved to New York to pursue a career as in art. Over the next ten years, Warhol worked successfully as an advertising artist. During this time, he created vivid advertisements for the shoe manufacturer Israel Miller, won prizes for his work, and started to become known for his unique style of design. Despite this early success, he longed to do something different.

In the early 1960s, Warhol's style began to evolve. Warhol came up with the idea of using easily recognized, commercial items in his art. Critics and artists called this style "Pop Art," and it became an influential artistic movement. Warhol also began to use screen printing, which is a way of producing art that allows the artist to reprint the same image several times. One of Warhol's early uses of this technique was on his famous Campbell's Soup cans, where Warhol printed again and again the image of a can of Campbell's Chicken Noodle Soup. Sometimes he repeated the same image, but in different, brighter colors. He also became known for his prints of famous people, like the superstar actress Marilyn Monroe.

Andy Warhol was a unique artist who sought his fame and fortune through art. He achieved this fame and fortune by bringing his art to the masses. Warhol made large quantities of his prints so that they were affordable to everyone. Nowadays, his paintings are an iconic part of American culture, with one piece of his even selling for nearly $200 million in 2022. Warhol's legacy is felt all around the world, but especially in his hometown. The Andy Warhol Museum, located in Pittsburgh, Pennsylvania, is the largest museum in North America dedicated to only one artist. Thousands of people visit the museum each year to appreciate the life and work of Andy Warhol.

1. This passage is mostly about
   (A) the history of Pop Art.
   (B) the Andy Warhol Museum.
   (C) the impact of art on society.
   (D) the life and legacy of a famous artist.

2. What would be the most appropriate title for this passage?
   (A) Art in Pittsburgh
   (B) Impressionist Painters
   (C) Pop Art: The Man Behind the Movement
   (D) The Best Art Colleges in the United States

3. According to the passage, which of the following is true?
   (A) The art of deceased artists is less valuable than that of living artists.
   (B) Warhol often worked at night or in the dark.
   (C) Warhol's signature style was realistic landscape paintings.
   (D) The more a piece of art is made available, the more affordable it will be.

4. The author states that The Andy Warhol Museum
   (A) is in New York City.
   (B) was closed in the early 2000s due to a massive fire.
   (C) is located in the artist's hometown.
   (D) is named after Andy Warhol and displays art made by numerous artists.

5. According to the facts in the passage,
   (A) as a child, Warhol was outgoing and loved to play outside.
   (B) Warhol worked as a professor at Carnegie Melon University.
   (C) Warhol himself launched the Andy Warhol Museum before his death.
   (D) early in his career, Warhol worked successfully in advertising.

6. Which of the following can be inferred from the passage?
   (A) Sydenham's chorea is a life-threatening disease.
   (B) Andy Warhol likely was not interested in art until after his job in advertising.
   (C) Andy Warhol's childhood influenced his future career as an artist.
   (D) Andy Warhol was interested in art primarily to make money.

7. It can be inferred from the passage that
   (A) Andy Warhol had a very successful career.
   (B) Andy Warhol's parents disapproved of his career choice.
   (C) Andy Warhol did not have as much of an impact on the art world as he had hoped.
   (D) Andy Warhol owed his fame to the invention of screen printing.

8. The author would most likely agree with which of the following statements?
   (A) Artists have little impact on culture.
   (B) Artists have similar personalities.
   (C) Anyone has the potential to become an artist.
   (D) Only people from wealthy backgrounds can become artists.

9. As it is used in the passage, the word "<u>prolific</u>" most nearly means
   (A) beautiful.
   (B) catastrophic.
   (C) productive.
   (D) reclusive.

10. As it is used in the passage, the word "<u>pursue</u>" most nearly means
   (A) avoid.
   (B) follow.
   (C) join.
   (D) run.

Expository Passage #6

With almost 5 million people visiting every year, the Grand Canyon is one of the most visited national parks in the United States. Located in northern Arizona, the Grand Canyon is an enormous, mile-deep gorge that runs over half the length of the state. The Grand Canyon was first protected as a nature reserve in 1893 by President Benjamin Harrison and later designated as a national monument in 1908 by President Theodore Roosevelt. Finally, in 1919, the Grand Canyon officially became a national park. At over 270 miles long and with some regions over 18 miles wide, it is one of the largest canyons in the world.

Scientists believe the canyon was formed around five to six million years ago through a process called erosion, in which the Colorado River carved a channel through layers of rock over many years. As a result of this process, the Grand Canyon exposes rock dated as far back as nearly two billion years. Since the canyon cuts so deep, scientists have been able to study the gradual evolution of the earth's crust over time.

The Grand Canyon is massive—bigger than the entire state of Rhode Island! In fact, it is so large that the size of the Grand Canyon can even influence the local weather. The elevation of the canyon ranges from 2,000 to 8,000 feet, which means that different parts of the canyon experience different weather conditions. This isn't the only mystery of the Grand Canyon, though.

Scientists have estimated that there are nearly 1,000 caves hidden in the canyon; only 335 of them have been documented. Even fewer have been mapped or explored. Of these caves, only one is open to tourists. While much of the Grand Canyon has been explored already, much it is still a mystery.

Whether you are interested in seeing the ancient rocks or the spectacular view, a visit to the Grand Canyon is sure to be an experience to remember.

1. This passage is mostly
   (A) a general overview of a famous national park.
   (B) about the best caves to explore in the Grand Canyon.
   (C) an explanation about what formed the Grand Canyon.
   (D) about how to maintain safety when hiking in the Grand Canyon.

2. What would be the most appropriate title for this passage?
   (A) National Parks of America
   (B) America's Grandest Canyon
   (C) Monuments in Arizona
   (D) Wildlife in National Parks

3. According to the passage, which of the following is true?
   (A) The number of visitors to the Grand Canyon each year is increasing.
   (B) The Grand Canyon is the most beautiful of all the national parks.
   (C) It is hard to estimate the number of visitors to the park each year.
   (D) The Grand Canyon attracts a higher number of visitors each year compared to many other national parks.

4. The author states that
   (A) the Colorado River continues to make the Grand Canyon deeper.
   (B) there are many caves in the Grand Canyon that visitors can explore.
   (C) there are many caves in the Grand Canyon, but only one is open to tourists.
   (D) except in winter, the weather in the Grand Canyon is predictable.

5. According to the facts in the passage, the Grand Canyon
   (A) was formed around two billion years ago.
   (B) is the youngest National Park.
   (C) is the oldest National Park.
   (D) was formed five to six million years ago.

6. The author would most likely agree with which of the following statements?
   (A) The Grand Canyon is worth visiting.
   (B) Only local people should visit the Grand Canyon.
   (C) The Grand Canyon is generally not open to visitors.
   (D) The caves are the best feature of the Grand Canyon.

7. It can be inferred from the passage that the
   (A) variety of wildlife that lives in the Grand Canyon is due to the plentiful rain.
   (B) the view from the top of the Grand Canyon is impressive.
   (C) the Grand Canyon is too dangerous to visit due to the variable weather
   (D) the Grand Canyon is shrinking due to wind erosion.

8. You would probably find this passage in
   (A) a diary.
   (B) a school newsletter.
   (C) a sports magazine.
   (D) a brochure for travelers.

9. As it is used in the passage, the word "gradual" most nearly means
   (A) abrupt.
   (B) giant.
   (C) slow.
   (D) final.

10. As it is used in the passage, the word "influence" most nearly means
   (A) convince.
   (B) impact.
   (C) suspend.
   (D) worry.

Expository Passage #7

Many people consider sharks dangerous sea monsters that prey on humans. In movies, they lurk under the surface of the water, waiting for the perfect moment to chomp down on unsuspecting surfers or swimmers. However, movies can be deceiving. Shark attacks on humans are actually quite uncommon. Despite this, humans continue to obsess over the dangerous reputation of sharks.

Sharks have inhabited the planet for at least 450 million years. They've been around so long that they shared the earth with dinosaurs! There are over 500 known species of sharks, with new species being discovered every year. Because there are so many different species, sharks vary in size and appearance. Some of the smallest species, such as the dwarf lantern shark, grow to be only a few inches in length. On the other hand, the whale shark can reach a whopping 39 feet! Still, most shark species are about the size of humans or slightly larger.

Only about 30 species of shark have ever been reported to have attacked any humans. When they do, it is usually a case of mistaken identity. All sharks are carnivores. Small sharks eat plankton and other small animals; large sharks eat fish, sea lions, and seals. Sharks sometimes misconstrue humans with their prey, and that is when attacks happen. Sharks also have an extraordinary sense of smell; they can smell a single drop of blood from around a quarter-mile away. However, just because they smell blood does not mean they will attack. Sharks only hunt when they are hungry. More people die each year from bee stings than shark attacks!

The unpleasant truth is that humans are far deadlier to sharks than sharks are to us. On average, fewer than 20 humans are killed by sharks each year. However, around 100 million sharks are killed by humans each year. This number is much higher than the sharks' recovery rate. This means that sharks are being killed faster than they can reproduce. Humans are putting many shark species at risk of extinction. Though the media portrays sharks as terrifying killing machines, they themselves are the real victims.

1. This passage is mostly about
   (A) shark attacks on humans.
   (B) the discovery of a species of shark.
   (C) movies about sharks.
   (D) debunking a common misconception.

2. What would be the most appropriate title for this passage?
   (A) Ancient Fossils
   (B) Deepwater Sharks
   (C) Great White Sharks
   (D) The Truth About Sharks

3. According to the passage, sharks
   (A) existed around the same time as dinosaurs.
   (B) are at risk of extinction due to pollution.
   (C) first appeared on earth 100 million years ago.
   (D) have a symbiotic relationship with humans.

4. The author states that
   (A) most shark species live in deep water.
   (B) the largest shark species is the Great White Shark.
   (C) shark species vary in appearance but not in size.
   (D) most sharks are approximately the size of a person.

5. According to the facts in the passage, sharks
   (A) only eat once per week.
   (B) only hunt when they are hungry.
   (C) need to eat continuously throughout the day.
   (D) only eat in the warm months and hibernate in the winter.

6. Which of the following can be inferred from the passage?
   (A) If sharks are not protected, they will eventually go extinct.
   (B) Sharks have highly developed eyesight.
   (C) Sharks are endangered because of their many predators.
   (D) You are likely to be involved in a shark attack if you swim in the ocean.

7. It can be inferred from the passage that
   (A) humans have a significant effect on shark populations.
   (B) most shark populations are increasing.
   (C) because they are predators, sharks are not at risk.
   (D) sharks have been on the earth for millions of years and will likely live millions more.

8. The author would most likely agree with which of the following statements?
   (A) Sharks are dangerous and aggressive.
   (B) There is not much difference between shark species.
   (C) Sharks do not deserve the negative reputation they have.
   (D) Scientists should stop studying sharks because doing so endangers them.

9. As it is used in the passage, the word "whopping" most nearly means
   (A) beautiful.
   (B) obvious.
   (C) gracious.
   (D) enormous.

10. As it is used in the passage, the word "misconstrue" most nearly means
    (A) eat.
    (B) confuse.
    (C) hunt.
    (D) decide.

Expository Passage #8

Early humans relied heavily on the natural world for survival. They hunted animals for food and used their skins to keep warm. They harvested wood and stone to build shelter and planted seeds for a balanced diet. In addition to making use of the earth's resources, they also looked to the heavens for help. The sun was useful in providing daylight for them to work and for nourishing their crops, but the night sky was also a guide in many ways. The cycles of the moon helped early humans know when to plant and harvest their crops, as well as to predict the oceans' tides. Early humans also used the stars as navigational tools. Sometimes, when they didn't understand a celestial event, they believed supernatural forces were at play. One of these fascinating occurrences in the sky was the eclipse.

An eclipse happens when one heavenly body obscures the light coming from another by passing in front of it. At times, both the sun or the moon can be eclipsed, appearing almost completely dark. Before science could help us explain how they worked, eclipses were a worrisome event to people on Earth who witnessed them. Today, astronomy helps us understand the movement of planets in our solar system and the reasons for eclipses. But people remain fascinated by them and even plan their lives so they might catch a glimpse of the rare event. Some eclipses, like one that occurred in November 2021, are even rarer.

The November 2021 eclipse occurred during the Beaver Full Moon, a phrase used to describe the full moon visible for three days every November. It is named for the time of year that beavers go into hibernation for the winter. The eclipse was only partial, because the moon was not completely blocked by Earth's shadow. Still, most of it was obscured, with only three percent of the moon left exposed to the direct sunlight. This slice of moon was the rusty color of most full lunar eclipses. What made the event rare was that it was the longest eclipse seen in over five centuries, clocking in at around six hours.

Most of North America was fortunate to get good views of the eclipse. Because it occurred from 1:00 AM to 7:03 AM on the East Coast, many needed to wake up in the middle of the night if they wanted to catch a glimpse of it! Fortunately, most areas of the US, except the Southeast and West Coasts, had clear skies for viewing. If you missed it, don't worry; there will be plenty of opportunities to see more eclipses in your lifetime!

1. This passage is mostly about
   (A) the difference between lunar and solar eclipses.
   (B) a recent common event that occurred in the night sky.
   (C) a fascinating astronomical phenomenon.
   (D) early man's limited understanding of Earth and other planets.

2. This article would most likely be found in
   (A) an encyclopedia.
   (B) a magazine.
   (C) a scientific journal.
   (D) an astronomy textbook.

3. According to the passage, early humans
   (A) Used wood and seeds for their survival.
   (B) Never utilized the stars or the moon.
   (C) Developed complex navigational tools like compasses and maps.
   (D) Drank oil and water.

4. As it is used in the passage, the word "supernatural" most nearly means
   (A) fake.
   (B) gravitational.
   (C) unusual.
   (D) magical.

5. As it is used in the passage, the word "obscures" most nearly means
   (A) conceals.
   (B) extinguishes.
   (C) dims.
   (D) shines.

6. It can be inferred from the passage that eclipses were "worrisome" to early man because
   (A) they disrupted their lives.
   (B) they did not understand the reason for their occurrence.
   (C) they were always followed by disasters.
   (D) their spiritual leaders told them their behavior caused eclipses.

7. According to the passage, how much of the moon was obscured during the November 2021 lunar eclipse?
   (A) 3%
   (B) 3.5%
   (C) 97%
   (D) 100%

8. According to the passage, the November 2021 lunar eclipse was uncommon because of
   (A) its length.
   (B) its rusty color.
   (C) the fact that it was only a partial eclipse.
   (D) the moon's closeness to Earth.

9. It can be inferred from the passage that
   (A) a full moon makes viewing an eclipse difficult.
   (B) an obsolete calendar makes viewing an eclipse difficult.
   (C) a poor night's rest makes viewing an eclipse difficult.
   (D) a cloudy sky makes viewing an eclipse difficult.

10. What would be the most appropriate title for this passage?
   (A) Life on Earth for Primitive Man
   (B) The Heavens: Nature's First GPS
   (C) A Fascinating Celestial Phenomenon
   (D) The Sun, Moon and Stars

Expository Passage #9

The California condor is best known for being the largest flying bird in North America. It is also known for almost going extinct. At one time, the California condor lived all along the western coast of North America, from Canada to Mexico. By the late 1970s, there were only a few dozen California condors living in the wild. By 1987, there were only ten left who weren't in captivity. The remaining birds caught by U.S. Fish & Wildlife Services, who brought back the species through a carefully calculated captive breeding program. Populations grew and California condors were released back into the wild in 1992.

Large black birds with bald heads, California condors are easy to spot in the wild. When they spread their wings, they can have a wingspan of up to ten feet! While flying, these birds can reach speeds of up to 55 miles per hour. California condors live in a variety of habitats, such as savannas, forests, and shrublands. They are scavengers and will travel up to 150 miles in a single day in their search for food. California condors have a poor sense of smell, so they rely on their keen eyesight to find food. As scavengers, they often eat food that would make other animals sick. They've evolved to have super strong immune systems that allow them to eat materials like decaying flesh without becoming ill. Another interesting fact about California condors is that they are one of the few species of birds that do not build nests. They lay their eggs directly on the ground in caves, on rocks, or in large trees.

Although the condor was brought back from the brink of extinction, they are still considered critically endangered. Only about 400 of these birds are alive today, with around 200 living in the wild. Their largest threat is the presence of poisonous substances in their food. Condors are frequently in danger of ingesting poison from hunters' bullets left inside the dead animals that condors eat. Condors are also threatened by poachers—people who illegally hunt endangered wild animals—and habitat loss. These animals also reproduce very slowly. Females only lay one egg every two years! Therefore, their population increase is slow even without outside dangers. While they have made a great recovery over the past few decades, California condors still have a long way to go before their population can be considered stable.

1. What would be the most appropriate title for this passage?
   (A) Protecting Endangered Birds
   (B) The Survival of the California Condor
   (C) Extinct Animals
   (D) Birds of North America

2. This passage is mostly about
   (A) birds that live in California.
   (B) bird species that have gone extinct.
   (C) the history of California condors and facts about their species.
   (D) California condors, the first species of bird to go extinct in North America.

3. According to the facts in the passage,
   (A) the number of California condors left in the wild is unknown.
   (B) there are fewer than 100 California condors left in the wild today.
   (C) at one point, there were only ten California condors living in the wild.
   (D) California condor populations increased without the help of humans.

4. According to the facts in the passage, California condors
   (A) build nests high in trees.
   (B) build nests in caves.
   (C) make nests out of sticks and dried brush.
   (D) do not build nests.

5. Based on the details of the passage, California condors are
   (A) similar in size to bald eagles.
   (B) large bald-headed birds who are primarily black.
   (C) the largest bird in the entire world.
   (D) large birds with gray and white feathers.

6. Which of the following can be inferred from the passage?
   (A) Humans should not interfere with nature.
   (B) The actions of humans have no effect on wild animal species.
   (C) California condors would have survived with or without human help.
   (D) The actions of humans can have both positive and negative impacts on wild animal species.

7. The author would most likely agree with which of the following statements?
   (A) California condors are not unique.
   (B) California condors are a threat to the environment.
   (C) California condors can only live in very specific climates.
   (D) California condors should be protected so their populations can continue to grow.

8. You would most likely find this passage in
   (A) a nature magazine.
   (B) a town newsletter.
   (C) a travel pamphlet.
   (D) a school newsletter.

9. As it is used in the passage, the word "keen" most nearly means
   (A) hungry.
   (B) eager.
   (C) accurate.
   (D) wise.

10. As it is used in the passage, the word "ingesting" most nearly means
   (A) eating.
   (B) finding.
   (C) smelling.
   (D) tempting.

Expository Passage #10

When you think about animals that live in the desert, snakes and lizards may come to mind. However, there are many other diverse species that inhabit deserts around the world. The fennec fox, sometimes called the "desert fox," is a species of fox living in North Africa, where it is hot and arid.

The fennec fox is the world's smallest species of fox. On average, they weigh between two and three pounds and stand eight inches tall. That is smaller than a typical housecat. However, fennec foxes are usually recognized by one distinctive physical feature: their extremely large ears. A fennec fox's ears can be between four and six inches long, which is half the size of the fox's body. These giant ears serve several purposes. They help the fox stay cool in the hot desert and to hear prey from far away. Fennec foxes are even able to hear prey that hides underground. The foxes have sand-colored fur that helps them blend in with their environment. This fur covers the fox's feet to protect them from the hot sand. The fennec fox's fur also helps it stay warm during the night.

Fennec foxes are nocturnal and avoid the daytime heat when possible. During the day, they sleep in burrows they've dug in the sand. Fennec foxes need water to survive but can go long periods without it. This trait makes them suited to living in the desert, where water sources are limited. Fennec foxes are omnivores. Their diet includes plants, rodents, birds, insects, and even small rabbits. Fennec foxes live in pairs or small groups. They mate for life, which means that a male and female pair stay together their entire lives. They typically have a litter of babies, called kits, once each year. The kits stay with their parents for several years, even after new litters are born. Fennec foxes are playful—even the adults! They bark, purr, and leap around while playing. The fennec fox is an example of an animal perfectly suited to its environment. Everything about the fennec fox, from its large ears to its fur, protects the fox and helps it thrive in the desert.

1. This passage is mostly about
   (A) a desert fox.
   (B) desert animals.
   (C) animals that live in Africa.
   (D) animals with unique features.

2. What would be the most appropriate title for this passage?
   (A) Animals of Africa
   (B) All About Foxes
   (C) Nocturnal Animals
   (D) The Tiny Fox of North Africa

3. According to the facts in the passage, fennec foxes' ears
   (A) help them keep their balance.
   (B) are important for attracting mates.
   (C) are large to help with their poor hearing.
   (D) help keep them cool in the desert heat

4. Based on the information in the second paragraph, fennec foxes
   (A) have no major features that differentiate them from other foxes
   (B) have unique physical qualities that protect them from the challenges of being a small animal.
   (C) have unique physical qualities that protect them from the challenges of living in a desert.
   (D) are not adapted to the environment in which they live.

5. According to the passage, which of the following is true?
   (A) Fennec foxes mate for life.
   (B) Fennec foxes kits leave the family after one year.
   (C) Fennec foxes are solitary and do not find mates.
   (D) Only fennec fox young are playful.

6. Which of the following can be inferred from the passage?
   (A) Fennec foxes are solitary.
   (B) Fennec foxes are social.
   (C) Fennec foxes are skittish.
   (D) Fennec foxes hibernate.

7. The author would most likely agree with which of the following statements?
   (A) Fennec foxes are unique.
   (B) Fennec foxes are just like other species of fox.
   (C) Fennec foxes are not well suited to living in the desert.
   (D) Fennec foxes are not as interesting to learn about as other desert animals.

8. It can be inferred from the passage that fennec foxes
   (A) have poor eyesight.
   (B) have a short lifespan.
   (C) prefer to be solitary.
   (D) have excellent hearing.

9. As it is used in the passage, the word "arid" most nearly means
   (A) dry.
   (B) expansive.
   (C) fruitful.
   (D) isolated.

10. As it is used in the passage, the word "distinctive" most nearly means
   (A) ambiguous.
   (B) similar.
   (C) unmistakable.
   (D) vague.

Expository Passage #11

Deep in rural South Dakota lies one of the most recognizable monuments in the United States—Mount Rushmore. Famous for the four enormous faces carved into its side, Mount Rushmore is no ordinary mountain. The faces are those of four former United States presidents: George Washington, Thomas Jefferson, Abraham Lincoln, and Theodore Roosevelt. The sculpture and surrounding area are together known as Mount Rushmore National Memorial.

Mount Rushmore is part of the Black Hills Mountain range. The mountain in which the faces are carved is about 5,725 feet tall, with each face in the sculpture nearly 60 feet in height! The sculpture is at the top of the mountain, making it easy for visitors to see. Visitors can get the best view of the monument from the Grand View Terrace, though there is also a hiking trail and a museum for tourists want to learn more about the history of Mount Rushmore.

The original idea for the sculpture came from a historian named Doane Robinson. Robinson came up with the idea in 1923 as a way to <u>promote</u> tourism in South Dakota. He thought the unique sculpture would <u>draw</u> tourists to the area. In 1924, Robinson convinced a sculptor named Gutzon Borglum to visit the Black Hills and determine if the sculpture was possible. Borglum agreed to do the sculpture, and the design process began. He chose four presidents that symbolized something different from the first 150 years of the United States. Washington represented the founding of the country. Jefferson represented growth. Lincoln represented the preservation of the country after the Civil War. And finally, Roosevelt represented strength. Work on the monument began in 1927. Workers used jackhammers, chisels, drills, and even dynamite to carve the faces. The monument was finally completed in 1941, after 14 years of work, around 450,000 tons of granite removed, and nearly $1 million in construction costs.

The monument has its secrets too. One famous one left by Borglum is the hidden room behind the head of Abraham Lincoln. Called the "Hall of Records," it contains records of the story of the monument and copies of famous American history documents like the Declaration of Independence and United States Constitution. As an iconic symbol of the United States, Mount Rushmore has appeared as a setting in countless books and movies. Upward of three million people visit the Mount Rushmore National memorial each year. It remains one of the most visited monuments in the United States and will likely remain so for years to come.

1. What would be the most appropriate title for this passage?
   (A) American Monuments
   (B) Visiting South Dakota
   (C) Faces on a Mountain
   (D) Famous Sculptors

2. This passage is mostly
   (A) a brief history and overview of a specific national monument.
   (B) an overview of how Borglum developed his skills as a sculptor.
   (C) about how the money was spent during construction of Mount Rushmore.
   (D) about the process of picking which presidents would be represented on Mount Rushmore.

3. According to the facts in the passage, the four presidents on Mount Rushmore
   (A) are not symbolic.
   (B) were chosen by a public vote.
   (C) are meant to represent the first 150 years of the United States.
   (D) were chosen so the design would be symmetrical.

4. According to the facts in the passage, Mount Rushmore is
   (A) found in the Black Hills mountains.
   (B) carved on an unnamed mountain.
   (C) part of the South Dakota mountains.
   (D) located on its own mountain called Dakota Hill.

5. According to the passage, which of the following is true?
   (A) There is a secret passageway in Mount Rushmore between the heads.
   (B) There is a hidden room in Mount Rushmore behind the head of Abraham Lincoln.
   (C) The notion of a hidden room in Mount Rushmore is an urban legend.
   (D) There are several rooms built behind Mount Rushmore but they are not hidden.

6. Which of the following can be inferred from the passage?
   (A) Mount Rushmore is a unique and historically significant landmark.
   (B) Mount Rushmore is not worth visiting.
   (C) Mount Rushmore may not allow visitors in the future.
   (D) Mount Rushmore is the only mountain you can visit in South Dakota.

7. You would probably find this passage in
   (A) a newspaper.
   (B) a college pamphlet.
   (C) a sports magazine.
   (D) a history magazine.

8. It can be inferred from the passage that Mount Rushmore
   (A) was finished very quickly.
   (B) took a long time to complete.
   (C) could have been finished faster if the artist chose a different mountain.
   (D) could have been finished more quickly if different tools were used.

9. As it is used in the passage, the word "promote" most nearly means
   (A) bribe.
   (B) encourage.
   (C) gauge.
   (D) worsen.

10. As it is used in the passage, the word "draw" most nearly means
   (A) attract.
   (B) elude.
   (C) provide.
   (D) sketch.

Expository Passage #12

As a form of therapy that uses the connection between people and horses to encourage healing, equine therapy has been around for hundreds of years. This type of therapy was first used in ancient Greece, where it was called "hippotherapy" after the ancient Greek word for "horse," which was "hippos." Today, the practice is more commonly called therapeutic riding or equine therapy. During equine therapy, patients interact with and ride horses. The purposes of equine therapy vary: altogether, the therapy helps different people reach different goals through work with horses.

Physically, riding a horse is great exercise. Many riders use equine therapy to build their physical strength, as well as their flexibility, coordination, and reflexes. Because riding exercises your heart and lungs, many riders have improved breathing and circulation. A horse's motion as it walks actually moves the rider similar to how humans walk. This is helpful for riders who are working on maintaining their balance while walking. Though everyone has different needs, nearly all riders benefit physically from equine therapy.

Equine therapy also has social and emotional benefits. Forming a bond with a horse can help people with low self-esteem or trouble socializing. This unique connection can give riders a sense of well-being and improve their confidence. In addition to forming friendships with horses, riders often develop friendships with other people in the same program, which improves their social skills. Working with horses requires patience, which can lead to increased patience in other areas of life. Riding horses also gives riders time to be around animals and nature, which reduces stress, anxiety, and depression, in addition to teaching riders to respect animals. In conclusion, equine therapy offers a variety of benefits for a variety of people, all of them changed through their work with horses.

1. This passage is mostly about
   (A) therapy for horses.
   (B) a unique form of therapy for people.
   (C) different forms of therapy.
   (D) how physical therapy benefits the mind.

2. What would be the most appropriate title for this passage?
   (A) Horses 101
   (B) Alternative Therapies
   (C) Healing with Horses
   (D) How to Become an Equestrian

3. According to the facts in the passage,
   (A) equine therapy has extremely limited use.
   (B) equine therapy is only for children.
   (C) both the physical and emotional aspects of equine therapy benefit patients.
   (D) during equine therapy, patients interact with horses but do not ride them.

4. The author states that riding horses is
   (A) only physically rewarding to the elderly.
   (B) good physical exercise.
   (C) too strenuous for children.
   (D) too much strain on horses but easy for the rider.

5. According to the passage, which of the following is true?
   (A) Being in nature increases stress, anxiety, and depression in most people.
   (B) Being around animals and nature presents more challenges than it fixes.
   (C) It is unknown if being around horses has any benefit different from being around other animals.
   (D) Being around animals and nature has been shown to reduce stress, anxiety, and depression.

6. Which of the following can be inferred from the passage?
   (A) People of any age can benefit from equine therapy.
   (B) Children see the best benefits of equine therapy.
   (C) Equine therapy is too difficult for the elderly.
   (D) Adults can participate in equine therapy without the help of a professional.

7. You would probably find this passage in
   (A) a diary.
   (B) a medical journal.
   (C) a school newsletter.
   (D) a style magazine.

8. It can be inferred from the passage that
   (A) the connection between humans and animals is special.
   (B) horses rely on humans for support.
   (C) animals can form connections with other animals, but not with people.
   (D) little is known about the benefits of equine therapy for humans.

9. As it is used in the passage, the word "<u>vary</u>" most nearly means
   (A) align.
   (B) differ.
   (C) motivate.
   (D) stay.

10. As it is used in the passage, the word "<u>bond</u>" most nearly means
    (A) balance.
    (B) equality.
    (C) relationship.
    (D) silence.

Narrative

Narrative Passage #1

"You start in the attic. I'll take the basement," Ben's mom said as she walked down the hallway of Ben's grandfather's house. "Remember, if you're unsure about what to keep or toss, just make two piles. I'll help you sort it out later."

Ben groaned as he trudged up the stairs. Opening the attic door, he was hit with a musty smell. He started to sneeze from the dust that covered everything.

"What a load of junk!" Ben thought. He wondered where to begin.

He decided to start by the window for fresh air and better light. He opened a dilapidated box on the floor that held dozens of vinyl records. He didn't recognize most of the artists—too old-school for him—but he knew some of the rock bands. "These have to be mom's," Ben thought. "No way grandpa listens to Pink Floyd."

He opened other boxes and started to make piles of their contents. So far, most of it looked worthless: trinkets, knickknacks, other old-person junk. He kept thinking about the records. Why was his mom keeping them here? Then Ben happened upon a box of photos. His curiosity took hold. Some seemed to be of his mom as a kid—dressed up for the holidays, taking a bath, being held by family members. By the time he got to the bottom of the box, the photos became more interesting—a tanned and muscular young man in a boxing ring; the same man, slightly older, with long hair, rocking a guitar and sweating under hot stage lights; then the man, now mustached, dressed in hiking gear, standing atop a huge boulder, with nothing but sky behind him.

"Could these be grandpa?" Ben thought of his grandfather as he knew him: quiet, frail, and definitely nothing like the guy in the pictures.

"How's it going?" Ben's mom appeared behind him.

"Well, I haven't gotten much done. I found this box of pictures, and I'm trying to figure out who this is."

Ben's mom shuffled through a couple of the photos. "That's your grandfather! Don't you recognize him?"

"Not really," Ben confessed.

His mom laughed. "Yeah, I guess you wouldn't! These were taken ages ago."

"So, wait," Ben said, "you're telling me that Grandpa used to box, play in a band, *and* scale mountains?"

"And more! He's lived a busy life. He started boxing when he was in the army, and he was tough to beat! And he loved rock music—that's his guitar over there." She pointed to an instrument leaning in a far corner of the attic. Ben must have missed it while cleaning. "He played bass. When I was little, your grandmother would take me to watch him play."

"How come Grandpa never mentioned this stuff?"

"You can ask him yourself when we get to the nursing home later!"

"I definitely will!" Ben grabbed the photos. Suddenly, he had a lot of questions for his once "boring" grandfather.

1. This story is mostly about
   (A) a mother and son's collaborative effort to help an elderly family member.
   (B) the problems that arise when families keep secrets from one another.
   (C) a boy's discovery of a family member's interesting past.
   (D) the challenges associated with moving to a new home.

2. As it is used in the story, the word "trudged" most nearly means
   (A) hurried.
   (B) plodded.
   (C) raced.
   (D) sped.

3. Which of the following can be inferred from the story?
   (A) Ben and his mom will be moving into the house.
   (B) Ben and his grandfather are very close.
   (C) Ben's mother used to be in a rock band.
   (D) No one had been in the attic for a long time.

4. As it is used in the story, the word "dilapidated" most nearly means
   (A) discarded.
   (B) forgotten.
   (C) heavy.
   (D) worn.

5. The bottom of the box of photos was likely "more interesting" to Ben because
   (A) Ben liked looking at old photos.
   (B) the photos at the bottom painted a different picture of his grandfather than Ben had in his mind.
   (C) Ben felt the photos had some monetary value and that he could make money from selling them.
   (D) playing in a rock band had always been one of Ben's dreams.

6. In the final paragraph, the narrator most likely puts "boring" in quotation marks to
   (A) show the contrast between Ben's initial and current view of his grandfather.
   (B) emphasize how uninterested Ben is in his grandfather's past.
   (C) reinforce Ben's initial opinion about his grandfather.
   (D) reveal Ben's reluctance about helping his mom with a chore.

7. By the end of the story, Ben would most likely agree with which of the following statements?
   (A) You can't teach an old dog new tricks.
   (B) Out of sight, out of mind.
   (C) Youth is wasted on the young.
   (D) You can't judge a book by its cover.

8. According to the story, Ben was surprised to learn all the following about his grandfather EXCEPT that
   (A) he had been a good boxer.
   (B) he used to go hiking.
   (C) he had served in the army.
   (D) he liked rock music.

C

9. The change in Ben's attitude toward the contents of his grandfather's attic can most appropriately be described as from
   (A) bored to fascinated.
   (B) nervous to excited.
   (C) skeptical to convinced.
   (D) tolerant to apathetic.

10. What would be the most appropriate title for this story?
    (A) Antiques for Sale
    (B) Ben's Bad Day
    (C) Grandpa's House
    (D) Surprises in the Attic

Narrative Passage #2

As he strutted down the hall wearing his brand-new Air Jordans, Ryan noticed the stares from his peers. He felt like a million bucks. Not only was he wearing the hottest sneakers, but he was also among the very small number of people who were even able to get their hands on a pair. He knew that the virtual lines for buying them online were really long, so he coded a bot that took up his space in line and bought multiple pairs for him so he wouldn't have to waste time waiting. He wanted to sell the extra pairs in his Sneaker Club's upcoming shoe auction so the other kids could get a chance to buy a pair of the sought-after sneaks for less than the retail cost. For now, though, he was enjoying showing off his unique flair.

As Ryan rummaged through his locker, he heard two students whispering near him. He could just barely understand what they were saying, and it sent his confidence spiraling to the ground.

"What kind of guy shows off his expensive sneakers at a time like this?" said the first student. "Some kids here lost their homes."

"I know!" said the other. "That hurricane did so much damage. So many people don't have their basic needs met, but he's still walking around flashing his privilege! How unthoughtful."

Ryan cleared his throat. The other students turned to find him standing there. All three were embarrassed.

"Um... Sorry. We didn't know you were there," stammered the first student.

The other one just shrugged his shoulders. By the time Ryan came back down to earth, they'd closed their lockers and walked away. Ryan felt like a fool. He couldn't believe he didn't think of how others would feel, watching him strut around like a peacock. He knew what he had to do. He went straight to Mr. Khan's room.

"Help me make this right," Ryan said, pointing to his feet.

Mr. Khan looked at Ryan quizzically.

"I feel like a jerk!" Ryan said. "I look so selfish and materialistic! I just wanted to help people, not hoard sneakers!"

With Mr. Khan's help, Ryan got students to donate their used sneakers. The Sneaker Club used its excess funds to buy up more sneakers online and hold several auctions; Ryan even donated his Jordans! The auctions, always very popular with both students and teachers, became even more so when word got out that all money collected would be donated to local charities who were helping families impacted by the hurricane.

This was the start of a tradition for the Sneaker Club. And just like that, Ryan felt like a million bucks again.

1. This story is mostly about
   (A) a change in focus for one boy and his extracurricular club.
   (B) a natural disaster that negatively impacted a small community.
   (C) the benefits of learning computer programming.
   (D) the immense popularity of a certain sneaker

2. According to the story, Ryan "felt like a million bucks" for all the following reasons EXCEPT that he
   (A) outsmarted the online purchasing process to get his new sneakers.
   (B) felt admired by his peers.
   (C) was wearing something that few other students could acquire for themselves.
   (D) came from a very wealthy family.

3. Based on the story, it can be inferred that Ryan was being stared at by his peers because
   (A) he was well liked.
   (B) they were shocked by his lack of awareness concerning the suffering of others.
   (C) he was a new student and everyone was curious about him.
   (D) they admired his new sneakers

4. As it is used in the story, the word "privilege" most nearly means
   (A) advantages.
   (B) clothing.
   (C) insensitivity.
   (D) wealth.

A

5. Based on the information in the story, it can be inferred that Mr. Khan
   (A) thinks Ryan should be punished for his thoughtlessness.
   (B) lost his home in the hurricane.
   (C) cares about and wants to help Ryan.
   (D) helped Ryan program his computer bot.

6. Which of the following can be assumed was the reason Ryan felt like a "fool" after his conversation with the other students?
   (A) His sneakers were no longer as rare as when he bought them.
   (B) He had been tricked into paying too much money for his sneakers.
   (C) His friends had betrayed him by talking behind his back.
   (D) He realized his peers did not perceive him the way he thought they did.

7. According to the story, Ryan wants to make "right"
   (A) his buying more sneakers than he needed.
   (B) his misunderstood focus on material items.
   (C) his lack of prior leadership in the Sneaker Club.
   (D) his faked concern with helping others.

8. As it is used in the story, the word "quizzically" most nearly means
   (A) inquiringly.
   (B) madly.
   (C) patiently.
   (D) testily.

9. The change in how Ryan feels like "a million bucks" at the start of the story versus the end can best be described as from
   (A) vain to insecure.
   (B) unaware to intelligent.
   (C) proud to fulfilled.
   (D) thoughtful to oblivious.

C

10. What would be the most appropriate title for this story?
   (A) The Bot Conspiracy
   (B) Sneakers for Good
   (C) Sneaker Club Drama
   (D) The Calm Before the Storm

Narrative Passage #3

Leyla threw her backpack on the floor and plopped onto the sofa, planting her feet on the coffee table. Her mom could tell from the look on her face—Leyla'd had a bad day.

"Okay, what happened?"

"My life is ruined!" Leyla said. "I'm going to fail theater, and I won't go to college, and I'll have to live with you and Dad for the rest of my life, and—"

"Why don't we take it one step at a time? What happened?"

Leyla hated it when her mom was rational; it made it so much harder to pout and complain.

"My group for the play stinks! Everyone has different ideas about everything. We can't even agree on a story! It's a disaster! I'm just going to write the play myself and forget about everyone else and their stupid ideas."

Leyla's mom didn't speak. She sat with her arms crossed and head tilted. She looked disappointed.

"Ugh! Okay! I can't stand it when you look like that! I'll talk to my group and try to figure it out," Leyla said. Obviously, her mom knew how to get to her.

Leyla's mom smiled. She knew her daughter would figure it out.. "What would you like for a snack?"

"Like I have time for that! I have to call my *lovely* group mates and figure this out!" Leyla rolled her eyes and walked to her room.

A week later, Leyla bounced into the house and threw her backpack on the floor again, Only this time, grinning widely and dancing around the kitchen.

Leyla's mom wryly smiled. "So, I'm guessing the play turned out alright?"

"Once I thought about it, I realized we were approaching it all wrong. We each have different strengths, but instead of focusing on them, we were all trying to do everything individually, from the writing to the acting to the directing. Too many of us wanted too much control! So we made a list of everyone's talents and divided the responsibilities from there, and it's working way better! Our teacher loves our ideas! I can't wait for you and Dad to see what we've done!"

"I'm glad it's turning out so well! Aren't you proud of yourself for not giving up?"

Leyla nodded. "Yeah, whatever." But she couldn't hide her delighted smile. Her life wasn't ruined like she'd thought it was—far from it.

1. This story is mostly about
   (A) an impossible group project.
   (B) one student's failed attempt to be a leader.
   (C) a family disagreement.
   (D) the power of cooperation.

2. As it is used in the story, the word "rational" most nearly means
   (A) curious.
   (B) impatient.
   (C) sensible.
   (D) understanding.

3. Leyla can be best described as
   (A) proud and insensitive.
   (B) careless and lazy.
   (C) passionate and ambitious.
   (D) diligent and shy.

4. According to Leyla, the group project is not coming together because
   (A) she is having to do all the work.
   (B) no one is willing to give up control of any task.
   (C) the other group members are not as smart as her.
   (D) the assignment is testing them on concepts they have not yet been taught.

5. How does Leyla feel about her classmates when she uses the word "*lovely*" to describe them?
   (A) empathetic
   (B) annoyed
   (C) affectionate
   (D) neutral

6. The difference between Leyla's arrival home in the beginning of the story versus the end can be described as from
   (A) frustrated then elated.
   (B) disgruntled then calmed.
   (C) doubtful then content.
   (D) outraged then disappointed.

7. As it is used in the story, the word "wryly" most nearly means
   (A) amusedly.
   (B) menacingly.
   (C) sarcastically.
   (D) weakly.

8. According to the story, the solution to the group's problem was to
   (A) divide up the work according to everyone's talents.
   (B) have everyone do a little of everything.
   (C) let Leyla finish the project on her own.
   (D) ask the teacher to assign new groups.

9. Based on the information in the story, it can be inferred that Leyla's mom
   (A) feels indifferent to the suffering of her daughter.
   (B) has a close relationship with her daughter.
   (C) prefers to solve her daughter's problems for her.
   (D) got Leyla's teacher to cancel the project.

10. What would be the most appropriate for this story?
   (A) No Time for a Snack!
   (B) Teacher's Pet
   (C) A Group Effort
   (D) All the World's a Stage

Narrative Passage #4

Maritza settled into her spot by the front window in the warm, filtered light of the afternoon. She pulled her sketchbook out of her bag and began drawing broad strokes across a clean page, first in black and white, then in color. She sketched with no plan in mind. Drawing helped her process her emotions. An image would develop without her even realizing it. The final product wasn't as important to Maritza as getting her feelings out onto the page. She needed that today.

With each stroke of her pencil, Maritza shaved down her feelings of loneliness, awkwardness, and embarrassment. She thought back to her first day at Komack High. She had been nervous, but things had turned out okay. Everyone seemed nice enough, she'd made it through her classes, and she sat with some classmates at lunch. The girls were friendly and curious, asking her about life in Germany. She had been a novelty.

But the novelty had since worn off. Now Maritza was just the odd foreign exchange student—her clothing, her hair and her accent were all just different enough to keep her from being part of a group. Now, Maritza continued to draw and, for the moment, some of her negative feelings left her.

Soon the custodian came in and made her leave. Maritza hurriedly scooped up her belongings and left for home.

The next morning, while getting her books from her locker, Maritza noticed Jasmine and Ethan striding toward her. Jasmine waved a piece of paper in the air.

"This is you, right?" Jasmine asked as the pair approached Maritza's locker.

Maritza nervously stammered. "Wh-what?"

"You did this, right?" Jasmine demanded. "Yes or no?"

Maritza recognized the sketch she had drawn the afternoon before. "Um…uh…yes. Yes, it's mine."

Maritza reached for the paper. Jasmine yanked it out of her grasp.

"Nope," Jasmine said. "You have to help us. Please! We're desperate!"

Ethan could sense that Maritza was feeling daunted. "Hey, it's okay. We really loved your sketch. You have nice coloring and shading. A cool modernist vibe. We wanted to ask you to help us create some art to liven up the gym for next week's dance. If you want."

Jasmine flashed a bright smile and linked her arm in Maritza's. "Of course she does! C'mon, we don't have time to waste!"

Maritza had found her group, or rather her group had found her. That day she officially became Lead Artist for the junior class Events Committee.

1. This story is mostly about
   (A) the difficulties of living in a foreign country.
   (B) a dispute between rival students.
   (C) the importance of belonging to a group.
   (D) the challenges of being an artist.

2. According to the story, all of the following are true about Maritza's drawing EXCEPT
   (A) she doesn't always know what she is drawing.
   (B) it's a new hobby for her.
   (C) it helps her feel better.
   (D) the image isn't as important as the process.

3. It can be inferred from the story that Maritza's "loneliness, awkwardness and embarrassment" are the result of her
   (A) excessive shyness.
   (B) being bullied by her peers.
   (C) refusal to try activities outside of her comfort zone.
   (D) not fitting in with the other students at school.

4. As it is used in the story, the word "<u>novelty</u>" most nearly means
   (A) stranger.
   (B) souvenir.
   (C) curiosity.
   (D) oddball.

5. Based on the details of the story, Martiza
   (A) was from Germany.
   (B) was preparing to move to Germany.
   (C) went to the same school her entire life.
   (D) has always felt at home in her new school.

6. According to Ethan, Martiza's art is all of the following EXCEPT
   (A) a style that he and Jasmine were attracted to.
   (B) going to be permanently on display in the gym.
   (C) a potential solution for a problem with the dance.
   (D) reflective of great talent and skill.

7. Jasmine most likely links her arm through Maritza's because she
   (A) wants to be Maritza's new best friend.
   (B) wants to make Ethan jealous.
   (C) feels bad for having ignored Maritza since her arrival at Komak High.
   (D) doesn't want to give Maritza a chance to turn down their request for help.

8. As it is used in the story, the word "<u>daunted</u>" most nearly means
   (A) dumbfounded.
   (B) intimidated.
   (C) depressed.
   (D) angry.

9. Based on the details in the passage, the story takes place
   (A) at Maritza's home.
   (B) in a gym.
   (C) at school.
   (D) in a lunch room.

10. What would be the most appropriate for this story?
   (A) The New Art Director
   (B) A Cool Modernist Vibe
   (C) The Foreign Exchange Student
   (D) Drawing for Dollars

Narrative Passage #5

As Seth entered the kitchen after school, there was no snack waiting for him on the counter. His mom wasn't smiling or asking him about his day, but leaning against the sink, her arms crossed over her chest. She frowned. Something was up.

"Um… Hi Mom," Seth said uneasily.

"Don't "hi" me," his mom replied testily. "Your guidance counselor emailed me about your grades."

Oh no.

"A C in History and a D in English? Several missing assignments? You *said* you had your classes under control!"

"I did, I swear, but—"

"You promised me you'd bring your grades up. You *said* you didn't need any help. Well now we know that you do. You're getting a tutor, mister."

Seth began to protest. "No way, Mom, I—"

"It's settled. I still have the contact information for the tutor I found last time we had this conversation. She's coming here tomorrow after school."

Seth knew there was no point protesting, but inside he was fuming. He didn't want to work with a stupid tutor. Why did his mom always have to butt in?

Sure enough, when he got home the next day, Seth heard chatting coming from the kitchen. His mom and the tutor were engaged in an animated conversation, sharing their war stories about the trials of raising teenagers. Seth groaned.

"There he is!" his mom said in the super friendly voice she used with strangers. "Nora, this is Seth. I have cleared the kitchen table for you to work together." Seth smiled weakly as Nora gestured for him to take a seat.

As soon as Nora left the house an hour later, Seth's mom began her questioning. "So, how was it?"

Seth looked sheepish. "I guess it was fine," he admitted. "She helped me make a plan for getting my missing assignments done, and she's going to help me figure out how to my research project. I didn't even know where to start."

His mom's shoulders dropped in relief. He hadn't realized it, but she'd been stressed about getting him help since she first saw his grades slipping a few months back. "Seth, why didn't you ask for assistance? From your teachers? From me? We all want you to succeed, you know."

"I know," he said. "Thank you, Mom. I really think I can do this now. With your help." She gave him a hug, and suddenly, all the promises he'd made about his grades and his homework seemed possible.

1. This story is mostly about
   (A) the importance of asking for help when you need it.
   (B) the consequences of irresponsibility.
   (C) the challenges of being a teenager.
   (D) an argument between a mother and son.

2. It can be inferred that Seth greets his mom "uneasily" because
   (A) he is worried that something bad has happened to his mom.
   (B) he knows he has been caught in a lie.
   (C) her behavior indicates something is wrong.
   (D) they still haven't made up after their previous arguments.

3. As it is used in the story, the word "testily" most nearly means
   (A) angrily.
   (B) cruelly.
   (C) meanly.
   (D) uncertainly.

4. It can be inferred from the story that
   (A) Seth has always been a good student.
   (B) Seth's mother is apathetic about his academic performance.
   (C) Seth frequently lies to his mother.
   (D) Seth's grades have been suffering for some time.

5. Based on the details in the story, which of the following is true?
   (A) Seth didn't realize his grades were so low.
   (B) Seth wanted a different tutor instead of Nora.
   (C) Seth and his mother previously discussed his poor academic performance.
   (D) Seth was already making strong academic progress before his mom decided to help him.

6. As it is used in the story, the word "fuming" most nearly means
   (A) complaining.
   (B) dismissing.
   (C) ignoring.
   (D) raging.

7. It can be inferred from the conversation between Seth's mom and the tutor that
   (A) the tutor has a teenager of her own.
   (B) Seth's mom and the tutor are longtime friends.
   (C) Seth is the first student the tutor will be working with.
   (D) the tutor is a former teacher of Seth's.

8. Based on the details in the story, Seth
   (A) struggled in math but excelled in English.
   (B) asked his teachers for assistance before his mom hired the tutor.
   (C) was reluctant to ask for academic help from anyone.
   (D) had a fleet of tutors for every subject.

9. The change in Seth's attitude toward working with a tutor can best be described as from
   (A) fearful to excited.
   (B) resistant to grateful.
   (C) hopeful to disappointed.
   (D) opposed to ambivalent.

10. What would be the most appropriate title for this story?
    (A) Lesson Learned—Just Ask!
    (B) The History Class Incident
    (C) Mom to the Rescue
    (D) The World's Best Tutor

Persuasive

Persuasive Passage #1

While trees are admired for their beauty, they serve a much greater purpose than just enhancing the landscape. Whether to the environment, animals, or humans, trees have a number of unique positive effects on the world around them. Planting a tree is one of the most beneficial ways you can support your local environment.

Like all plants, trees perform a process called photosynthesis. Through this process, trees absorb water and carbon dioxide to produce oxygen for humans and other animals to breathe. By absorbing carbon dioxide from the air, trees reduce the harmful effects caused by too much carbon. Trees also absorb odors and dangerous pollutants in the air. Scientists estimate that a single tree has the ability to absorb about 48 pounds of polluted air and release 260 pounds of oxygen each year. Finding ways to prevent air pollution is a major part of fighting climate change, and planting trees is a great way to help.

Providing clean air is not the only thing trees do for the environment. Trees support their ecosystems by providing shelter and food for animals. Birds, squirrels, and other animals make their homes in trees. Many trees produce nuts and fruits that some animals depend on for food. If you want to help support wildlife near you, you can always hang a bird house or feeder from a tree to encourage more little critters to visit!

Though humans may not make their homes in trees, we benefit from their continued presence as well. Studies have shown that being around trees can have a positive impact on a person's mental and physical health. Particularly in urban areas, having a view of trees has been shown to reduce stress, anxiety, and even crime rates. This is why trees are often planted in the middle of cities. You don't need an entire forest near you to benefit from the healing properties of trees. Even hospitals can use small tree gardens to help keep patients' spirits high during the healing process!

Planting a tree is one of the easiest things you can do to have a positive impact on the world around you. All you need is a shovel, sapling, and a place to plant. Trees are an amazing natural gift; they protect the environment, support animals, and even help make our day-to-day lives better. Trees can live for centuries—once you plant one, you give a gift that future generations will benefit from for years to come.

1. This passage is mostly about
   (A) how trees are being rapidly cut down.
   (B) different species of trees and their different effects on the world around them.
   (C) the types of animals that live in trees.
   (D) why planting trees is a good thing to do.

2. What would be the most appropriate title for this passage?
   (A) Climate Change
   (B) The Harm of Deforestation
   (C) The Gift of a Sapling
   (D) Tree Species of North America

C

3. According to the passage, which of the following is true?
   (A) Trees are in danger of extinction.
   (B) Trees aren't the only living thing to perform photosynthesis.
   (C) Trees are beautiful to look at but do not benefit humans in any way.
   (D) Trees are difficult to plant because of their large size.

4. According to the facts in the passage,
   (A) trees have trouble surviving in urban areas.
   (B) only certain species of trees are helpful to the environment.
   (C) trees help the environment but have no effect on humans.
   (D) trees can positively affect both mental and physical health.

5. Based on the information in the passage, planting a tree
   (A) is a relatively easy way for one to help support their local environment.
   (B) is illegal in some areas.
   (C) should only be done on farms and near other trees.
   (D) is a difficult task best left to professionals.

6. You would most likely find this passage in
   (A) a diary.
   (B) a historical magazine.
   (C) a newspaper ad.
   (D) an environmental newsletter.

7. Which of the following does the author use to advance their argument?
   (A) Personal stories.
   (B) Scientific information.
   (C) Fairy tales.
   (D) Historical details.

8. The author would most likely agree with which of the following statements?
   (A) Protecting the environment is a good thing.
   (B) We should build more bird houses.
   (C) We shouldn't care so much about planting trees.
   (D) Air pollution has no effect on the environment.

9. As it is used in the passage, the word "estimate" most nearly means
   (A) assume.
   (B) believe.
   (C) guess.
   (D) hope.

C

10. As it is used in the passage, the word "impact" most nearly means
   (A) collision.
   (B) importance.
   (C) influence.
   (D) push.

Persuasive Passage #2

Decades ago, if you wanted a new book to read, you went to your local bookstore or library. In today's world, there are many more options. Large bookstore chains like Barnes & Noble are still the main way many people buy books. Stores like Walmart and Target, as well as shopping websites such as Amazon.com, have played a huge role in changing how and where readers buy books. Many people have given up paper books altogether, opting instead for digital copies on e-readers. These changes to the way readers buy and read their books have a profound impact on local independent bookstores.

Independent bookstores are usually modest and often owned by individuals or small groups. They exist all over the world, from small towns to big cities. Unfortunately, many of these small bookstores are struggling to stay in business. In 2020, around 20% of independent bookstores in the United States were at risk of closing. Small bookstores often cannot compete with the low prices and convenience offered by online booksellers like Amazon.com, which allow buyers to shop from their own homes. Since many customers choose to shop online, small bookstores are losing sales.

The effects of independent bookstore closures are felt in several ways. If the stores close, the employees who work there will lose their jobs. The local economy will suffer from the loss of a business. New authors may even have difficulty finding readers.

When you shop at an independent bookstore, you support your community. As it eliminates the shipping process, which can often be bad for the environment, shopping local is also an environmentally friendly choice. This is because it eliminates the shipping process of ordering a book online. An independent bookstore also often has more of a unique flair than large box stores like Barnes & Noble or Walmart. You are more likely to discover new authors or rare books in an independent bookstore. You might even find antique first editions in the used section. The experience of shopping at a small, local store is invaluable. If independent bookstores close, that experience may become a memory of the past. Although is the convenience of ordering a book online is tempting, the only way to save independent bookstores is by supporting them.

1. This passage is mostly about
   (A) shopping on Amazon.com.
   (B) supporting independent bookstores.
   (C) the pros and cons of paper books versus e-readers.
   (D) making environmentally friendly shopping choices.

2. What would be the most appropriate title for this passage?
   (A) Buy More Books!
   (B) Why Reading is Good for You
   (C) The Case for Shopping at Independent Bookstores
   (D) How to Get the Best Deals at Bookstores

3. According to the passage, which of the following is true?
   (A) Authors are unaffected by independent bookstores closing.
   (B) Established authors will benefit from independent bookstores closing.
   (C) Online platforms are the best ways for new authors to sell their books.
   (D) The closing of independent bookstores could make it difficult for new authors to succeed.

4. The author states that
   (A) independent bookstores do not affect the local economy.
   (B) small bookstores are not as important as other types of businesses.
   (C) shopping at local bookstores is not environmentally friendly.
   (D) shopping at an independent bookstore helps your community.

5. According to the facts in the passage,
   (A) new authors do not put their books in independent bookstores.
   (B) independent bookstores are more likely to carry new authors.
   (C) independent bookstores are less likely to carry new authors.
   (D) shopping online or in a small bookstore has no effect on what kind of books you discover.

6. Which of the following can be inferred from the passage?
   (A) Many people value low prices and convenience.
   (B) Shopping is inconvenient no matter how you do it.
   (C) Convenience is not an important factor to most people who shop.
   (D) People do not care one way or another about the price of items they buy.

7. It can be inferred from the passage that large companies
   (A) hurt small businesses.
   (B) help small businesses.
   (C) have no effect on small businesses.
   (D) attract different groups of shoppers than small businesses.

8. The author would most likely agree with which of the following statements?
   (A) Digital books are better than paper books.
   (B) It is better to buy new books than used books.
   (C) People who love books should support independent bookstores.
   (D) The popularity of online shopping does not affect small stores.

9. As it is used in the passage, the word "modest" most nearly means
   (A) desperate.
   (B) current.
   (C) bashful.
   (D) small.

10. As it is used in the passage, the word "invaluable" most nearly means
   (A) appropriate.
   (B) extensive.
   (C) irreplaceable.
   (D) unimportant.

Persuasive Passage #3

Since it began in Italy around the year 1500, ballet has developed a reputation as an extremely elegant and complex style of dance. The name "ballet" comes from the Italian word "ballare," which means "to dance." After beginning in Italy, the form developed in France and Russia, where the style of dance became notorious for the great technical skill and grace it required of its dancers. Even for non-dancers, though, ballet is a rewarding physical activity with numerous benefits, both physical and personal.

The most widely-spoken benefits of practicing ballet are usually physical; although the dance may look delicate, it is very physically demanding and requires great athleticism. Ballet is a fantastic cardio exercise, meaning it works out the heart in addition to the muscles. Ballet also builds strength—continued training in the dance often produces the same results as training with light weights. Ballet dancers develop their endurance as well. Endurance training makes every day activities (like jogging up a flight of stairs) easier, allowing their bodies to be active for longer without getting tired. Ballet dancers are also more flexible and have better posture than the average person.

While there are many physical benefits of ballet, there are a number of mental and emotional benefits as well. By helping dancers understand their bodies better, ballet helps many people develop their confidence. Ballet also requires a great deal of focus—because of the complexity of the form, dancers must always concentrate on what they are doing. Though developing this type of concentration can take a lot of practice, dancing ballet can increase the dancer's ability to focus in many other areas of their life. Taking ballet lessons introduces a dancer to a group of people who all enjoy the same art form. Ballet, like any art form, has a diverse and wide-ranging community, with plenty of friends to be made.

Overall, ballet offers a number of benefits for dancers and non-dancers alike. While dancers may focus on developing their skill, non-dancers may feel a new sense of accomplishment at trying something new, in addition to the wide range of other benefits ballet offers. Anyone looking to improve themselves physically or personally can find something beneficial in ballet!

1. What would be the most appropriate title for this passage?
   (A) How to Become a Ballerina
   (B) Benefits of Ballet
   (C) Ballet Dancing in Italy
   (D) The Most Popular Forms of Dance

2. This passage is mostly about
   (A) the pros and cons of trying a new activity.
   (B) why ballroom dancing is slowly declining in popularity.
   (C) why ballet should only be practiced by professionals.
   (D) how taking up a specific form of dance might benefit someone.

3. According to the passage, which of the following is true?
   (A) Ballet is poor exercise.
   (B) Ballet weakens a dancer's posture.
   (C) Ballet is a good exercise for cardio and strength.
   (D) Ballet exercises a dancer's heart, but does not build strength.

4. According to the facts in the passage,
   (A) the primary physical goal of ballet is to lose weight.
   (B) professional ballet dancers are only from France and Russia.
   (C) practicing ballet involves running up a lot of stairs.
   (D) ballet is a great way to strengthen one's ability to focus.

5. The author states that
   (A) starting ballet is difficult.
   (B) ballet is a great way to make friends.
   (C) ballet is only beneficial if you start it as a child.
   (D) the ballet community is small and restricting.

6. Which of the following can be inferred from the passage?
   (A) Ballet is a popular form of dance.
   (B) Ballet dancing has declined in popularity since the 1500s.
   (C) Ballet dancers make terrific basketball players.
   (D) Ballet dancers speak Italian.

7. It can be inferred from the passage that ballet is
   (A) too difficult for anyone that isn't a professional dancer to try.
   (B) often challenging but rewarding.
   (C) better exercise than most sports.
   (D) one of the easiest dances to learn.

8. You would probably find this passage in
   (A) a travel journal.
   (B) a college brochure.
   (C) a zoo pamphlet.
   (D) a health magazine.

9. As it is used in the passage, the word "notorious" most nearly means
   (A) dangerous.
   (B) despised.
   (C) famous.
   (D) obscure.

10. As it is used in the passage, the word "athleticism" most nearly means
   (A) clumsiness.
   (B) hunger.
   (C) power.
   (D) irritability.

Persuasive Passage #4

People of all ages love listening to music. rom modern pop to classic rock, listening to music has a wide range of benefits for a wide range of people—even babies in the womb! Early in a mother's pregnancy, babies gain the ability to hear sound from outside the womb. Once this happens, they can hear nearly everything their mother hears—voices, sounds, and even music. Listening to music has been shown to help babies and mothers alike, and is a unique way for a mother to have a positive impact on her baby before they're even born.

While babies grow in the womb, their brains are constantly developing. Listening to music during this process can actually stimulate the brain and boost the process of development. Some women even report feeling their babies move around and kick in response to hearing music—this activity helps the babies improve their strength and motor skills before they're even born. The benefits extend beyond the womb, too—some studies show that babies remember music they listened to in the womb for up to four months after birth.

Babies who listened to music in the womb also sleep better, both before and after they are born. This is not just a benefit to the baby, but to the parents as well! Pregnant women often experience high levels of stress, which can negatively impact a baby's development. Listening to music can be a soothing experience for both a mother and her baby, calming and destressing both, which can contribute to the bond shared by the two.

One thing for pregnant women who want to play music for their baby to consider is to never put headphones directly on their bellies. Though it's an understandable impulse, doing this will create a volume and vibration that is too intense for the baby. Instead, mothers should listen to music at a soft, normal volume; the baby will be able to hear it. Expectant mothers should consider listening to music while pregnant—if it can be so beneficial, why not try?

1. What would be the most appropriate title for this passage?
   (A) Pregnancy: Week to Week
   (B) Music for Different Ages
   (C) Infant Development After Birth
   (D) The Benefits of Music During Pregnancy

2. This passage is mostly about
   (A) the stages of development of babies in the womb.
   (B) the best ways to get babies to sleep through the night.
   (C) how music can benefit babies and mothers alike.
   (D) ways for pregnant women to relieve stress during pregnancy.

3. According to the passage, which of the following is true?
   (A) Babies cannot hear in the womb.
   (B) Babies benefit from music the most when it's played loud.
   (C) Early in their development, babies gain the ability to hear sounds outside the womb.
   (D) Babies can only hear things happening inside the mother's body.

4. According to the facts in the passage, listening to music
   (A) causes babies to move around in the womb.
   (B) causes babies to plug their ears in the womb.
   (C) has no effect on babies after they're born.
   (D) makes babies more likely to become musicians when they grow up.

5. The author states that
   (A) listening to music in the womb excites babies too much to sleep.
   (B) babies who listen to music in the womb may sleep better.
   (C) mothers who listen to music while pregnant will sleep less.
   (D) mothers who listen to music while pregnant will be more active.

6. Which of the following can be inferred from the passage?
   (A) Babies in the womb prefer classic rock to modern pop.
   (B) Listening to music while pregnant has no effect on mothers.
   (C) Babies who were exposed to music in the womb often have a number of advantages over babies who weren't.
   (D) The type of music a mom listens to has an enormous effect on the quality of the baby's musical taste.

7. It can be inferred from the passage that
   (A) a calm environment is best for babies in the womb.
   (B) babies in the womb are not affected by the mother's stress.
   (C) the environment outside the womb has no effect on the baby.
   (D) a noisy environment is best for the development of a baby's hearing.

8. The author would most likely agree with which of the following statements?
   (A) Babies remember everything their mother heard while pregnant.
   (B) Pregnant women should consider playing music for their babies.
   (C) Babies who listen to calm music in the womb may become dangerously less active.
   (D) Babies in the womb enjoy the vibration of headphones on the mother's belly.

9. As it is used in the passage, the word "<u>stimulate</u>" most nearly means
   (A) accept.
   (B) activate.
   (C) limit.
   (D) open.

10. The words "<u>soothing</u>" most nearly means
   (A) addictive.
   (B) dreary.
   (C) gorgeous.
   (D) relaxing.

Vocabulary

Overview

The last 22 questions in the Reading section test vocabulary. Students are presented with a short phrase with one word underlined and asked to choose an answer that has the same meaning as the underlined word.

Tutorverse Tips!

When trying to determine the meaning of the underlined word, consider the other words that are given in the phrase. These can give you valuable clues to the meaning of the underlined word. Remember as well to consider root words and prefixes. Does the word seem to have a positive, negative, or neutral meaning, as used in the phrase? Eliminate the choices that do not make sense and you'll arrive at the correct answer!

Vocabulary Exercises

1. Troubled by the problematic situation
   (A) appropriate
   (B) desirable
   (C) helpful
   (D) worrisome

2. An unimaginable outcome
   (A) correct
   (B) debatable
   (C) inconceivable
   (D) luminous

3. To swelter in the heat
   (A) chill
   (B) feel
   (C) relax
   (D) sweat

4. Disliked his abrasive personality
   (A) caustic
   (B) delightful
   (C) innocent
   (D) pleasant

5. A vitriolic attack against his character
   (A) appreciative
   (B) malicious
   (C) newfound
   (D) obvious

6. Felt bitter about being left out
   (A) appreciative
   (B) determined
   (C) resentful
   (D) wonderful

7. Jealous of her belongings
   (A) aware
   (B) envious
   (C) genius
   (D) heroic

8. A desolate desert town
   (A) barren
   (B) celebrated
   (C) even
   (D) fearsome

9. A glance in his direction
   (A) annoyance
   (B) guess
   (C) peek
   (D) question

10. To tamper with evidence
    (A) annoy
    (B) behave
    (C) interfere
    (D) mold

11. A tedious journey home
    (A) dull
    (B) shining
    (C) troubling
    (D) worrisome

12. An encroaching danger
    (A) elegant
    (B) flattering
    (C) imminent
    (D) lovely

13. A soothing bubble bath
    (A) aggressive
    (B) frightening
    (C) limiting
    (D) relaxing

14. To <u>authorize</u> a decision
    (A) aid
    (B) guess
    (C) permit
    (D) stretch

15. They <u>smuggled</u> in goods
    (A) appeased
    (B) fried
    (C) ignored
    (D) stole

16. To <u>covet</u> valuable things
    (A) desire
    (B) explain
    (C) plan
    (D) queue

17. <u>Extract</u> poison from a bite
    (A) hide
    (B) imitate
    (C) remove
    (D) solve

18. An <u>avid</u> fan
    (A) deceitful
    (B) eager
    (C) forgotten
    (D) lost

19. An oppressive <u>tyrant</u>
    (A) challenger
    (B) gift
    (C) oppressor
    (D) town

20. It <u>spanned</u> generations
    (A) bridged
    (B) dismissed
    (C) irritated
    (D) pleased

21. A <u>lucrative</u> investment
    (A) actual
    (B) demanding
    (C) profitable
    (D) ready

22. To <u>contradict</u> the rules
    (A) allow
    (B) counter
    (C) elaborate
    (D) hide

23. The <u>decorative</u> details on the building
    (A) altered
    (B) inevitable
    (C) ornamental
    (D) pungent

24. An <u>essential</u> worker
    (A) dreamy
    (B) geriatric
    (C) necessary
    (D) unwelcome

25. A <u>temperamental</u> attitude
    (A) confusing
    (B) excitable
    (C) mounting
    (D) newfound

26. A <u>questionable</u> life decision
    (A) dubious
    (B) effervescent
    (C) unending
    (D) verified

27. He <u>lazily</u> dawdled
    (A) bravely
    (B) recklessly
    (C) slowly
    (D) tenderly

28. They <u>pondered</u> their decision
    (A) applied
    (B) considered
    (C) pulled
    (D) rendered

29. The <u>frigid</u> winter weather
    (A) arctic
    (B) determined
    (C) unpleasant
    (D) warm

30. A <u>scathing</u> remark
    (A) biting
    (B) creative
    (C) eminent
    (D) forgetful

31. A <u>thorough</u> review
    (A) banned
    (B) detailed
    (C) defenseless
    (D) pathetic

32. To <u>apprehend</u> the outlaw
    (A) catch
    (B) defend
    (C) harass
    (D) liberate

33. To <u>evoke</u> a memory
    (A) dismiss
    (B) found
    (C) misinterpret
    (D) recall

34. Rebel against <u>tyranny</u>
    (A) dictatorship
    (B) friendship
    (C) history
    (D) wellness

35. A <u>vengeful</u> plot
    (A) easy
    (B) feasible
    (C) implicit
    (D) vindictive

36. Her <u>explosive</u> anger
    (A) dim
    (B) eruptive
    (C) gentle
    (D) meager

37. The <u>attentive</u> pupils
(A) alert
(B) delirious
(C) disrespectful
(D) disappointed

38. To <u>abstain</u> from the vote
(A) avert
(B) learn
(C) operate
(D) refuse

39. A <u>charitable</u> donation
(A) benevolent
(B) devolved
(C) egregious
(D) selfish

40. The <u>absence</u> of fear
(A) celebration
(B) dearth
(C) event
(D) resource

41. The <u>culpable</u> criminal
(A) kind
(B) guilty
(C) handy
(D) ignoble

42. The <u>dissatisfied</u> customer
(A) behaved
(B) only
(C) resourceful
(D) unhappy

43. To <u>puncture</u> a balloon
(A) avoid
(B) mirror
(C) pierce
(D) specialize

44. Her <u>punctual</u> arrival
(A) avoidable
(B) durable
(C) prompt
(D) unpleasant

45. His <u>disheveled</u> appearance
(A) daunting
(B) helpful
(C) messy
(D) orated

46. An entertaining <u>diversion</u>
(A) distraction
(B) dread
(C) exam
(D) package

47. An unexpected <u>departure</u>
(A) apparent
(B) exit
(C) rebellion
(D) riot

48. To <u>abbreviate</u> a long word
(A) behave
(B) decide
(C) plummet
(D) shorten

49. An <u>honorable</u> soldier
(A) disrespectful
(B) ignorant
(C) respected
(D) tender

50. The <u>pleasantly</u> warm day
(A) belligerently
(B) delightfully
(C) frighteningly
(D) violently

51. A <u>robust</u> feast
(A) acceptable
(B) hearty
(C) limited
(D) weary

52. To <u>exaggerate</u> one's achievements
(A) elaborate
(B) forget
(C) generate
(D) hound

53. Delete <u>extraneous</u> details
(A) important
(B) obvious
(C) quaint
(D) unnecessary

54. To hold <u>confidential</u> secrets
(A) ambitious
(B) confident
(C) derivative
(D) private

55. A <u>concealed</u> weapon
(A) apparent
(B) hidden
(C) prestigious
(D) weird

56. A <u>prominent</u> public figure
(A) conditional
(B) famous
(C) invisible
(D) unknown

57. A <u>pious</u> religious leader
(A) confusing
(B) devout
(C) evident
(D) unread

58. The <u>prodigious</u> artist
(A) apparent
(B) jealous
(C) limited
(D) wonderful

59. Mortified about his mistake
(A) embarrassed
(B) grateful
(C) hateful
(D) loving

60. To procrastinate making a decision
(A) paint
(B) ready
(C) stall
(D) verify

61. A sympathetic friend
(A) compassionate
(B) demonstrative
(C) invisible
(D) lavish

62. A comfortable domicile
(A) destiny
(B) event
(C) residence
(D) strain

63. The king's dominion
(A) appreciation
(B) bundle
(C) loss
(D) rule

64. An unremarkable childhood
(A) avid
(B) caustic
(C) normal
(D) obvious

65. Her affectionate children
(A) capable
(B) mature
(C) obvious
(D) sweet

66. To decline a request
(A) burn
(B) demonstrate
(C) imagine
(D) spurn

67. An ingenious invention
(A) anxious
(B) false
(C) innovative
(D) questionable

68. A controversial decision
(A) tangential
(B) terrifying
(C) tinted
(D) tough

69. A contentious issue
(A) bland
(B) candid
(C) efficient
(D) problematic

70. A sonorous singing voice
(A) amusing
(B) devised
(C) resounding
(D) unveiled

71. To memorize verbatim
(A) commonly
(B) exactly
(C) friendly
(D) quality

72. An overly verbose speaker
(A) quiet
(B) undone
(C) valid
(D) wordy

73. A charismatic conversationalist
(A) caustic
(B) charming
(C) closed
(D) common

74. Let the events commence
(A) begin
(B) explode
(C) fizzle
(D) lose

75. A belligerent bully
(A) aggressive
(B) cultured
(C) kind
(D) mindful

76. Live under imminent danger
(A) basic
(B) edible
(C) looming
(D) lovely

77. A gruesome scene of violence
(A) decadent
(B) disturbing
(C) dominant
(D) dull

78. To depict in a painting
(A) devise
(B) embalm
(C) founder
(D) portray

79. A corrupt government
(A) celebratory
(B) dreamy
(C) final
(D) unethical

80. An <u>inspirational</u> speaker
    (A) malevolent
    (B) meaningless
    (C) moving
    (D) murky

81. A <u>motivational</u> speech
    (A) apparent
    (B) complicated
    (C) inaudible
    (D) stimulating

82. An <u>impulsive</u> decision
    (A) abundant
    (B) fabulous
    (C) hidden
    (D) spontaneous

83. To <u>narrate</u> a story
    (A) appropriate
    (B) flatter
    (C) gyrate
    (D) tell

84. A <u>resilient</u> survivor
    (A) adaptable
    (B) invalid
    (C) pathetic
    (D) weak

85. To <u>belittle</u> one's existence
    (A) derange
    (B) disparage
    (C) exist
    (D) express

86. Of <u>indispensable</u> value
    (A) essential
    (B) disruptive
    (C) general
    (D) unnecessary

87. A <u>persuasive</u> argument
    (A) appropriate
    (B) influential
    (C) radiant
    (D) stylish

88. To <u>validate</u> one's feelings
    (A) confirm
    (B) enthuse
    (C) grow
    (D) imitate

89. A <u>panoramic</u> view of the mountains
    (A) genial
    (B) precious
    (C) questionable
    (D) surrounding

90. A <u>balmy</u> spring day
    (A) challenging
    (B) destructive
    (C) temperate
    (D) unpleasant

91. A <u>disgruntled</u> demeanor
    (A) edible
    (B) fanatical
    (C) irritable
    (D) kindred

92. <u>Avoid</u> one's responsibilities
    (A) enjoy
    (B) find
    (C) ignore
    (D) mend

93. A lake <u>teeming</u> with fish
    (A) shining
    (B) shrinking
    (C) spinning
    (D) swarming

94. A <u>bounty</u> of a kindness
    (A) approval
    (B) dismissal
    (C) generosity
    (D) verification

95. Highways <u>congested</u> with traffic
    (A) aloft
    (B) crowded
    (C) decorated
    (D) deranged

96. An <u>inconceivable</u> mystery
    (A) acceptable
    (B) knowable
    (C) pleasant
    (D) unbelievable

97. A lucky <u>talisman</u>
    (A) bedlam
    (B) charm
    (C) hygiene
    (D) omen

98. Perform with a <u>flourish</u>
    (A) benefit
    (B) comment
    (C) gesture
    (D) stage

99. To live in <u>solitude</u>
    (A) altar
    (B) bohemian
    (C) loneliness
    (D) valor

100. <u>Confide</u> in a trusted friend
    (A) betray
    (B) divulge
    (C) hate
    (D) vie

101. Make a <u>snide</u> remark
    (A) bright
    (B) material
    (C) miraculous
    (D) rude

102. A <u>boisterous</u> laugh
   (A) animated
   (B) dreadful
   (C) odious
   (D) unpleasant

103. The <u>generic</u> brand of medicine
   (A) basic
   (B) forgotten
   (C) harmful
   (D) old

104. An <u>impending</u> doom
   (A) cheerful
   (B) forthcoming
   (C) hopeful
   (D) merry

105. An <u>omitted</u> word
   (A) abrasive
   (B) colorful
   (C) excluded
   (D) invisible

106. To <u>possess</u> a home
   (A) abject
   (B) imagine
   (C) own
   (D) vile

107. Meet at a <u>juncture</u>
   (A) child
   (B) judgement
   (C) point
   (D) speed

108. A <u>loquacious</u> speaker
   (A) candid
   (B) imperfect
   (C) obvious
   (D) talkative

109. An <u>insatiable</u> appetite
   (A) appropriate
   (B) incorrect
   (C) perfect
   (D) voracious

110. A <u>delectable</u> box of chocolates
   (A) apparent
   (B) disgusting
   (C) mouthwatering
   (D) veritable

Language Skills

On the Actual Test

In the Language section of the HSPT, you will encounter four types of questions:

- Punctuation and Capitalization
- Usage
- Spelling
- Composition

There will be 60 questions on the actual Verbal Skills section, which you will have 25 minutes to complete.

In This Practice Book

The practice questions in this section of the workbook *are not* structured like an actual HSPT exam. Instead, these sections contain many exams' worth of materials to help you practice. This will allow you to drill for each type of question you will find on the Language section.

There may be additional instructions and recommendations at the beginning of each section, which you should review before starting.

Remember: there are detailed answer explanations available online at www.thetutorverse.com/books. Be sure to obtain permission before going online.

Punctuation and Capitalization

Overview

The Punctuation and Capitalization questions present four sentences and ask that you pick the sentence with a mistake in the use of punctuation or capitalization. If there is no mistake in any of the sentences, choose D, indicating no error.

- Punctuation
  - Periods, commas, semicolons, and colons
  - Quotes in sentences
  - Correct ending punctuation for the sentence
  - Apostrophe use with possession and contractions
- Capitalization
  - Proper nouns
  - Titles
  - Days, months, and holidays
  - First word of a sentence
  - Cities, countries, nationalities, and languages

We recommend that you practice at least 15-20 questions per week in preparing for the exam.

How to Use This Section

As determined by your study plan, including the results of your diagnostic tests, we encourage you to focus on the topics that are most challenging to you. This section will give you exposure to the different types of questions that are presented in Punctuation and Capitalization, and give you the practice to finding the path to the correct answer. If you find that you are challenged by this area and need additional help, remember to reach out to a trusted educator. Don't get discouraged! Take the materials to a teacher or tutor if you need additional enrichment in any given topic.

Tutorverse Tips!

Develop a list of the types of punctuation and capitalization questions that tend to trick you. This will give you a better idea of what you need to keep an eye out for when evaluating the questions on the real test.

Punctuation and Capitalization Exercises

Choose the sentence that contains an error in punctuation or capitalization. If there is no error, select choice (D).

1. (A) The state animal of California is the grizzly bear.
   (B) The student council agreed to meet on Thursdays.
   (C) Australia and New Zealand have many similarities.
   (D) No mistake.

2. (A) Let's pretend that the room is empty.
   (B) Throughout her life she had only owned one car.
   (C) You'll succeed if you continue to work hard.
   (D) No mistake.

3. (A) In the month of May, Jesse ran fifty miles.
   (B) The tree's bark was ruined by insects.
   (C) Despite her excuses; Elena still had to jog during gym class.
   (D) No mistake.

4. (A) What was the temperature on the hottest day of summer?
   (B) Lemonade's made with just a few simple ingredients.
   (C) They agreed on a date; they would meet on the fourth of January.
   (D) No mistake.

5. (A) The garbage collectors turned down Leopold Street.
   (B) The city was ravaged by Hurricane Sandy.
   (C) The capital of Maine is Augusta.
   (D) No mistake.

6. (A) Las Vegas is a city full of casinos and clubs.
   (B) Clarissa's favorite genre of music was hip hop.
   (C) Marcel didn't trust anyone but his brother.
   (D) No mistake.

7. (A) If, and only if, they escape, then they will be free.
   (B) Her memory's were mostly pleasant.
   (C) Although she was finished, she still felt like she had more work to do.
   (D) No mistake.

8. (A) Brown eyes are the most common; green eyes are the most rare.
   (B) Despite losing his job, Damon was in high spirit's.
   (C) The joke's effect was lost on the audience.
   (D) No mistake.

9. (A) The only person left in line was Tom.
   (B) The entire school was flooded after the storm.
   (C) Marie couldn't believe that i wouldn't help her cheat.
   (D) No mistake.

10. (A) The university's mascot was the Texas Longhorn.
    (B) Harry missed the Austrian Cuisine of his childhood.
    (C) George lost his history textbook.
    (D) No mistake.

11. (A) Her Birthday was on the last day of November.
    (B) Simon was dreading his school field trip to the Guggenheim Museum.
    (C) The Louvre is a famous museum in Paris, France.
    (D) No mistake.

12. (A) She wished her brother had brought back Souvenirs from Thailand.
    (B) The largest city in the United States in New York City.
    (C) The town closest to them was called Perryville.
    (D) No mistake.

13. (A) The only species of frogs in the Jungle is endangered.
    (B) He dreamed of climbing Mount Everest.
    (C) Julia was learning how to play the guitar.
    (D) No mistake.

14. (A) They couldn't understand her.
    (B) They braided each other's hair.
    (C) Only he could defeat the emperor.
    (D) No mistake.

15. (A) The eagle's wingspan was impressive.
(B) She knows it's for the best.
(C) How long will it take until they reach their destination.
(D) No mistake.

16. (A) Mondays were Luisa's least favorite day of the week.
(B) They informed their landlord that they'd be moving out at the end of June.
(C) The street fair happened the first wednesday of each month.
(D) No mistake.

17. (A) Im going to the store to get some milk.
(B) Elijah's suit was neatly pressed.
(C) The frames on the wall hadn't fallen during the earthquake.
(D) No mistake.

18. (A) The most capable swimmer on the school team was Felipe Gomez.
(B) They met in the cafeteria every Tuesday and Thursday.
(C) The store was closed for the entire Month of February.
(D) No mistake.

19. (A) The Dutch painter moved to the south of France.
(B) Seth was terrified of watching horror movies.
(C) They ordered their Persian rug from a vendor.
(D) No mistake.

20. (A) She looked forward to Hanukkah every year.
(B) They watched the parade on Lunar New Year.
(C) They went to Church on Easter Sunday.
(D) No mistake.

21. (A) The Christmas dance was festive.
(B) Priscilla told her Mom about the dance on Saturday.
(C) Katrina picked up her homework from her teacher.
(D) No mistake.

22. (A) They visited the childrens hospital on Monday.
(B) Only a doctor's opinion would be heard.
(C) The operation's success depended on the surgeon's skill.
(D) No mistake.

23. (A) Penguins can be found on that Continent.
(B) Mo dreamed of riding a camel in Egypt.
(C) May is the fifth month of the year.
(D) No mistake.

24. (A) Well, there isn't another solution.
(B) Although they fought they always made up in the end.
(C) Because of her brother's mistake, she had to serve detention.
(D) No mistake.

25. (A) He offered to teach his friend how to fish.
(B) Jorge buys coffee every morning; he doesn't like making coffee at home.
(C) The mayor's decision was final.
(D) No mistake.

26. (A) The volcano posed an imminent threat to the villagers.
(B) They decided to try and visit every National Park.
(C) The biggest island of Hawaii is a popular travel destination.
(D) No mistake.

27. (A) A magician never reveal's his secrets.
(B) Esther's not the only witch in town.
(C) This'll be a quick journey.
(D) No mistake.

28. (A) She kept tapping on her mother's kitchen table.
    (B) We don't know who changed the lock's.
    (C) Zachariah's favorite cheese is parmesan.
    (D) No mistake.

29. (A) Dean couldn't decide what costume to wear for Halloween.
    (B) Gerard hoped he'd get a scooter for his Birthday.
    (C) A variety of flavors were offered in every bag.
    (D) No mistake.

30. (A) Margaret's favorite flowers are Peonies.
    (B) Leona couldn't wait for Valentine's Day.
    (C) The monarch butterfly migrates long distances.
    (D) No mistake.

31. (A) The houses' windows were all broken.
    (B) Marie's sister bought a bicycle.
    (C) Luis' scored well in math, reading, and science.
    (D) No mistake.

32. (A) "I'm being framed," cried Jacob!
    (B) "You're right," admitted Bella.
    (C) "I can't believe this!" exclaimed Edward.
    (D) No mistake.

33. (A) In October Tracy auditioned for the school play and got the part.
    (B) When is the first day of rehearsal?
    (C) Each character's motive was clear.
    (D) No mistake.

34. (A) The prisoner's cell was tiny.
    (B) Each person's locker was locked.
    (C) John was patient kind and smart.
    (D) No mistake.

35. (A) She was running late; she likely wouldn't make it on time.
    (B) The tedious, lengthy lecture seemed to last forever.
    (C) Tim raced his brother, but his brother was really fast.
    (D) No mistake.

36. (A) Winter was long; summer was brief.
    (B) A variety of goods' were sold at the store.
    (C) She doesn't know what to do next.
    (D) No mistake.

37. (A) Classic hollywood films are sometimes played in modern theaters.
    (B) The United States Postal Service promises to deliver mail in all types of weather.
    (C) The star of the film was none other than Marilyn Monroe.
    (D) No mistake.

38. (A) Country music is very popular in Nashville.
    (B) One of the most popular religions in the world is christianity.
    (C) Harriet was especially fond of art class.
    (D) No mistake.

39. (A) The Professor chastised her students for being on their phones.
    (B) The decision was made by President Barack Obama.
    (C) The colonies revolted against King George III.
    (D) No mistake.

40. (A) The school, which was located in town, was very large.
    (B) The smoothies ingredients included strawberries, bananas, and apples.
    (C) The party's guests were dressed formally.
    (D) No mistake.

41. (A) She exclaimed, "what a beautiful rainbow!"
(B) The television show had been sold to Showtime.
(C) The bridge was built over one hundred years ago.
(D) No mistake.

42. (A) Katy sent her sister a postcard from Denver.
(B) The play had been canceled due to an Emergency.
(C) Paris is a popular travel destination for couples.
(D) No mistake.

43. (A) "Stop!" shouted Greg.
(B) The shiny, expensive car was a gift.
(C) Only Summer's dog was properly trained.
(D) No mistake.

44. (A) The judge refused to listen to the defense's argument.
(B) Ted's journey—which had been long and arduous, was finally complete.
(C) Aaron's favorite part of the week was here; he could finally play basketball.
(D) No mistake.

45. (A) He stopped on his way out to ask Professor Wells a question.
(B) Both of Jeremiah's parents disapproved of his major.
(C) She took the train North to see Niagara Falls.
(D) No mistake.

46. (A) On Saturdays they met for brunch in the city.
(B) "I'm so tired," whined Sage.
(C) The senator's speech brought the crowd to tears.
(D) No mistake.

47. (A) Students return to school after two months of summer vacation.
(B) She couldn't wait to run in the Marathon on Sunday.
(C) People often confuse the climates of Iceland and Greenland.
(D) No mistake.

48. (A) Rudy made an appointment with the doctor on Thursday.
(B) They asked their parents, "Are we there yet?"
(C) Bobby surprised his Girlfriend with a bouquet of flowers.
(D) No mistake.

49. (A) Maine's Senator agreed to vote for the bill.
(B) Eleanor Roosevelt is one of the most admired first ladies in history.
(C) Volunteers urged residents to call their local representatives.
(D) No mistake.

50. (A) The childrens' shared bedroom is dirty.
(B) The evening's selection of shows was exciting.
(C) Mariah, who was tired, went to bed.
(D) No mistake.

51. (A) Robert's only concern was how he would make it home.
(B) A guitar has six string's.
(C) "Are you coming to the party?" asked Jerome.
(D) No mistake.

52. (A) The Australian flag has similar colors to the United Kingdom's flag.
(B) Birthdays were celebrated with cake in the office.
(C) Julia's favorite band was playing at Madison Square Garden.
(D) No mistake.

53. (A) Which choice should he make?
(B) They werent ready for the test.
(C) "Who's there?" asked Juan.
(D) No mistake.

54. (A) The cat's tail kept twitching.
(B) The curtains' fabric was made of linen.
(C) They left; which is what they were planning.
(D) No mistake.

55. (A) Charlie know's that he can't convince his dad to change his mind.
(B) There was only one thing left to do: take out the trash.
(C) Her mother, who was a gardener, loved the outdoors.
(D) No mistake.

56. (A) He had always admired Harry Houdini.
(B) She hopes to be a marine biologist when she grows up.
(C) The students went on spring break in March.
(D) No mistake.

57. (A) The book wasn't hers.
(B) Zach was a teacher; Melissa was a professor.
(C) Rebecca couldnt complete the marathon.
(D) No mistake.

58. (A) Cassandra said to her sister, "don't forget your backpack."
(B) Her cousin sent them a postcard from San Francisco, California.
(C) Ramadan is a holiday in the religion of Islam.
(D) No mistake.

59. (A) Her stuffed animal's were carefully placed on a shelf.
(B) She was doctor; she saved lives every day.
(C) Micah's shoes were untied.
(D) No mistake.

60. (A) She celebrated her cousin's graduation.
(B) Even though she was tired, she completed the race.
(C) So that she wouldn't forget anything she wrote everything down.
(D) No mistake.

61. (A) The basket contained jams, cheeses, and crackers.
(B) James exclaimed, "That's enough!"
(C) At a food stand, an ice cream cone costs $2.
(D) No mistake.

62. (A) Einstein was a highly respected scientist.
(B) Doctors who specialize in skin are called dermatologists.
(C) The kid's favorite superhero was Spiderman.
(D) No mistake.

63. (A) The speech, in its entirety, was an hour long.
(B) It's only a matter of time before she quits.
(C) It's a long way home from here.
(D) No mistake.

64. (A) She was afraid to ski in the Rocky mountains.
(B) The only lake she hadn't visited was Lake Huron.
(C) Her sister lived in Sacramento, California.
(D) No mistake.

65. (A) They were running; they had to get there on time.
(B) Miranda asked, "Where are the boots that match this belt"?
(C) The laughed, cried, and slept.
(D) No mistake.

66. (A) She was musical yet she hated classical music.
(B) She couldn't feel her legs.
(C) He was ready: he was going to high school.
(D) No mistake.

67. (A) She dreamed of owning a siberian husky.
(B) Only her sister, Chanel, could fix her door.
(C) She needed help from her dad to finish her homework.
(D) No mistake.

68. (A) Both of the teachers were tired.
(B) The lesson plan focused on Chinese history.
(C) She stayed late to ask professor Wu a question.
(D) No mistake.

69. (A) They visited the Metropolitan Museum of Art last week.
(B) Her last name was Smith but her husband's was gregson.
(C) Amy's favorite season was winter.
(D) No mistake.

70. (A) The first time she saw snow, she cried.
(B) Her favorite television show was canceled.
(C) The fifteenth of may was her mother's birthday.
(D) No mistake.

71. (A) Elsa and Anya both loved folk music.
(B) The band was called Iron Maiden.
(C) Carnegie hall is a famous music venue.
(D) No mistake.

72. (A) My brother's birthday is in April.
(B) Steve looks forward to Halloween every year.
(C) Helen wants to visit Japan, even though she is studying italian.
(D) No mistake.

73. (A) "We're going to have so much fun!" exclaimed Crystal.
(B) They're not too far from the finish line.
(C) She carefully placed the items in her bag, a sandwich, a crystal, and her favorite book.
(D) No mistake.

74. (A) She took a trip to Rehoboth Beach.
(B) Her favorite subject in school was geography.
(C) Her uncle lives on Staten island.
(D) No mistake.

75. (A) "Are you there" asked Selma?
(B) They couldn't accept the truth.
(C) I am just so excited to finally be here!
(D) No mistake.

76. (A) Her least favorite weather happened during April.
(B) The best season for harvesting is Autumn.
(C) Memorial Day happens at the end of May.
(D) No mistake.

77. (A) She was musical yet she hated classical music.
(B) She couldn't feel her legs.
(C) He was ready: he was going to high school.
(D) No mistake.

78. (A) She wants to travel to the south of france one day.
(B) Why does Rebecca want to go to the store?
(C) He needed to finish her project before she can watch television.
(D) No mistake.

79. (A) None of the student had plans for the weekend.
    (B) Her favorite cuisine is Chinese food.
    (C) She asked for a recommendation from professor Herndon.
    (D) No mistake.

80. (A) They made a trip to the Ronald Reagan Presidential Library last week.
    (B) She was surprised to discover her best friend's last name was crawford.
    (C) Jill's favorite season was fall.
    (D) No mistake.

81. (A) The very first thing she did was eat.
    (B) Her favorite play was coming to Broadway.
    (C) The thirteenth of june was her anniversary.
    (D) No mistake.

82. (A) Charlie and his cat love to look out the window.
    (B) The band was originally named the Silver Beetles.
    (C) The Eiffel tower is beautiful at night.
    (D) No mistake.

83. (A) I go back to school in August.
    (B) Chandra looks forward to Christmas every year.
    (C) Lilly finds Chinese difficult to learn, but she is getting a perfect grade in spanish.
    (D) No mistake.

84. (A) "We're about to go over the edge!" exclaimed Douglas.
    (B) They're not too far from their destination.
    (C) She packed everything she needed for the trip, a thermos, a book, and a picture of her family.
    (D) No mistake.

85. (A) Wayne took at trip to Myrtle Beach.
    (B) Her favorite subject in school was literature.
    (C) They visited the twins on Long island.
    (D) No mistake.

86. (A) "Why don't you answer" asked Peter?
    (B) They couldn't find what they were looking for.
    (C) I so happy I could jump for joy!
    (D) No mistake.

87. (A) She loves how the plants bloom in March.
    (B) The best season for using snowshoes is Winter.
    (C) President's Day happens at the end of February.
    (D) No mistake.

88. (A) Everybody's got a reason.
    (B) Theyre not done yet.
    (C) The dance is done; we have to go home.
    (D) No mistake.

89. (A) She wished he hadn't given up.
    (B) "Will we ever win" asked Nate.
    (C) All was lost; the game was over.
    (D) No mistake.

90. (A) Every day; she got to work early.
    (B) She's the only child of the family.
    (C) He's the oldest of his siblings.
    (D) No mistake.

91. (A) "I'm so done" screamed Jesse.
    (B) Eva asked her brother, "Are you done?"
    (C) There was rain, thunder, and lightning.
    (D) No mistake.

92. (A) "Is it all gone" asked Marissa.
    (B) They're not all bad.
    (C) It's time to finish the class.
    (D) No mistake.

94. (A) After turning left onto Grand Street, walk three blocks and then turn right on Main Street:
    (B) Since they left, they could no longer come back.
    (C) Her favorite season was summer: it was so sunny every day.
    (D) No mistake.

95. (A) The French people have excellent cuisine.
    (B) Her mother only spoke a bit of english.
    (C) It wasn't in her nature to stay in during spring.
    (D) No mistake.

96. (A) Her aunt promised to give her lots of money.
    (B) The shortest month of the year is February.
    (C) The largest States were California, Texas, and Alaska.
    (D) No mistake.

97. (A) Keisha promised to clean her sister's truck.
    (B) Only the Professor could explain the theory.
    (C) She loved to watch old film noir movies.
    (D) No mistake.

98. (A) The capital of Alaska is not very populated.
    (B) She couldn't wait for thanksgiving in November.
    (C) The last time she saw the ocean, she was in Greece.
    (D) No mistake.

99. (A) She believed in Santa Claus.
    (B) The Holidays were Jake's favorite time of year.
    (C) She waited to put the Christmas tree up in December.
    (D) No mistake.

100. (A) The fourth day of July is Independence Day.
    (B) Raul couldn't remember the name of alicia's favorite movie.
    (C) She addressed Chief Smith with great respect.
    (D) No mistake.

101. (A) The Atlantic Ocean is a large distance to cover.
    (B) Her favorite actress was Eliza Maria.
    (C) Casey ordered a burger for Lunch on Friday.
    (D) No mistake.

Usage

Overview

This section gives you practice in finding errors in correct English language usage.

Usage topics tested include:

- Comparative and superlative words
- Subject and direct object pronouns
- Verb tenses
- Relative pronouns (like who, whom, and which)
- Double negatives
- Sentence fragments

We recommend that you practice at least 15-20 questions per week in preparing for the exam.

How to Use This Section

As determined by your study plan, including the results of your diagnostic tests, we encourage you to focus on the topics that are most challenging to you. This section will give you exposure to the different types of questions that are presented in English usage, and give you the practice to finding the path to the correct answer. If you find that you are challenged by this area and need additional help, remember to reach out to a trusted educator. Don't get discouraged! Take the materials to a teacher or tutor if you need additional enrichment in any given topic.

Tutorverse Tips!

English usage can present some challenges. Try making mental categories as you practice the questions and take notes about the types of usage questions that challenge you the most. Practice and you will get the hang of it in no time!

Usage Exercises

Choose the sentence that contains an error in usage. If there is no error, select choice (D).

1. (A) New York city is the most biggest city in the country.
   (B) Her yard was the greenest in the neighborhood.
   (C) The butterfly had the longest antennae.
   (D) No mistake.

2. (A) The violinist stood and bowed.
   (B) The bigger the piano, the better it sounds.
   (C) She stood and walked to the door.
   (D) No mistake.

3. (A) The audience members found themselves clapping along.
   (B) The cat ran away but then they came home.
   (C) She gave the books to Sylvia and me.
   (D) No mistake.

4. (A) Maine is further north than Massachusetts.
   (B) He is more braver than his brother.
   (C) The test was the hardest exam that year.
   (D) No mistake.

5. (A) The movie that the sisters chose was hilarious.
   (B) Mr. Jacobs was the teacher who won the competition.
   (C) Murray is a man which loves to play the piano.
   (D) No mistake.

6. (A) They apply for every college in the state last year.
   (B) She takes the train to work every day.
   (C) He forgot to do the dishes yesterday.
   (D) No mistake.

7. (A) His favorite song was shorter than hers.
   (B) He released the most successful album of the year.
   (C) The lamp was the most brightest in the store.
   (D) No mistake.

8. (A) The restaurant was very fancy.
   (B) The story was told dramatically.
   (C) They crossed the river fast.
   (D) No mistake.

9. (A) The afternoon was hotter than the morning.
   (B) Nathan played flute more better than Kacey.
   (C) She was the youngest in her grade.
   (D) No mistake.

10. (A) She passed the notes over to him.
    (B) He's a doctor which likes to be sure.
    (C) Annie's cat came running to her.
    (D) No mistake.

11. (A) Only one jar of peanut butter sit on the shelf.
    (B) Most of the eggs in the carton are broken.
    (C) The only milk available is soy milk.
    (D) No mistake.

12. (A) Each person takes a tray and then moves along the line.
    (B) All of the raisins were tossed into the garbage.
    (C) She expected the doctor and the dentist to say the same thing.
    (D) No mistake.

13. (A) He plays soccer powerfully.
    (B) He writes real well.
    (C) She was feeling defensive.
    (D) No mistake.

14. (A) I am going to the store today.
    (B) They gave us back our ball.
    (C) Jane gave the assignment to Bob and I.
    (D) No mistake.

15. (A) His shoes were cleaner than mine.
    (B) She is the strictest teacher in the school.
    (C) He was training to swim more faster.
    (D) No mistake.

16. (A) Next year, I will go to Japan.
    (B) Bob went to the store yesterday.
    (C) My parents are coming to visit today.
    (D) No mistake.

17. (A) Her favorite movie wasn't available to stream.
    (B) Her was crying; he couldn't believe it was over.
    (C) She wasn't ready to move on.
    (D) No mistake.

18. (A) They couldn't find Paul nowhere.
    (B) She couldn't turn down dessert.
    (C) Elena wasn't lost.
    (D) No mistake.

19. (A) He was the most charming realtor at his firm.
    (B) He was the most speediest turtle ever.
    (C) She was the most competitive lawyer in the city.
    (D) No mistake.

20. (A) Bertie can't finish the project without the help of his partner.
    (B) The furniture at her grandma's house are covered in cat hair.
    (C) The elite school for boys is known for having prestigious clubs.
    (D) No mistake.

21. (A) He was taller than his father.
    (B) February is the most shortest month of the year.
    (C) Anthony was angrier than his siblings.
    (D) No mistake.

22. (A) Jesse almost forgot to turn in his homework.
    (B) The cheerleader was late but she still showed up.
    (C) His son was the kid that was always late.
    (D) No mistake.

23. (A) On Saturday, I will walk my friend's dog, water my neighbor's plants, and washing my dad's car.
    (B) They wanted to go to Hawaii and surf in the ocean.
    (C) She was already the strongest and now she was also the fastest.
    (D) No mistake.

24. (A) The robot had a mobile body, a head with cameras, and having two arms.
    (B) She entered the classroom and walked up to the teacher.
    (C) She wanted to eat food and drink water.
    (D) No mistake.

25. (A) She's hardly been outside all day.
    (B) Her headphones finally stopped working.
    (C) He barely never went swimming.
    (D) No mistake.

26. (A) It doesn't hurt that bad.
    (B) The presentation was boring.
    (C) His lunch tasted bland.
    (D) No mistake.

27. (A) Each of her kids have a daily chore to complete after school.
    (B) That is not enough money to buy a car.
    (C) The roof of the garage is slowly caving in.
    (D) No mistake.

28. (A) She felt very dizzy.
    (B) They asked questions avidly.
    (C) She typed very quick.
    (D) No mistake.

29. (A) The song was finally over.
    (B) The cherries were too bitter.
    (C) After school she studying for tests.
    (D) No mistake.

30. (A) She made sure her brother got to his class first.
    (B) He drove way too dangerous.
    (C) Her mother makes the most delicious pies.
    (D) No mistake.

31. (A) He was bewildered by the play.
    (B) He sang very beautiful.
    (C) The actor was so dramatic.
    (D) No mistake.

32. (A) Every day was sunny, was full of activities, and busy.
    (B) They survived the good times and they survived the bad times.
    (C) They spent the night dancing and having fun.
    (D) No mistake.

33. (A) Her aunt felt badly about the delay.
    (B) Her roller-skating skills are impressive.
    (C) He is an athletic soccer player.
    (D) No mistake.

34. (A) She gave Christie's hair clip back to them.
    (B) She couldn't hear her own voice.
    (C) His guitar was scratched.
    (D) No mistake.

35. (A) She whispered her secret quiet.
    (B) Her career was impressive.
    (C) The dishes were very fragile.
    (D) No mistake.

36. (A) She swears she hasn't got any diamonds.
    (B) He won't never get hurt while skiing.
    (C) The bartender wouldn't stop serving them drinks.
    (D) No mistake.

37. (A) They barely never went to the zoo.
    (B) March never has more than thirty-one days.
    (C) She couldn't find her shoes anywhere.
    (D) No mistake.

38. (A) Lawrence left the house and going to school.
    (B) She ran and made it on time.
    (C) The bus sped by them.
    (D) No mistake.

39. (A) Jane is the smartest pupil.
    (B) He has more marbles than his brother.
    (C) She has the tidier desk out of all her roommates.
    (D) No mistake.

40. (A) The tigers watched the visitors.
    (B) The elephant, after eating dinner, walking around the zoo.
    (C) The zoo closed early.
    (D) No mistake.

41. (A) She locked herself out.
    (B) They promised to keep the secret.
    (C) Her town was very tiny.
    (D) No mistake.

42. (A) They hoped to learn how to paint and how to draw.
    (B) This morning, I rode my bike to work and I got some exercise.
    (C) Tomorrow, I will need to wash the car, clean the air conditioners, and resealing the drive.
    (D) No mistake.

43. (A) Janet and her brother make dinner together.
    (B) Fiona can't remember the last time she slept.
    (C) The group of artists create a new piece together.
    (D) No mistake.

44. (A) There was a team of engineers whom designed a robot.
    (B) She gave her sister her old pair of boots.
    (C) His horse galloped faster than her horse.
    (D) No mistake.

45. (A) The kids were being uncooperative.
    (B) The soup was too spicy.
    (C) She spells really excellent.
    (D) No mistake.

46. (A) They already painted those walls.
    (B) She qualifies for nationals last year.
    (C) He will go to school in the fall.
    (D) No mistake.

47. (A) She couldn't never sing on tune.
    (B) They couldn't see the horizon.
    (C) She had never eaten meat before.
    (D) No mistake.

48. (A) The band members were talented.
    (B) The chorus sang very loud.
    (C) Only the pianist was quiet.
    (D) No mistake.

49. (A) The museum is closed every Tuesday.
(B) Maria walk to her exam.
(C) Josh and Sam are best friends.
(D) No mistake.

50. (A) Her friend is a more capable host.
(B) She runs the most faster.
(C) He sings the most beautifully.
(D) No mistake.

51. (A) Jeremiah's favorite show is the one with the corrupt detective.
(B) Marina and her father are on their way to the train station.
(C) Dorothy annoyed her mom when she forgot her passport and were late for the flight.
(D) No mistake.

52. (A) The drawing was very colorful.
(B) The bed was so comfortable.
(C) She handled the issue smooth.
(D) No mistake.

53. (A) The racecar was the most fastest ever made.
(B) The journey was the most dangerous she'd ever been on.
(C) Her professor was more intelligent than her.
(D) No mistake.

54. (A) They couldn't make it last forever.
(B) There was barely a drop of juice in the glass.
(C) He was hardly never sad during summer.
(D) No mistake.

55. (A) The very first student receives a reward.
(B) The cars enter the parking lot one by one.
(C) Each person do a great deal of work.
(D) No mistake.

56. (A) The librarian's job was amazing.
(B) The center's offices were locked.
(C) She craved her sister's approval.
(D) No mistake.

57. (A) The elephant refused to eat our dinner.
(B) The zoo keeper was exhausted after his long day of work.
(C) The birds flew into their cages.
(D) No mistake.

58. (A) The coffee and the tea are piping hot.
(B) All of her jackets are waterproof.
(C) She can't remember where she left her keys.
(D) No mistake.

59. (A) John is younger than Sarah.
(B) Suzie is the quietest person in class.
(C) Dave is the most smartest person in his family.
(D) No mistake.

60. (A) Its not her fault they lost.
(B) Her sister's brother is there.
(C) "I'm so tired," complained her mom.
(D) No mistake.

61. (A) They danced, sang, and ate.
(B) Her parents wanted to go on vacation and relax.
(C) She went to the store and bought so many groceries.
(D) No mistake.

62. (A) She can never make up her mind.
(B) He aren't the only one who arrived early.
(C) The ocean waves push various sea creatures onto the beach.
(D) No mistake.

63. (A) She washed, conditioned, and brushed her hair every single morning.
    (B) I was worried that the car would be stopped by authorities and taking away.
    (C) They hurried to finish cleaning and polishing every window on the building.
    (D) No mistake.

64. (A) Chloe was an excellent student.
    (B) Please drive careful.
    (C) They didn't behave politely.
    (D) No mistake.

65. (A) Halloween always happens before Thanksgiving.
    (B) Her favorite tire swing finally broke.
    (C) The house on the corner has incredible Christmas decorations last year.
    (D) No mistake.

66. (A) Both of the sisters are excellent at math.
    (B) It is widely accepted that he will become a doctor.
    (C) All of the gold are going to be turned into watches.
    (D) No mistake.

67. (A) She hated summer but she loving fall.
    (B) She wanted new shoes, clothes, and accessories.
    (C) The forest was impossibly dense and wide.
    (D) No mistake.

68. (A) Our mom suggested that we stay inside, having drank hot chocolate, and relax.
    (B) The coach was inspirational and encouraging to his team members.
    (C) The sky darkened rapidly and then rain poured from the clouds.
    (D) No mistake.

69. (A) Mandy's house is ancient.
    (B) Roma thoughtfully crafted a gift for her mom.
    (C) Kim ran quick around the track.
    (D) No mistake.

70. (A) They won't even consider the option.
    (B) The Earth won't never stop turning.
    (C) He said he'd never do that.
    (D) No mistake.

71. (A) One of her favorite songs play on that radio station every day.
    (B) Sarah and Mike cannot lift the car without tools.
    (C) Rachel has one of the dogs that was saved from the house fire.
    (D) No mistake.

72. (A) Told me that I would have to see the dentist.
    (B) Katy forgot to turn in her homework.
    (C) She ran quickly.
    (D) No mistake.

73. (A) Candy is sweet and delicious, but it is also addicting.
    (B) Working as a physician is very lucrative but not very rewarding.
    (C) The lamp was both very bright, pretty, and colorful.
    (D) No mistake.

74. (A) The dancer refused to quit dancing.
    (B) Olive wishes she didn't have to go.
    (C) He'd buy lunch but he hasn't got no money.
    (D) No mistake.

75. (A) Her eyelashes were lovely.
    (B) The rest of the class was tired.
    (C) She practiced knitting very careful.
    (D) No mistake.

76. (A) The chef cooked the meal and brought it to the customers.
    (B) My brother likes working out and to eat breakfast before school.
    (C) A squirrel finds a nut, buries it in the ground, and returns for it later.
    (D) No mistake.

77. (A) He was the strongest boxer on the team.
    (B) He was one of the most greatest authors of his time.
    (C) Keith was a funnier comedian than Chase.
    (D) No mistake.

78. (A) All managers were present at tomorrow's conference.
    (B) Arthur's son has an important presentation at work tomorrow.
    (C) The eggs fell out of the fridge and broke last night.
    (D) No mistake.

79. (A) The dog won't never leave its yard.
    (B) She hung on to every word.
    (C) His heart wouldn't stop beating.
    (D) No mistake.

80. (A) Michelle is a person who can't stand spicy foods.
    (B) The teacher gave the students back her papers.
    (C) Margaret paid her sister the money she owed her.
    (D) No mistake.

81. (A) Every time she went.
    (B) This could be the last one.
    (C) She was close to the end.
    (D) No mistake.

82. (A) The office lights so bright.
    (B) The singing was off key.
    (C) Their chorus was very talented.
    (D) No mistake.

83. (A) Everyone at the party is tired of hearing the same song on repeat.
    (B) She loves driving in her car when there is no traffic.
    (C) New York is the city that were the first to build a large subway system.
    (D) No mistake.

84. (A) The park, the playground, and the library were free to go to.
    (B) They fell in love and they got married.
    (C) They built a skyscraper then they tearing it down.
    (D) No mistake.

85. (A) She was the most oldest in her class.
    (B) The movie was funnier than the book.
    (C) The scholar was the most experienced.
    (D) No mistake.

86. (A) Learning is very important to your future, so it is imperative that you prioritize studying.
    (B) When it comes to figure skating, jumps and spinning can be difficult to master and dangerous to attempt.
    (C) I know that I should take the job in Sydney and relocate to Australia.
    (D) No mistake.

87. (A) Only taller kids could see the board.
    (B) Before sunrise the cat meowing loudly.
    (C) The rooster was aggressive.
    (D) No mistake.

88. (A) The sun was glaring in her eyes.
    (B) If it will get mended today.
    (C) They kept dancing all night.
    (D) No mistake.

89. (A) The dog ran away, but they soon came back.
    (B) Their cats were so hungry.
    (C) Her house had a chimney.
    (D) No mistake.

90. (A) They can't never catch a break.
(B) Soon they would be running away from here.
(C) The lamp never stopped shining.
(D) No mistake.

91. (A) It took the camp counselors hours to find Tony, who will hide under the bed.
(B) Decide now to avoid confusion and save time and money later on.
(C) The planets will continue to orbit the sun forever.
(D) No mistake.

92. (A) The frogs hop along the river bank.
(B) Everybody in Naomi's class were afraid of snakes.
(C) The science teacher changed the class project.
(D) No mistake.

93. (A) The first movement was enchanting.
(B) They went to the theater to see a play.
(C) The museum was full of tourists.
(D) No mistake.

94. (A) The daisies grew faster than the roses.
(B) He made it back sooner than his dad.
(C) She is more intelligenter than he is.
(D) No mistake.

95. (A) The waitress showed the family to their table then gave them menus.
(B) She tipped her manicurist before she did an excellent job.
(C) I will fix the hole in the wall before I hang up the new television.
(D) No mistake.

96. (A) She drank too much soda.
(B) A very competitive team.
(C) Her brother was annoying.
(D) No mistake.

97. (A) Orville can't eat any kind of dairy.
(B) Paul has hardly seen no birds today.
(C) February doesn't ever have more than twenty-nine days.
(D) No mistake.

98. (A) Only the richest voters will be able to vote from home next fall.
(B) The first person to find the last egg will receive a reward.
(C) The professional magician will perform after the folk musician.
(D) No mistake.

99. (A) The circus was in town for four weeks next year.
(B) She couldn't avoid the traffic this morning.
(C) He released his album after working on it for two years.
(D) No mistake.

100. (A) The cat won't never come down from that tree.
(B) Maggie refused to turn in her essay.
(C) She had attended hardly any games.
(D) No mistake.

101. (A) She is an excellent host and greets every guest with a smile.
(B) A pound of vegetables and bread satisfy two people.
(C) For twenty people, you will need ten gallons of milk.
(D) No mistake.

102. (A) The family members took their leftovers home.
(B) Sandy couldn't believe she had lost her phone.
(C) I am just grateful I don't have school tomorrow.
(D) No mistake.

103. (A) It was cloudy.
(B) The weather is horrible.
(C) Raining so bring an umbrella.
(D) No mistake.

104. (A) Every person has their own unique personality.
(B) Some of the marbles is lost under the bed.
(C) All of the trees are swaying in the wind.
(D) No mistake.

105. (A) The critic wasn't sure whether or not he liked the painting.
(B) The students spent hours painting and building all of the set pieces.
(C) School will be cancelled on Wednesday, Thursday, and on Friday.
(D) No mistake.

106. (A) They weren't never tired of dancing.
(B) The school never closed for snow days.
(C) She refused to accept his apology.
(D) No mistake.

107. (A) She stole his fancy car from him.
(B) The coaches worked on the soccer player's skills in preparation for our big game.
(C) She verified the information that was presented to her.
(D) No mistake.

108. (A) Musicians are never tired of new music.
(B) The banker never promised not to steal.
(C) The giraffe was not too tall for the enclosure.
(D) No mistake.

109. (A) The blue car is fast.
(B) The teacher random drew names out of a hat.
(C) My best friend easily completed today's homework.
(D) No mistake.

110. (A) Donovan had prepared for the big test by studying diligently.
(B) I love to sing, to dance, and to play loud music.
(C) I was washing, rinsing, and curled my hair.
(D) No mistake.

111. (A) Sarah can't eat any kind of seafood.
(B) She can never go back there.
(C) The school never fully reopened.
(D) No mistake.

112. (A) She is going to change the calendar last week.
(B) Each day begins with a long train ride to work.
(C) Her laundry will be done in about an hour.
(D) No mistake.

113. (A) She walked over the bridge to Manhattan tomorrow.
(B) The Golden Gate Bridge enters San Francisco from the north.
(C) Her grandparents lived in Alabama.
(D) No mistake.

114. (A) The teacher had the loudest voice in the school.
(B) December is colder than March.
(C) Ali told the most scariest story at the campfire.
(D) No mistake.

115. (A) The book club planned to meet next Friday at the café.
(B) The pond was filled with fish after it will be restocked.
(C) His phone broke after he lost his phone case.
(D) No mistake.

116. (A) When she started the race, she runs too fast due to excitement.
(B) After work, she picked up her kids from school.
(C) Before February, she needs to finish all of her projects.
(D) No mistake.

117. (A) The book that the club chose was amusing.
(B) The car sped away, but then she crashed.
(C) The library returned my lost glasses to me.
(D) No mistake.

Spelling

Overview

In this section, students are given three sentences and asked to choose the one that contains a word with a spelling error. If there is no error in any of the sentences, the correct choice is "no mistake."

We recommend that you practice at least 15-20 questions per week in preparing for the exam.

How to Use This Section

As determined by your study plan, including the results of your diagnostic tests, we encourage you to focus on the topics that are most challenging to you. This section will give you exposure to the different types of questions that are presented in spelling, and give you the practice to finding the path to the correct answer. If you find that you are challenged by this area and need additional help, remember to reach out to a trusted educator. Don't get discouraged! Take the materials to a teacher or tutor if you need additional enrichment in any given topic.

Tutorverse Tips!

Remember to look at all of the sentences for an obvious spelling error before examining any individual word too closely. There may be a very challenging word that you are unfamiliar with and you may not be sure if it is spelled correctly or not. Look ahead to the other choices and see if there is a familiar word spelled wrong that stands out. There's the answer!

Consider creating a list of words that are tested in this section. Simply writing down the word with the correct spelling can help you remember it next time it is encountered in a question.

Spelling Exercise

Choose the sentence that contains an error in spelling. If there is no error, select choice (D).

1. (A) She was remembering the voyage she had just made from India.
   (B) Her favorite time of day was the early mourning.
   (C) She stared out of the window with a thoughtful and troubled look.
   (D) No mistake.

2. (A) The weather was incredibly hot and humid.
   (B) Clarissa remembered a lesson she learned in school.
   (C) He excelled in his grammer lessons.
   (D) No mistake.

3. (A) She whispered quietly in the dark.
   (B) He was too impatient to find out what happend next.
   (C) The material was incredibly soft and fluffy.
   (D) No mistake.

4. (A) She was only fourty years old.
   (B) Every day brought a new challenge.
   (C) She had known that she would have to go also.
   (D) No mistake.

5. (A) He was confident he would win the competition.
   (B) She was troubled by her thougts.
   (C) Luis's favorite sport was, without a doubt, football.
   (D) No mistake.

6. (A) Though she was only seven years old, she played piano very well.
   (B) He could no longer stand the harrassment on the train.
   (C) She could not verify whether his statement was accurate.
   (D) No mistake.

7. (A) She went on a vacation to avoid the bad whether.
   (B) It was only rational to move out of the country.
   (C) She was surprised it was already dark outside.
   (D) No mistake.

8. (A) She had seen other children depart for school.
   (B) It was a large lovely garden with soft green grass.
   (C) She couldn't wait for school to start in autumn.
   (D) No mistake.

9. (A) The young students were too noisy.
   (B) She forgot to grade they're papers.
   (C) They no longer have a place to play.
   (D) No mistake.

10. (A) The lights were visible from outer space.
    (B) He was suprised by the expression on his sister's face.
    (C) She kept interrupting him while he spoke.
    (D) No mistake.

11. (A) They never even said goodbye.
    (B) It made her feel unappreciated.
    (C) She was so greatful for every gift.
    (D) No mistake.

12. (A) They had everything they could have ever wanted.
    (B) Her favorite movie actually had terrible reviews.
    (C) The incedent was gossiped about in the office.
    (D) No mistake.

13. (A) She was known for being very talkative.
    (B) The grandmother stopped tending her garden.
    (C) Both children were increadibly polite.
    (D) No mistake.

14. (A) She loved to memorize the constelations.
    (B) He did not believe in the existence of aliens.
    (C) Maria dreamed of being an astronaut someday.
    (D) No mistake.

15. (A) They were so releived to get out of school early.
    (B) The road was too rough to ride down.
    (C) The sign was only visible at night.
    (D) No mistake.

16. (A) The two people had nothing to talk about.
    (B) She was finaly able to read the board now that she had glasses.
    (C) The tragedy was on the news for an entire year.
    (D) No mistake.

17. (A) The leafs all fell from the tree at once.
(B) The writer's profession had taken an unfortunate turn.
(C) The poor children had now nowhere to play.
(D) No mistake.

18. (A) These stories made life more interesting.
(B) Abe can't go out without permission.
(C) He lived a very long time ago in anceint Greece.
(D) No mistake.

19. (A) He wasn't that serius about his studies.
(B) There are many famous fables.
(C) They took their time verifying the details.
(D) No mistake.

20. (A) The story was ment to teach children to treat others nicely.
(B) Not every winter storm is a blizzard.
(C) Some people do not like when their food touches other food.
(D) No mistake.

21. (A) Japan built many railroads in the 1800s.
(B) The president's office was always guarded.
(C) They are sold all over the world.
(D) No mistake.

22. (A) National parks are an important part of America.
(B) People enjoy sightseeing and visiting nature.
(C) Many turists visit New York City every year.
(D) No mistake.

23. (A) They ended the arguement without reaching a resolution.
(B) The warmth of spring gave people hope again.
(C) The athlete was ousted after starting a fight.
(D) No mistake.

24. (A) They saw spring as a fresh start for themselves, too.
(B) She was the pop star's number one fan.
(C) People still beleive in making resolutions to have a better year.
(D) No mistake.

25. (A) He hated having to deliver bad news.
(B) The train returned to the begining of the track.
(C) They are examples of crops that people plant in the spring.
(D) No mistake.

26. (A) The sun came out after months of darkness.
(B) The traditiun of making resolutions began.
(C) The crops became mature and ready for harvest.
(D) No mistake.

27. (A) Parents always tell their children to eat their vegatables.
(B) The seeds exist so the plant can reproduce.
(C) People say you can't judge a book by its cover.
(D) No mistake.

28. (A) Volunteering is as simple as deciding to help another person.
(B) There are many ways to volunteer in your hometown.
(C) They donated canned goods to the homless shelter.
(D) No mistake.

29. (A) The presure of the atmosphere is impossible to live in.
    (B) You can create a better life for yourself and others.
    (C) The writing sample will be used by schools to assess a student's writing skills.
    (D) No mistake.

30. (A) Lisa was too spiteful toward her brothers.
    (B) The acceptance letter came in the mail the next day.
    (C) Write your notes on a seperate piece of paper.
    (D) No mistake.

31. (A) In a chess set, there is one black piece to every one white piece.
    (B) There are still milions of animals that are strays or live in shelters.
    (C) Pet adoption makes sense for humans and animals.
    (D) No mistake.

32. (A) They struggled to dance to the unsteady rhthym.
    (B) The kids were so excited for the snow storm.
    (C) Bringing a pet into your home can be good for you.
    (D) No mistake.

33. (A) He delivered the package promptly.
    (B) Chores can help children learn good habbits.
    (C) Their children were busy doing their homework.
    (D) No mistake.

34. (A) She accused him of cheating on the exam.
    (B) The winter weather was frigid.
    (C) He wasn't that exited for the party.
    (D) No mistake.

35. (A) There was a nice breeze blowing.
    (B) He hoisted the kite up into the air.
    (C) They headed strait to the airport.
    (D) No mistake.

36. (A) The children shouted on the playground during recess.
    (B) The intern was completly overwhelmed with work.
    (C) The skyscrapers blocked the sun from reaching the streets.
    (D) No mistake.

37. (A) Doctors know that having a healthy diet isn't easy.
    (B) The gargoyles on the mansion were a frightening site to see.
    (C) The mayor was unfortunately not reelected.
    (D) No mistake.

38. (A) The magazine was no longer being sold in stores.
    (B) They had always played together and been fond of each other.
    (C) They were embarking on a journy to a new home.
    (D) No mistake.

39. (A) In about a week, I was tired of seeing the sights.
    (B) He shouldn't travel because he is in poor physicle condition.
    (C) The narrator's use of tone is quite impressive.
    (D) No mistake.

40. (A) The king's actions were atrocious.
    (B) She hid all of her most precious belongings.
    (C) The game had apparently already been finished.
    (D) No mistake.

41. (A) Her companion apeared quite frightened.
    (B) They reveled in the sights and sounds of the outdoors.
    (C) The siblings were bonded by the experience of encountering danger.
    (D) No mistake.

42. (A) They turned off from the track accordingly.
    (B) They sollemnly paid their respects.
    (C) We made our way across the hills toward home.
    (D) No mistake.

43. (A) There is an air of easy conversation among the guests.
    (B) Their was only one way they could survive.
    (C) Suddenly she whirled from the window and stood before her mirror.
    (D) No mistake.

44. (A) They woke up at nine and went down the shore.
    (B) The narrator implies that the hero might actually be the villain.
    (C) They spent their vacations visiting amusement parques.
    (D) No mistake.

45. (A) They broght an extravagant air to an otherwise casual event.
    (B) The teacher illustrated her point with a personal anecdote.
    (C) Luisa threw herself into her father's arms.
    (D) No mistake.

46. (A) She described a problem and recommended a solution.
    (B) Each generation can make life better for the next.
    (C) People should focus on themselfs and not worry about others.
    (D) No mistake.

47. (A) The roses bloomed before spring even arrived.
    (B) Mark and Abel were still feeling the affects of the long trip.
    (C) The rumor spread through town like wildfire.
    (D) No mistake.

48. (A) Ancient sculptors are more skilled than today's sculptors.
    (B) Desserts are not an appropriate environment for statues.
    (C) Even the greatest accomplishments will eventually be lost or forgotten.
    (D) No mistake.

49. (A) The author was famous for her populer historical novel.
    (B) Their journey was abruptly cut short.
    (C) Their neighbors were incredibly reliable and helpful.
    (D) No mistake.

50. (A) Her father's choice was difficult to comprehend.
    (B) She should reflect upon it in the peacefulness of nature.
    (C) He liked to spend time contemplating life's mysteries.
    (D) No mistake.

51. (A) She always kept a personal journal or diary.
    (B) There are other requirements to be fulfiled.
    (C) Artist should be as creative and inventive as possible.
    (D) No mistake.

52. (A) Voter turnout would remain largely the same.
    (B) America would reestablish its position as a global superpower.
    (C) It was wonderful to see all the cats happy and frolicking in the garden.
    (D) No mistake.

Composition

Overview

The Composition section has a variety of questions testing a student's ability with the correct forms of English and writing.

Students are challenged with tasks including:

- finding the most clearly written sentence
- determining the best transition word to connect thoughts
- choosing the sentence that does not fit with a theme
- understanding sentence placement in paragraphs
- picking a suitable topic that would fit a one-paragraph essay

We recommend that you practice at least 15-20 questions per week in preparing for the exam.

How to Use This Section

As determined by your study plan, including the results of your diagnostic tests, we encourage you to focus on the topics that are most challenging to you. This section will give you exposure to the different types of questions that are presented in composition, and give you the practice to finding the path to the correct answer. If you find that you are challenged by this area and need additional help, remember to reach out to a trusted educator. Don't get discouraged! Take the materials to a teacher or tutor if you need additional enrichment in any given topic.

Tutorverse Tips!

When asked to fill in a blank, consider your own answer first and then look at the choices provided. One may jump out as a matching answer. Consider the relationships between sentences in this section to arrive at the correct choice!

Composition Exercises

1. Choose the word that best completes the sentence.

   Sammy was __________ calm after being injured during her soccer game.

   (A) carefully
   (B) nervously
   (C) surprisingly
   (D) jokingly

2. Which sentence does *not* belong in the paragraph?

   (1) Dalmatians are a unique breed of dog known for their spotted black and white coats. (2) These special canines are also highly intelligent and make great companion animals. (3) They are highly trainable and can even be used as service dogs. (4) Some people are allergic to dogs.

   (A) Sentence 1
   (B) Sentence 2
   (C) Sentence 3
   (D) Sentence 4

3. Choose the group of words that best completes the sentence.

   Nicole felt most prepared for her tests when she ________________.

   (A) was regular studying
   (B) studied regularly
   (C) did studying regular
   (D) none of these

4. Which of the following sentences offers the *least* support for the topic "Learning to Ride a Bike"?

   (A) Training wheels are one of the early steps for new riders.
   (B) Riding a bike requires good balance.
   (C) It is normal to fall when you are learning, but do not let that discourage you.
   (D) The bicycle was invented in 1817.

5. Choose the group of words that best completes the sentence.

   After his car broke down, ________________.

   (A) taking the bus is what Shawn did.
   (B) Shawn took the bus.
   (C) the bus is what Shawn took.
   (D) taking the bus will Shawn.

6. Choose the best word or words to join the thoughts together.

   I am very full from dinner;__________ I would still like dessert.

   (A) in contrast
   (B) nevertheless
   (C) in addition
   (D) none of these

7. Which of these sentences expresses the idea most clearly?

   (A) Freddie enjoyed walking his dog after school.
   (B) Walking his dog after school is what Freddie enjoyed.
   (C) After school, walking his dog is what Freddie enjoyed.
   (D) Freddie, after school, enjoyed walking his dog.

8. Choose the word that best completes the sentence.

   __________ waiting for his brother to get home from school, Lawrence made a snack.

   (A) While
   (B) Since
   (C) Never
   (D) Until

9. Which of these sentences expresses the idea most clearly?

   (A) Emily, when she grows up, wants to be a scientist.
   (B) Emily wants to be a scientist when she grows up.
   (C) Being a scientist is what Emily wants when she grows up.
   (D) When she grows up, being a scientist is what Emily wants.

10. Which of the following themes could be effectively explored in a one-paragraph passage?

    (A) Medicine
    (B) Algebra
    (C) How to Build a Telescope
    (D) none of these

11. Which of the following themes could be effectively explored in a one-paragraph passage?

(A) Politics
(B) Psychology
(C) How to Slice an Apple
(D) none of these

12. Where should the sentence, "You can even pick apples in your own backyard by planting an apple tree." be placed in the paragraph below?

(1) Apple picking is a fun activity that anyone can enjoy. (2) The best time to pick apples is in the fall. (3) Many local farms offer apple picking to the public for a fee.

(A) Between sentences 1 and 2
(B) Between sentences 2 and 3
(C) After sentence 3
(D) The sentence does not fit in this paragraph.

13. Choose the best word or words to join the thoughts together.

Tony studied every night; __________ Kaylie never studied.

(A) for example,
(B) in contrast,
(C) however,
(D) none of these

14. Choose the best word or words to join the thoughts together.

Olivia did not water her plant as often as she should; __________ it still grew.

(A) therefore,
(B) in addition,
(C) surprisingly,
(D) none of these

15. Choose the best word or words to join the thoughts together.

Mary was excited to see her older brother; __________ she was looking forward to playing baseball with him.

(A) in addition,
(B) nevertheless,
(C) however,
(D) none of these

16. Which sentence does *not* belong in the paragraph?

(1) Visiting the dentist regularly is an important part of maintaining dental health. (2) During a cleaning, the dentist will remove plaque and tartar from your teeth and identify any problems you may be having. (3) Doctors must go through many years of school and training. (4) Always let your dentist know if you have any concerns about your teeth or gums.

(A) Sentence 1
(B) Sentence 2
(C) Sentence 3
(D) Sentence 4

17. Choose the word that best completes the sentence.

Tori was __________ surprised that she won the contest.

(A) frightfully
(B) nervously
(C) pleasantly
(D) jokingly

18. Which of the following pairs of sentences fits best under this topic sentence?

Buying a house is a great investment.

(A) Neighborhoods are great places to live. There are many sidewalks, playgrounds, and trees.
(B) However, there are also risks that buyers should be aware of. Many houses come with unforeseen problems and repairs may be needed.
(C) Homes come in many different styles. There is something for everyone's tastes.
(D) none of these

19. Which of the following pairs of sentences fits best under this topic sentence?

Sewing is a fun hobby and a great skill to have.

(A) Hobbies are a great way to spend time. There are many different hobbies to choose from.
(B) Once you know how to sew, you can make quilts, clothing, and more. Sewing your own items allows you to make exactly what you want.
(C) Craft stores are a great place to buy hobby materials. There are craft stories in most towns and cities.
(D) none of these

20. Which of these sentences expresses the idea most clearly?

(A) Karate practice on Thursday, Makhi looked forward to.
(B) Every Thursday, karate practice is what Makhi looked forward to.
(C) Makhi looked forward to karate practice every Thursday.
(D) Makhi, every Thursday, looked forward to karate practice.

21. Choose the best word that best completes the sentence.

Max waited ___________ his hot chocolate had cooled before he began drinking.

(A) first
(B) since
(C) after
(D) until

22. Which of these sentences expresses the idea most clearly?

(A) Jill's favorite activity is baking cookies with her mom.
(B) With her mom, baking cookies is Jill's favorite activity.
(C) Jill's favorite activity, with her mom, is baking cookies.
(D) Baking cookies is Jill's favorite activity with her mom.

23. Choose the word that best completes the sentence.

Patrick closed his eyes and relaxed on the hammock, ___________ swinging back and forth.

(A) peacefully
(B) nervously
(C) surprisingly
(D) badly

24. Which of these sentences expresses the idea most clearly?

(A) On the hill, the castle is where the Queen lived.
(B) The Queen, on the hill, lived in the castle.
(C) The castle on the hill is where the Queen lived.
(D) The Queen lived in the castle on the hill.

25. Choose the group of words that best completes the sentence.

    Before cutting the grass, ______________________.

    (A) Justin filled the lawnmower up with gasoline.
    (B) filling the lawnmower with gasoline is what Justin did.
    (C) the lawnmower was full of gasoline, Justin made sure.
    (D) fill the lawnmower with gasoline was first for Justin.

26. Choose the group of words that best completes the sentence.

    Most doctors will agree that it is essential ________________.

    (A) often to hydrate
    (B) to hydrate often
    (C) for hydrating often
    (D) often hydrating

27. Which choice most clearly expresses the intended meaning?

    (A) John took the cookies out of the oven when they were done.
    (B) The cookies John took out of the oven when they were done.
    (C) When the cookies were done, out of the oven John took them.
    (D) The cookies, when done, were taken out of the oven by John.

28. Choose the word that best completes the sentence.

    The boy looked ____________ at the broken vase; he feared there would be consequences for breaking it.

    (A) happily
    (B) effortlessly
    (C) nervously
    (D) alarmingly

29. Which choice most clearly expresses the intended meaning?

    (A) Caleb and his dad, on Saturday, went to the museum.
    (B) Caleb and his dad went to the museum on Saturday.
    (C) On Saturday, the museum is where Caleb and his dad went.
    (D) The museum is where Caleb and his dad went on Saturday.

30. Which of the following best fits under the topic, "How to Build a Jigsaw Puzzle"?

    (A) It is great to build puzzles with family and friends.
    (B) Puzzles are a great winter activity.
    (C) Use the picture on the box to sort the pieces based on which section of the puzzle they belong in.
    (D) Puzzles come in many shapes and sizes.

31. Choose the group of words that best completes the sentence.

    After eating dinner, __________________________.

    (A) washing his plate is what Leo did.
    (B) Leo washed his plate.
    (C) his plate was washed, Leo made sure.
    (D) the plate was washed by Leo.

32. Which choice most clearly expresses the intended meaning?

    (A) The clothes were folded neatly by Michael.
    (B) The clothes folded by Michael were neat.
    (C) Michael folded the clothes neatly.
    (D) Michael's clothes, when folded, were neat.

33. Choose the best word that best completes the sentence.

    Ellie knew that recess was _________ lunch.

    (A) beside
    (B) since
    (C) after
    (D) until

34. Choose the word that best completes the sentence.

    Tatiana sat ___________ at her desk; she knew she was prepared for the exam.

    (A) confidently
    (B) anxiously
    (C) uneasily
    (D) alarmingly

35. Which of these sentences would best fit at the end of the paragraph?

    (1) Whales are some of the largest creatures on the planet. (2) They are actually mammals, not fish, and are known to be highly intelligent. (3) Whales live in large family groups called *pods* and communicate with each other using echolocation.

    (A) Whales do not belong in zoos.
    (B) Whales truly are amazing creatures.
    (C) The ocean is home to many animals, including whales.
    (D) Baby whales grow very slowly.

36. Which choice most clearly expresses the intended meaning?

    (A) The birds made a safe nest for their eggs.
    (B) The nest was made safe for their eggs by the birds.
    (C) The eggs, in the nest, were made safe by the birds.
    (D) The nest made by the birds was safe for their eggs.

37. Choose the word that is a clear connective to complete the sentence.

    An hour before the football game, it started to storm; ___________ the game was cancelled.

    (A) excitedly,
    (B) unfortunately,
    (C) hopefully,
    (D) none of these

38. Choose the word that is a clear connective to complete the sentence.

    The heat was unbearable; ___________ we were able to find a spot at the pool.

    (A) luckily,
    (B) sadly,
    (C) carefully,
    (D) none of these

39. Which of the following themes could be effectively explored in a one-paragraph passage?

    (A) Genetics
    (B) Art History
    (C) Becoming a Published Author
    (D) none of these

40. Which sentence does *not* belong in the paragraph?

    (1) Tigers are unique animals. (2) Their black stripes and orange coat distinguish them from other big cats and help them camouflage in their habitat. (3) Unlike some big cats that live in family groups, tigers are solitary, meaning they prefer to live alone. (4) Cats make great companions.

    (A) Sentence 1
    (B) Sentence 2
    (C) Sentence 3
    (D) Sentence 4

41. Where should the sentence, "There are several steps to take when building a garden." be placed in the paragraph below?

(1) To begin, make sure your soil is fluffy and well-draining. (2) Assess how much sun and shade the area gets to help determine what you can plant there. (3) Finally, dig holes for your seeds, cover them with soil, and water.

(A) Before sentence 1.
(B) Between sentences 1 and 2.
(C) Between sentences 2 and 3.
(D) After sentence 3.

42. Which of the following pairs of sentences fits best under this topic sentence?

Sharks are as fascinating as they are misunderstood.

(A) Often thought of as man-eating monsters, most shark species are afraid of humans. In fact, humans are much more dangerous to sharks than they are to us.
(B) Many fish are carnivores, meaning they eat other fish or animals to survive. They are part of a food chain.
(C) Many divers enjoy looking for sharks while underwater. It takes years of training to become a deep-sea diver.
(D) none of these

43. Which of the following pairs of sentences fits best under this topic sentence?

The ocean is a vast habitat and home to many different plants and animals.

(A) The study of plants and animals in their environment is called ecology. It is all about ecosystems and how species interact with each other.
(B) Surfing is a highly competitive ocean sport. Many people compete in surfing competitions every year.
(C) Scientists believe that over one million different species live in the ocean. However, much of the ocean is still unexplored.
(D) none of these

44. Choose the word that best completes the sentence.

Martin walked to the shed ________ his house to put away his gardening tools.

(A) above
(B) beneath
(C) behind
(D) far

45. Which of the following sentences offers the *least* support for the topic "Why Pine Grove Middle School Needs a Computer Room"?

(A) Pine Grove Middle School does not have a computer room.
(B) Every other middle school in the area has a computer room.
(C) The students at Pine Grove Middle School need a place to do research, practice typing, and play educational games.
(D) Many students have computers at home.

46. Choose the word that best completes the sentence.

    Elizabeth __________ peered into the birds' nest to see if there were eggs inside.

    (A) curiously
    (B) anxiously
    (C) confidently
    (D) warily

47. Which sentence does *not* belong in the paragraph?

    (1) Reading is an excellent hobby and a wonderful way to learn. (2) Reading has been proven to improve memory and enrich vocabulary. (3) Reading can even help you relax. (4) Hobbies are a great way for people to spend their time.

    (A) Sentence 1
    (B) Sentence 2
    (C) Sentence 3
    (D) Sentence 4

48. Choose the word that best completes the sentence.

    Candace slid _________ the covers and was cozy in bed.

    (A) above
    (B) beneath
    (C) behind
    (D) away

49. Which of the following sentences offers the *least* support for the topic "Why Malls are Going Extinct"?

    (A) Many people do their shopping online.
    (B) Some people prefer the convenience of box stores such as Walmart and Target.
    (C) Malls are decorated beautifully during the holidays.
    (D) Some malls are far for people to travel to.

50. Choose the words that are a clear connective to complete the sentence.

    The boy spent every afternoon studying and always turned his homework in on time; __________ he was a good student.

    (A) because,
    (B) nevertheless,
    (C) in other words,
    (D) none of these

51. Which sentence does *not* belong in the paragraph?

    (1) Turkeys are a unique species of bird. (2) They are best known for their large size and the distinct "gobble" sound they make, which can be heard from up to a mile away. (3) Turkeys also have incredible eyesight; they can see three times as well as humans can. (4) Eyesight is an important sense.

    (A) Sentence 1
    (B) Sentence 2
    (C) Sentence 3
    (D) Sentence 4

52. Choose the words that are a clear connective to complete the sentence.

    Thomas forgot to pay his electric bill on time; __________ he had to pay a late fee.

    (A) because,
    (B) however,
    (C) consequently,
    (D) none of these

Practice Test 1

Overview

The practice test is designed to assess your understanding of key skills and concepts. It is important to take the final practice test after completing the diagnostic tests and after you have spent time studying and practicing.

The main difference between the practice tests and the actual test is that the practice tests are scored differently from how the actual exam is scored. On the actual exam, your score will be determined by how well you did compared to other students in your grade. On the practice tests, however, we will score every question in order to gauge your mastery over skills and concepts.

Format

The format of the practice test is similar to that of the actual test. The number of questions included in each section mirror those of the actual test. This is done by design, in order to help familiarize you with the actual length of the test.

In addition to the reading, verbal, and language concepts reviewed in this workbook, this practice test also includes mathematics and quantitative reasoning material, similar to what will be on the actual exam. If you feel you need more practice on the math concepts covered in this test, consider consulting our other book, "HSPT Mathematics and Quantitative Reasoning: 1,300+ Practice Problems," which is available for purchase at www.thetutorverse.com/books.

The practice test includes the following sections:

Diagnostic Test Section	**Questions**	**Time Limit**
Verbal Skills	60	16 minutes
Quantitative Skills	52	30 minutes
Reading Comprehension	62	25 minutes
Mathematics	64	45 minutes
Language	60	25 minutes
Total	**298**	**2h 21 minutes**

Breaks: Generally, 2 brief breaks are given between sections of the test; however, the timing and duration of the breaks are determined by the individual school that is administering the exam.

Calculators

Students are not permitted to use calculators on the HSPT. **To ensure the results of the practice test are as accurate as possible, do not use a calculator on this exam.** If you have a diagnosed learning disability which requires the use of a calculator, contact your testing site to organize special accommodations and continue to practice with a calculator as needed.

Answering

Use the answer sheet provided on the next several pages to record your answers. You may wish to tear these pages out of the workbook.

Practice Test Answer Sheet

[Carefully tear or cut out this page.]

Section 1: Verbal Skills

1 ⒶⒷⒸⒹ	13 ⒶⒷⒸⒹ	25 ⒶⒷⒸⒹ	37 ⒶⒷⒸⒹ	49 ⒶⒷⒸ
2 ⒶⒷⒸⒹ	14 ⒶⒷⒸⒹ	26 ⒶⒷⒸⒹ	38 ⒶⒷⒸⒹ	50 ⒶⒷⒸⒹ
3 ⒶⒷⒸⒹ	15 ⒶⒷⒸⒹ	27 ⒶⒷⒸⒹ	39 ⒶⒷⒸ	51 ⒶⒷⒸⒹ
4 ⒶⒷⒸⒹ	16 ⒶⒷⒸⒹ	28 ⒶⒷⒸ	40 ⒶⒷⒸⒹ	52 ⒶⒷⒸⒹ
5 ⒶⒷⒸⒹ	17 ⒶⒷⒸⒹ	29 ⒶⒷⒸⒹ	41 ⒶⒷⒸⒹ	53 ⒶⒷⒸⒹ
6 ⒶⒷⒸⒹ	18 ⒶⒷⒸⒹ	30 ⒶⒷⒸⒹ	42 ⒶⒷⒸⒹ	54 ⒶⒷⒸ
7 ⒶⒷⒸⒹ	19 ⒶⒷⒸ	31 ⒶⒷⒸⒹ	43 ⒶⒷⒸⒹ	55 ⒶⒷⒸⒹ
8 ⒶⒷⒸ	20 ⒶⒷⒸⒹ	32 ⒶⒷⒸⒹ	44 ⒶⒷⒸⒹ	56 ⒶⒷⒸⒹ
9 ⒶⒷⒸⒹ	21 ⒶⒷⒸⒹ	33 ⒶⒷⒸⒹ	45 ⒶⒷⒸⒹ	57 ⒶⒷⒸ
10 ⒶⒷⒸⒹ	22 ⒶⒷⒸⒹ	34 ⒶⒷⒸⒹ	46 ⒶⒷⒸ	58 ⒶⒷⒸⒹ
11 ⒶⒷⒸⒹ	23 ⒶⒷⒸⒹ	35 ⒶⒷⒸ	47 ⒶⒷⒸⒹ	59 ⒶⒷⒸⒹ
12 ⒶⒷⒸ	24 ⒶⒷⒸⒹ	36 ⒶⒷⒸⒹ	48 ⒶⒷⒸⒹ	60 ⒶⒷⒸⒹ

Section 2: Quantitative Skills

61 ⒶⒷⒸⒹ	72 ⒶⒷⒸⒹ	83 ⒶⒷⒸⒹ	94 ⒶⒷⒸⒹ	105 ⒶⒷⒸⒹ
62 ⒶⒷⒸⒹ	73 ⒶⒷⒸⒹ	84 ⒶⒷⒸⒹ	95 ⒶⒷⒸⒹ	106 ⒶⒷⒸⒹ
63 ⒶⒷⒸⒹ	74 ⒶⒷⒸⒹ	85 ⒶⒷⒸⒹ	96 ⒶⒷⒸⒹ	107 ⒶⒷⒸⒹ
64 ⒶⒷⒸⒹ	75 ⒶⒷⒸⒹ	86 ⒶⒷⒸⒹ	97 ⒶⒷⒸⒹ	108 ⒶⒷⒸⒹ
65 ⒶⒷⒸⒹ	76 ⒶⒷⒸⒹ	87 ⒶⒷⒸⒹ	98 ⒶⒷⒸⒹ	109 ⒶⒷⒸⒹ
66 ⒶⒷⒸⒹ	77 ⒶⒷⒸⒹ	88 ⒶⒷⒸⒹ	99 ⒶⒷⒸⒹ	110 ⒶⒷⒸⒹ
67 ⒶⒷⒸⒹ	78 ⒶⒷⒸⒹ	89 ⒶⒷⒸⒹ	100 ⒶⒷⒸⒹ	111 ⒶⒷⒸⒹ
68 ⒶⒷⒸⒹ	79 ⒶⒷⒸⒹ	90 ⒶⒷⒸⒹ	101 ⒶⒷⒸⒹ	112 ⒶⒷⒸⒹ
69 ⒶⒷⒸⒹ	80 ⒶⒷⒸⒹ	91 ⒶⒷⒸⒹ	102 ⒶⒷⒸⒹ	
70 ⒶⒷⒸⒹ	81 ⒶⒷⒸⒹ	92 ⒶⒷⒸⒹ	103 ⒶⒷⒸⒹ	
71 ⒶⒷⒸⒹ	82 ⒶⒷⒸⒹ	93 ⒶⒷⒸⒹ	104 ⒶⒷⒸⒹ	

Section 3: Reading

113 ⒶⒷⒸⒹ	121 ⒶⒷⒸⒹ	129 ⒶⒷⒸⒹ	137 ⒶⒷⒸⒹ	145 ⒶⒷⒸⒹ
114 ⒶⒷⒸⒹ	122 ⒶⒷⒸⒹ	130 ⒶⒷⒸⒹ	138 ⒶⒷⒸⒹ	146 ⒶⒷⒸⒹ
115 ⒶⒷⒸⒹ	123 ⒶⒷⒸⒹ	131 ⒶⒷⒸⒹ	139 ⒶⒷⒸⒹ	147 ⒶⒷⒸⒹ
116 ⒶⒷⒸⒹ	124 ⒶⒷⒸⒹ	132 ⒶⒷⒸⒹ	140 ⒶⒷⒸⒹ	148 ⒶⒷⒸⒹ
117 ⒶⒷⒸⒹ	125 ⒶⒷⒸⒹ	133 ⒶⒷⒸⒹ	141 ⒶⒷⒸⒹ	149 ⒶⒷⒸⒹ
118 ⒶⒷⒸⒹ	126 ⒶⒷⒸⒹ	134 ⒶⒷⒸⒹ	142 ⒶⒷⒸⒹ	150 ⒶⒷⒸⒹ
119 ⒶⒷⒸⒹ	127 ⒶⒷⒸⒹ	135 ⒶⒷⒸⒹ	143 ⒶⒷⒸⒹ	151 ⒶⒷⒸⒹ
120 ⒶⒷⒸⒹ	128 ⒶⒷⒸⒹ	136 ⒶⒷⒸⒹ	144 ⒶⒷⒸⒹ	152 ⒶⒷⒸⒹ

(Section 3: Reading continued on reverse)

153 ⒶⒷⒸⒹ	158 ⒶⒷⒸⒹ	163 ⒶⒷⒸⒹ	168 ⒶⒷⒸⒹ	173 ⒶⒷⒸⒹ
154 ⒶⒷⒸⒹ	159 ⒶⒷⒸⒹ	164 ⒶⒷⒸⒹ	169 ⒶⒷⒸⒹ	174 ⒶⒷⒸⒹ
155 ⒶⒷⒸⒹ	160 ⒶⒷⒸⒹ	165 ⒶⒷⒸⒹ	170 ⒶⒷⒸⒹ	
156 ⒶⒷⒸⒹ	161 ⒶⒷⒸⒹ	166 ⒶⒷⒸⒹ	171 ⒶⒷⒸⒹ	
157 ⒶⒷⒸⒹ	162 ⒶⒷⒸⒹ	167 ⒶⒷⒸⒹ	172 ⒶⒷⒸⒹ	

Section 4: Mathematics

175 ⒶⒷⒸⒹ	188 ⒶⒷⒸⒹ	201 ⒶⒷⒸⒹ	214 ⒶⒷⒸⒹ	227 ⒶⒷⒸⒹ
176 ⒶⒷⒸⒹ	189 ⒶⒷⒸⒹ	202 ⒶⒷⒸⒹ	215 ⒶⒷⒸⒹ	228 ⒶⒷⒸⒹ
177 ⒶⒷⒸⒹ	190 ⒶⒷⒸⒹ	203 ⒶⒷⒸⒹ	216 ⒶⒷⒸⒹ	229 ⒶⒷⒸⒹ
178 ⒶⒷⒸⒹ	191 ⒶⒷⒸⒹ	204 ⒶⒷⒸⒹ	217 ⒶⒷⒸⒹ	230 ⒶⒷⒸⒹ
179 ⒶⒷⒸⒹ	192 ⒶⒷⒸⒹ	205 ⒶⒷⒸⒹ	218 ⒶⒷⒸⒹ	231 ⒶⒷⒸⒹ
180 ⒶⒷⒸⒹ	193 ⒶⒷⒸⒹ	206 ⒶⒷⒸⒹ	219 ⒶⒷⒸⒹ	232 ⒶⒷⒸⒹ
181 ⒶⒷⒸⒹ	194 ⒶⒷⒸⒹ	207 ⒶⒷⒸⒹ	220 ⒶⒷⒸⒹ	233 ⒶⒷⒸⒹ
182 ⒶⒷⒸⒹ	195 ⒶⒷⒸⒹ	208 ⒶⒷⒸⒹ	221 ⒶⒷⒸⒹ	234 ⒶⒷⒸⒹ
183 ⒶⒷⒸⒹ	196 ⒶⒷⒸⒹ	209 ⒶⒷⒸⒹ	222 ⒶⒷⒸⒹ	235 ⒶⒷⒸⒹ
184 ⒶⒷⒸⒹ	197 ⒶⒷⒸⒹ	210 ⒶⒷⒸⒹ	223 ⒶⒷⒸⒹ	236 ⒶⒷⒸⒹ
185 ⒶⒷⒸⒹ	198 ⒶⒷⒸⒹ	211 ⒶⒷⒸⒹ	224 ⒶⒷⒸⒹ	237 ⒶⒷⒸⒹ
186 ⒶⒷⒸⒹ	199 ⒶⒷⒸⒹ	212 ⒶⒷⒸⒹ	225 ⒶⒷⒸⒹ	238 ⒶⒷⒸⒹ
187 ⒶⒷⒸⒹ	200 ⒶⒷⒸⒹ	213 ⒶⒷⒸⒹ	226 ⒶⒷⒸⒹ	

Section 5: Language Skills

239 ⒶⒷⒸⒹ	251 ⒶⒷⒸⒹ	263 ⒶⒷⒸⒹ	275 ⒶⒷⒸⒹ	287 ⒶⒷⒸⒹ
240 ⒶⒷⒸⒹ	252 ⒶⒷⒸⒹ	264 ⒶⒷⒸⒹ	276 ⒶⒷⒸⒹ	288 ⒶⒷⒸⒹ
241 ⒶⒷⒸⒹ	253 ⒶⒷⒸⒹ	265 ⒶⒷⒸⒹ	277 ⒶⒷⒸⒹ	289 ⒶⒷⒸⒹ
242 ⒶⒷⒸⒹ	254 ⒶⒷⒸⒹ	266 ⒶⒷⒸⒹ	278 ⒶⒷⒸⒹ	290 ⒶⒷⒸⒹ
243 ⒶⒷⒸⒹ	255 ⒶⒷⒸⒹ	267 ⒶⒷⒸⒹ	279 ⒶⒷⒸⒹ	291 ⒶⒷⒸⒹ
244 ⒶⒷⒸⒹ	256 ⒶⒷⒸⒹ	268 ⒶⒷⒸⒹ	280 ⒶⒷⒸⒹ	292 ⒶⒷⒸⒹ
245 ⒶⒷⒸⒹ	257 ⒶⒷⒸⒹ	269 ⒶⒷⒸⒹ	281 ⒶⒷⒸⒹ	293 ⒶⒷⒸⒹ
246 ⒶⒷⒸⒹ	258 ⒶⒷⒸⒹ	270 ⒶⒷⒸⒹ	282 ⒶⒷⒸⒹ	294 ⒶⒷⒸⒹ
247 ⒶⒷⒸⒹ	259 ⒶⒷⒸⒹ	271 ⒶⒷⒸⒹ	283 ⒶⒷⒸⒹ	295 ⒶⒷⒸⒹ
248 ⒶⒷⒸⒹ	260 ⒶⒷⒸⒹ	272 ⒶⒷⒸⒹ	284 ⒶⒷⒸⒹ	296 ⒶⒷⒸⒹ
249 ⒶⒷⒸⒹ	261 ⒶⒷⒸⒹ	273 ⒶⒷⒸⒹ	285 ⒶⒷⒸⒹ	297 ⒶⒷⒸⒹ
250 ⒶⒷⒸⒹ	262 ⒶⒷⒸⒹ	274 ⒶⒷⒸⒹ	286 ⒶⒷⒸⒹ	298 ⒶⒷⒸⒹ

Verbal Skills

Questions 1-60, 16 Minutes

1. Which word does *not* belong with the others?
   (A) apartment
   (B) house
   (C) mansion
   (D) store

2. Bathing suit is to swimming as tracksuit is to
   (A) jacket
   (B) lake
   (C) running
   (D) sleeping

3. Invaluable most nearly means
   (A) expensive
   (B) fancy
   (C) priceless
   (D) uninteresting

4. Which word does *not* belong with the others?
   (A) beverage
   (B) juice
   (C) soda
   (D) coffee

5. Intense most nearly means
   (A) amusing
   (B) complicated
   (C) confusing
   (D) severe

6. Angry is to argument as calm is to
   (A) discussion
   (B) emotion
   (C) fight
   (D) peaceful

7. Majestic means the opposite of
   (A) expensive
   (B) pathetic
   (C) royal
   (D) serious

8. Jessica hates sundaes. Sundaes contain cherries. Jessica must hate cherries. If the first two statements are true, then the third is
   (A) True
   (B) False
   (C) Uncertain

9. Propose is to idea as prove is to
   (A) detective
   (B) discover
   (C) scientist
   (D) theory

10. Which word does *not* belong with the others?
    (A) bed
    (B) couch
    (C) dresser
    (D) furniture

11. Bliss means the opposite of
    (A) belief
    (B) happiness
    (C) sadness
    (D) undone

12. All flowers need photosynthesis to live. Daffodils are a type of flower. Daffodils need photosynthesis to live. If the first two statements are true, then the third is
    (A) True
    (B) False
    (C) Uncertain

13. Which word does *not* belong with the others?
    (A) campaign
    (B) debate
    (C) election
    (D) politics

14. Designer is to fashion as architect is to
    (A) art
    (B) buildings
    (C) career
    (D) sketch

15. Mediocre means the opposite of
    (A) bland
    (B) medium
    (C) special
    (D) tired

16. Eligible most nearly means
    (A) creative
    (B) employed
    (C) qualified
    (D) unable

17. Which word does *not* belong with the others?
(A) ask
(B) assume
(C) interrogate
(D) question

18. Proposal most nearly means
(A) denial
(B) marriage
(C) problem
(D) suggestion

19. Julian is afraid of sharks. Sharks live in the ocean. Julian never swims in the ocean. If the first two statements are true, then the third is
(A) True
(B) False
(C) Uncertain

20. Which word does *not* belong with the others?
(A) crayon
(B) marker
(C) paper
(D) pencil

21. Abandon most nearly means
(A) haunt
(B) leave
(C) locate
(D) rescue

22. Poised is to clumsy as intriguing is to
(A) dull
(B) graceful
(C) interesting
(D) personality

23. Which word does *not* belong with the others?
(A) assessment
(B) quiz
(C) study
(D) test

24. Casual most nearly means
(A) careful
(B) informal
(C) serious
(D) strict

25. Hamper means the opposite of
(A) arrange
(B) estimate
(C) facilitate
(D) suppress

26. Which word does *not* belong with the others?
(A) painter
(B) photographer
(C) professor
(D) sculptor

27. Which word does *not* belong with the others?
(A) cotton
(B) fabric
(C) silk
(D) wool

28. Janette is faster than Peter. Maria is faster than Peter. Maria is faster than Janette. If the first two statements are true, then the third is
(A) True
(B) False
(C) Uncertain

29. Irate is to angry as ecstatic is to
(A) electric
(B) emotion
(C) frustrated
(D) happy

30. Which word does *not* belong with the others?
(A) chips
(B) nuts
(C) popcorn
(D) snacks

31. Fierce most nearly means
(A) friendly
(B) pretty
(C) scared
(D) vicious

32. Spurn means the opposite of
(A) accept
(B) disdain
(C) rebuff
(D) scorn

33. Which word does *not* belong with the others?
(A) exercise
(B) health
(C) sleep
(D) vitamins

34. Sheepish most nearly means
(A) furry
(B) invisible
(C) outgoing
(D) shy

35. Rats are rodents. Most people consider rats as pests. All rodents are pests. If the first two statements are true, then the third is
(A) True
(B) False
(C) Uncertain

36. Mortify most nearly means
(A) embalm
(B) embarrass
(C) harm
(D) terminate

37. Iron is to metal as diamond is to
(A) beauty
(B) gem
(C) jewelry
(D) ruby

38. Ornate means the opposite of
(A) adorned
(B) complex
(C) elaborate
(D) simple

39. All arachnids have eight legs. Spiders are arachnids. All spiders have eight legs. If the first two statements are true, then the third is
(A) True
(B) False
(C) Uncertain

40. Which word does *not* belong with the others?
(A) ice
(B) smoke
(C) steam
(D) water

41. Consolidate most nearly means
(A) compare
(B) organize
(C) separate
(D) unite

42. Eruption is to volcano as avalanche is to
(A) dangerous
(B) disaster
(C) mountain
(D) skiing

43. Tolerance means the opposite of
(A) acceptance
(B) composure
(C) impatience
(D) submission

44. Which word does *not* belong with the others?
(A) beat
(B) melody
(C) music
(D) rhythm

45. Immense most nearly means
(A) energetic
(B) enormous
(C) passionate
(D) quick

46. Airports are very busy during holidays. Holidays can be stressful for some people. Flying is more dangerous during the holidays. If the first two statements are true, then the third is
(A) True
(B) False
(C) Uncertain

47. Florist is to flowers as chef is to
(A) cook
(B) kitchen
(C) restaurant
(D) vegetables

48. Prosper means the opposite of
(A) achieve
(B) derive
(C) flounder
(D) succeed

49. Stephany hates cold weather. Sweden is a country that has very cold winters. Stephany does not want to live in Sweden. If the first two statements are true, then the third is
(A) True
(B) False
(C) Uncertain

50. Sensation most nearly means
(A) destination
(B) emptiness
(C) feeling
(D) vacation

51. Obtuse most nearly means
(A) dull
(B) jagged
(C) misuse
(D) obvious

52. Dismiss is to accept as repair is to
(A) destroy
(B) fix
(C) tool
(D) work

53. Keen means the opposite of
    (A) acute
    (B) imperceptive
    (C) sensitive
    (D) sharp

54. Judith loves rock music. Oasis is a rock band. Judith loves Oasis. If the first two statements are true, then the third is
    (A) True
    (B) False
    (C) Uncertain

55. Which word does *not* belong with the others?
    (A) microwave
    (B) shower
    (C) stove
    (D) toaster

56. Which word does *not* belong with the others?
    (A) annoying
    (B) irritating
    (C) obnoxious
    (D) pleasurable

57. Percy loves coffee. Cafes sell coffee. Percy likes to hang out at cafes. If the first two statements are true, then the third is
    (A) True
    (B) False
    (C) Uncertain

58. Feasible most nearly means
    (A) attainable
    (B) edible
    (C) frightening
    (D) hopeless

59. Trite most nearly means
    (A) banal
    (B) delicious
    (C) fresh
    (D) original

60. Which word does *not* belong with the others?
    (A) bus
    (B) subway
    (C) train
    (D) transfer

Quantitative Skills

Questions 61-112, 30 Minutes

61. In the sequence $1, -1, -2, 2, 4...$, what number comes next?
(A) -8
(B) -4
(C) 4
(D) 8

62. Examine I, II, and III and find the *best* answer when x and y are both positive.

I. $4x + y$
II. $-1(-x - y)$
III. $x + 4y$

(A) I and III are equal
(B) I is greater than III
(C) III is greater than II
(D) III is greater than I

63. In the sequence $-40, 10, -\frac{1}{4}, \frac{1}{16}...$, what number should come next?
(A) $-\frac{1}{32}$
(B) $-\frac{1}{64}$
(C) $\frac{1}{64}$
(D) $\frac{1}{32}$

64. What number added to the sum of 8 and 9 is equal to the product of 10 and 4?
(A) 3
(B) 22
(C) 23
(D) 57

65. In the sequence 10.6, 10.3, 10.0, 9.7..., what number should come next?
(A) 9
(B) 9.2
(C) 9.3
(D) 9.4

66. What number subtracted from the difference of 21 and 10 is equal to the range of the numbers 10, 7, 9, 15, and 6?
(A) 2
(B) 3
(C) 4
(D) 5

67. Examine I, II, and III and find the *best* answer:

KEY

Large House = 10 houses

Small House = 1 house

I.
II.
III.

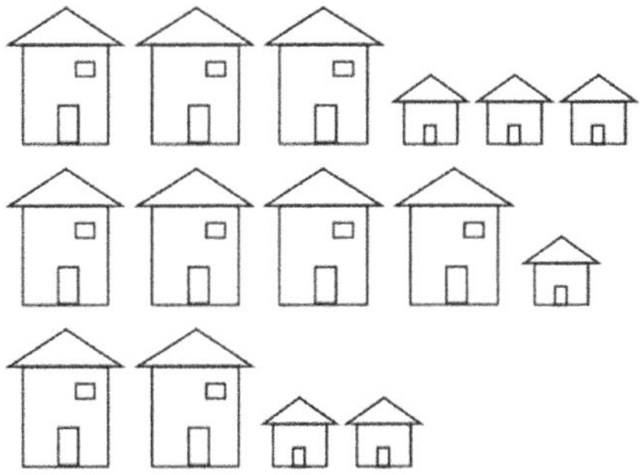

(A) I > II > III
(B) I = II > III
(C) III < II < I
(D) II > I > III

68. What number added to 37 is the product of 8 and 7?
(A) 15
(B) 19
(C) 21
(D) 22

69. Examine I, II, and III and find the best answer.

I. the y-intercept of $2x + y = 1$
II. the y-intercept of $y = 2x - 1$
III. the y-intercept of the line shown

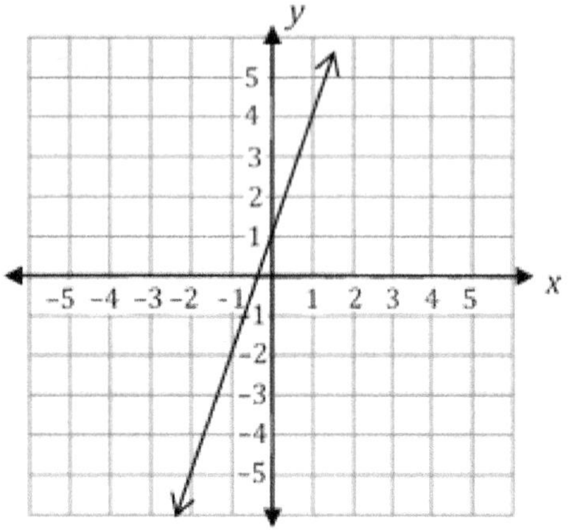
y
x
-5 -4 -3 -2 -1 1 2 3 4 5
5 4 3 2 1 -1 -2 -3 -4 -5

(A) I is less than II
(B) I is greater than III
(C) II is greater than III
(D) III is greater than II

70. Which number should come next in this series: 144, 72, 24, 12, ___?
(A) 2
(B) 3
(C) 4
(D) 6

71. Examine the angles below and find the *best* answer.

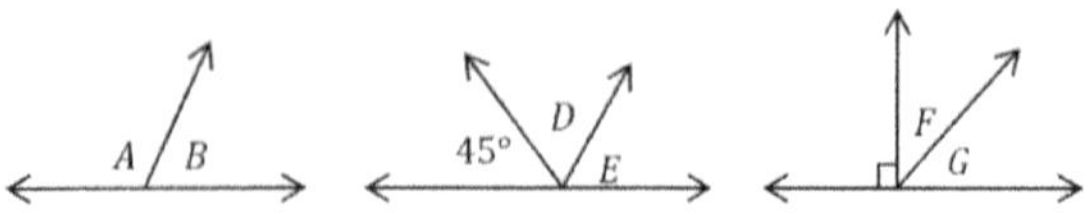
A
B
45°
D
E
F
G

(A) $\angle F + \angle G < \angle D + \angle E < \angle B + \angle A$
(B) $\angle D + \angle E > \angle B + \angle A$
(C) $\angle F + \angle G > \angle B + \angle A$
(D) $\angle D + \angle E = \angle F + \angle G$

72. In the sequence 1.3, 1.2, 1.1, 1..., what number should come next?
(A) −1
(B) 0
(C) 0.5
(D) 0.9

73. The following graph shows how many hours Ellie and Tara spent playing video games each day of the week. Find the *best* answer.

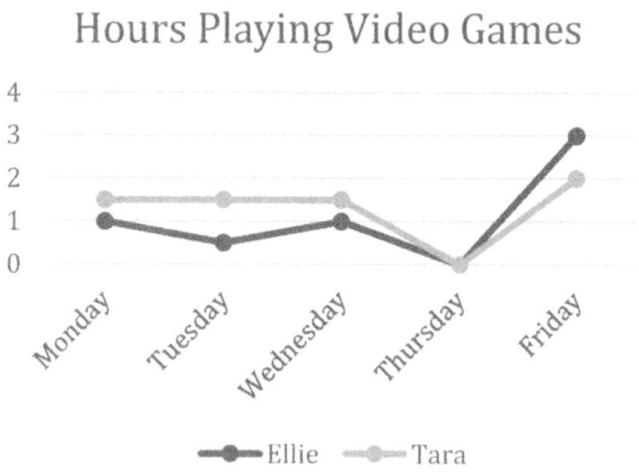
Hours Playing Video Games
4
3
2
1
0
Monday
Tuesday
Wednesday
Thursday
Friday
Ellie
Tara

(A) Ellie played more hours on Monday than Tara did.
(B) Neither Ellie nor Tara played video games on Thursday.
(C) Both Ellie and Tara played more than one hour on Wednesday.
(D) Tara played more hours on Friday than Ellie did.

74. What number divided by 2^3 is 20% of 45?
(A) 40
(B) 64
(C) 72
(D) 81

75. Examine I, II, and III and find the *best* answer when x and y are both positive.

I. $2(2y)$
II. $-x + 2y - 3y$
III. $-x - y$

(A) II and III are equal, and both are greater than I
(B) II is greater than I
(C) III is greater than II
(D) II and III are equal, and both are less than I.

76. What number subtracted from 31 makes 8 more than 13?
(A) 8
(B) 10
(C) 26
(D) 52

77. Examine the following and find the best answer.

I. The perimeter of the rectangle
II. The perimeter of the triangle
III. The perimeter of the hexagon

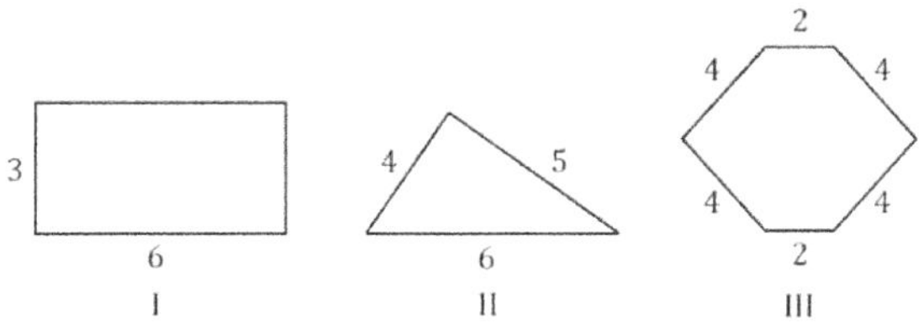
3
6
I
4
5
6
II
2
4
4
4
4
2
III

(A) I is less than II, and II is less than III
(B) I is less than III, and III is less than II
(C) III is greater than I, and I is greater than II
(D) I and III are equal, and both are greater than II

78. What number subtracted from 22 makes 12 less than 26?
(A) 4
(B) 6
(C) 8
(D) 10

79. Examine I, II, and III, and find the *best* answer.

I. 300% of 7
II. 50% of 50
III. 15% of 100

(A) I < II = III
(B) III < I < II
(C) I = II > III
(D) III > I > II

80. In the sequence 2, 1, 0.5, 0.25, ... what number should come next?
(A) 0.0125
(B) 0.05
(C) 0.1
(D) 0.125

81. Examine the following and find the best answer:

I. 11×2^2
II. $35 + 9$
III. $88 \div 2^1$

(A) I, II, and III are equal
(B) I is greater than II, which is greater than III
(C) I is smaller than II, which is smaller than III
(D) II is greater than III, which is greater than I

82. What number is 50% of 30% of 200?
(A) 10
(B) 15
(C) 30
(D) 40

83. Examine I, II, and III and find the best answer.

I. the y-intercept of the line shown
II. the y-intercept of $4x + 2y = 8$
III. the y-intercept of $y = -x - 6$

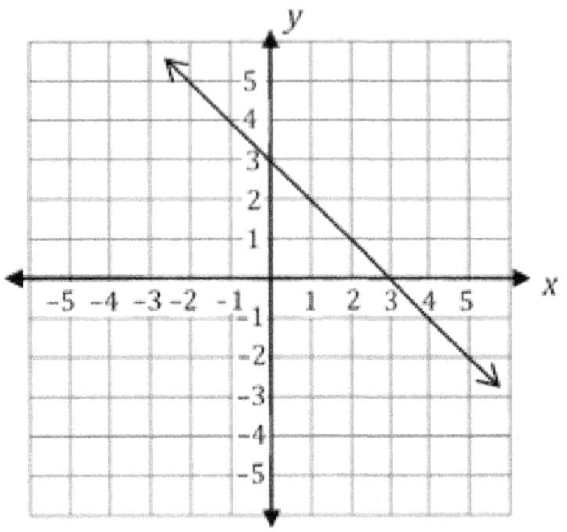
y
x
5
4
3
2
1
-1
-2
-3
-4
-5
-5 -4 -3 -2 -1
1 2 3 4 5

(A) I is equal to III
(B) I is less than III
(C) II is greater than III
(D) III is greater than II

84. What number when subtracted from $\frac{3}{4}$ of 20 is $\frac{1}{2}$ of 12?
(A) 4
(B) 6
(C) 9
(D) 15

85. What number subtracted by 5 is $\frac{2}{3}$ of 18?
(A) 1
(B) 11
(C) 14
(D) 17

86. The graph below shows how many pushups Jason is able to do each day. Find the *best* answer.

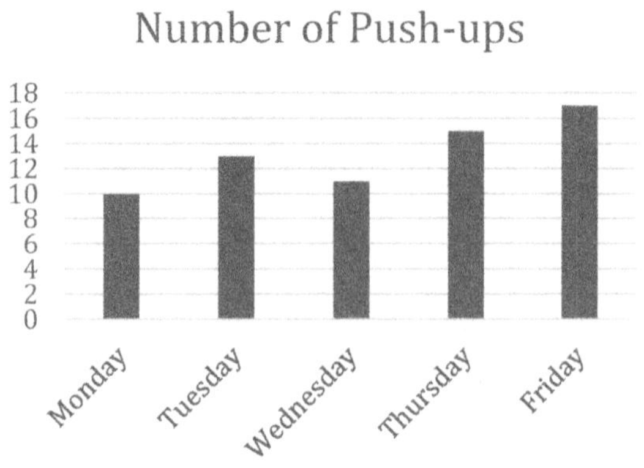
Number of Push-ups
18
16
14
12
10
8
6
4
2
0
Monday
Tuesday
Wednesday
Thursday
Friday

(A) Jason did more pushups on Wednesday than he did on Monday
(B) Jason did more pushups on Thursday than he did on Friday
(C) Jason did the same number of pushups on Tuesday and Thursday
(D) Jason did the least number of pushups on Friday

87. What number should fill in the blank in this series: 13, 22, 30,____,47?
(A) 37
(B) 38
(C) 39
(D) 40

88. Examine I, II, and III and find the *best* answer.

I. 4 months
II. 8 months
III. 1 year

(A) I is less than III, and III is less than II
(B) The sum of I and II is equal to III
(C) II is less than III, and III is less than I
(D) The sum of I and III is less than II

89. Examine I, II, and III and find the *best* answer.

I. Half-hour
II. 15 minutes
III. 30 minutes

(A) II < III = I
(B) II + III < I
(C) III > I > II
(D) III - II = I

90. Given that m is parallel to n, examine angles A, B, C, D, E, F, G, and H and find the best answer.

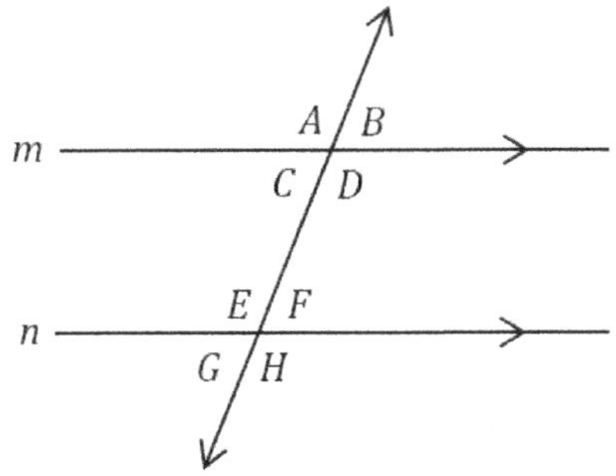
m
n
A
B
C
D
E
F
G
H

(A) $\angle A = \angle G$
(B) $\angle E + \angle C = \angle D + \angle F$
(C) $\angle D = \angle F$
(D) $\angle B + \angle C = \angle E + \angle G$

91. Examine the following and find the best answer.

I. The perimeter of an equilateral triangle with a side length of 7
II. The perimeter of a square with side length of 6
III. The perimeter of a regular octagon with a side length of 3

(A) II and III are equal, and both are greater than I
(B) I is greater than II, and II is greater than III
(C) III is less than II, and II is equal to I
(D) II and III are equal, and both are less than I

92. Examine I, II, and III and find the *best* answer.

I. 1 hour and 25 minutes
II. 1.25 hours
III. 125 minutes

(A) I and II and III are all equal
(B) III is greater than I, and I is greater than II
(C) III is greater than II, and II is greater than I
(D) I and II are equal, and both are less than III

93. Examine I, II, and III and find the *best* answer:

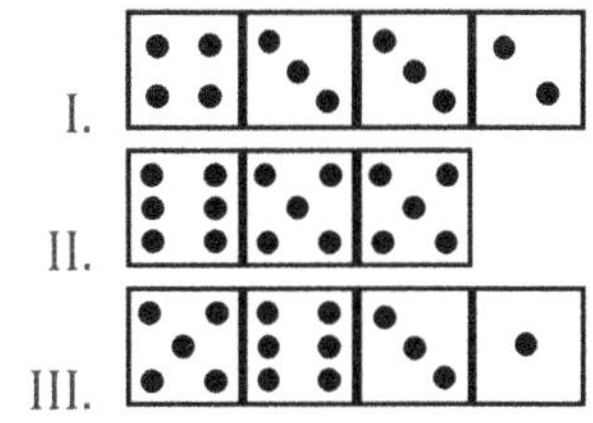
I.
II.
III.

(A) I is equal to III, which is less than II
(B) I and II are equal, and their difference is greater than III
(C) I and II are equal, and their sum is less than III
(D) I is less than III which is less than II

94. What is $\frac{1}{4}$ of the sum of $\sqrt{64}$ and 16?

(A) 2
(B) 6
(C) 8
(D) 12

95. Examine the following and find the best answer:

I. $6 \times (3 - 5)$
II. $(6 \times -5) + 3$
III. $(6 \times -3) + 5$

(A) I is greater than II
(B) I and III are equal
(C) I is smaller than III
(D) II is greater than III

96. Examine I, II, and III and find the *best* answer:

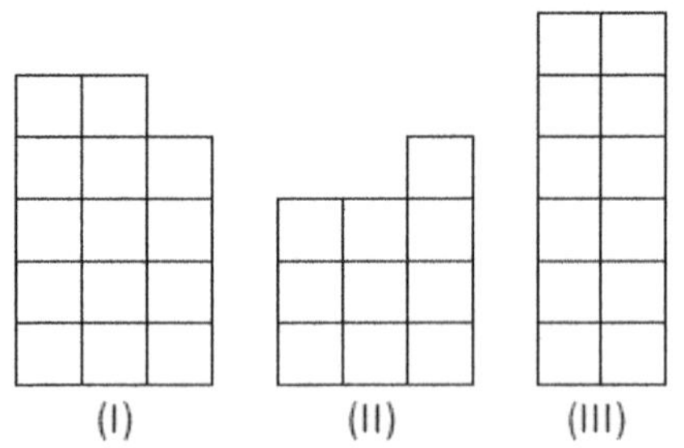
(I)
(II)
(III)

(A) III is less than II which is less than I
(B) III is greater than II, but it is less than I
(C) I, II, and III are equal
(D) II is greater than III, but it is less than I

97. In the sequence 350, 343, 49, 42..., what number should come next?
(A) 6
(B) 7
(C) 35
(D) 39

98. Examine the following and find the best answer.

I. The perimeter of the rectangle
II. The perimeter of the square
III. The perimeter of the rectangle

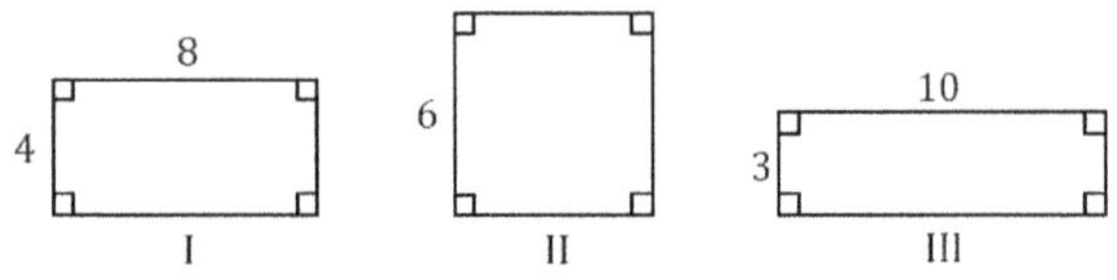
8
4
I
6
II
10
3
III

(A) III is less than I, and I is less than II
(B) I and II are equal, and both are less than III
(C) II is less than III, and III is less than I
(D) I and II are equal, and both are greater than III

99. Examine I, II, and III and find the *best* answer when x and y are both positive.

I. $3x - y - x$
II. $-2(y - x)$
III. $3x + y$

(A) I is less than both II and III
(B) I and II are equal
(C) III is greater than I, and I is greater than II
(D) III is less than II

100. Examine I, II, and III and find the *best* answer:

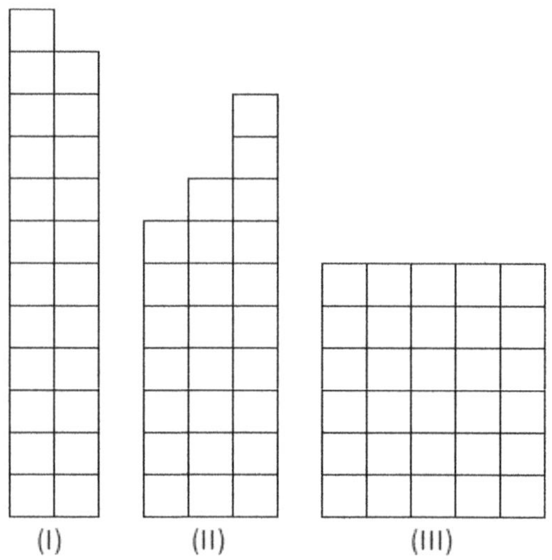
(I)
(II)
(III)

(A) II and III are equal, and both are less than I
(B) I is less than II which is less than III
(C) I is greater than II and less than III
(D) II and III are equal, and both are greater than I

101. Examine I, II, and III and find the *best* answer when x and y are both positive.

I. $2x + y$
II. $2(x - y)$
III. $x + 2x$

(A) I and III are greater than II
(B) I and III are equal
(C) III is less than II
(D) III is less than I

102. In the sequence $-1, -\frac{1}{2}, 0, \frac{1}{2}...$, what number should come next?
(A) $-1\frac{1}{2}$
(B) 0
(C) 1
(D) $1\frac{1}{2}$

103. Examine the angles and find the *best* answer.

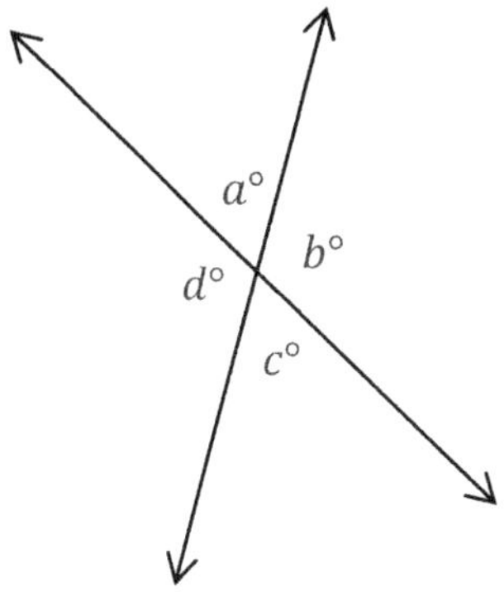

a°
b°
d°
c°

(A) $a + d = b + c$
(B) $c = d$
(C) $a + c > b + d$
(D) $a = b = c$

104. Examine I, II, and III, and find the *best* answer.

I. 6% of 40
II. 4% of 60
III. 20% of 15

(A) I = II < III
(B) I = II > III
(C) I = II = III
(D) I < III < II

105. In the sequence 2.4, 3.2, 4.0, 4.8..., what number should come next?
(A) 5
(B) 5.2
(C) 5.4
(D) 5.6

106. In the sequence $-0.3, -0.6, -0.12, -0.24...$, what number should come next?
(A) -0.30
(B) -0.46
(C) -0.48
(D) -0.72

107. Examine the line graph and find the *best* answer.

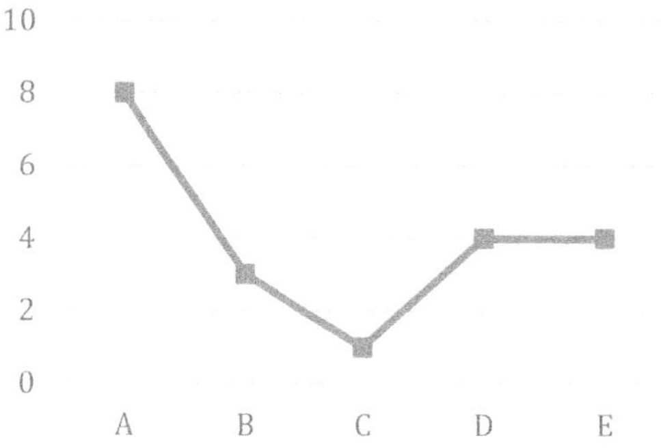

10
8
6
4
2
0
A
B
C
D
E

(A) B equals D
(B) A equals E
(C) Twice B equals E
(D) B plus C plus D equals A

108. Examine the following and find the best answer:

I. $11 \times -(3 + 1)$
II. 11×-4
III. $(11 \times -3) - 11$

(A) I is greater than II, which is greater than III
(B) I, II, and III are equal
(C) I is smaller than II, which is smaller than III
(D) II is greater than III, which is greater than I

109. Examine I, II, and III, and find the *best* answer.

I. 40% of 20
II. 25% of 36
III. 10% of 80

(A) III > I = II
(B) III > II > I
(C) III = II = I
(D) II > III = I

110. Examine I, II, and III and find the best answer.

I. the slope of $y = -3x - 3$
II. the slope of the line shown
III. the slope of $4x + y = 8$

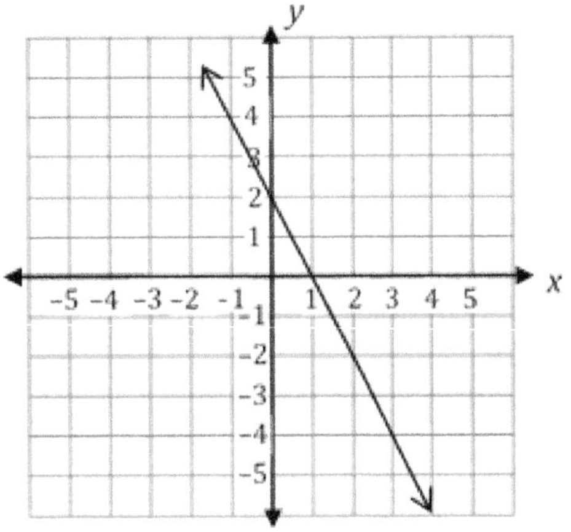
y
x
5
4
3
2
1
-5 -4 -3 -2 -1
1 2 3 4 5
-1
-2
-3
-4
-5

(A) II < I < III
(B) III < I < II
(C) I = II < III
(D) III < I = II

111. Examine I, II, and III, and find the *best* answer.

I. $\frac{2}{5}$ of 15
II. $\frac{1}{3}$ of 19
III. $\sqrt{36}$

(A) I < II < III
(B) II < I < III
(C) II < I = III
(D) II > I = III

112. In the sequence $3, 1, \frac{1}{3}, \frac{1}{9}, \ldots$, what number should come next?

(A) $\frac{1}{12}$
(B) $\frac{1}{18}$
(C) $\frac{1}{21}$
(D) $\frac{1}{27}$

Reading

Questions 113-174, 25 Minutes

Every four years, thousands of households tune in to catch the Olympics, a global competition honoring some of the best athletes in the world. But many families have no idea how or why the Olympics even started. The Olympics date back over 3,000 years and, at first, featured only one event. Now, athletes from over 200 countries compete in nearly 500 different events. Over time this basic athletic competition has evolved into the major sporting event we enjoy today.

The exact origin of the game is unknown; by this point, the history of the game has become inseparable from the myth, making it impossible to divide fact from fantasy. According to legend, in the 8th century BCE, the half-mortal, half-god Hercules held the first Olympic games in honor of his father, Zeus, king of the gods. He named the games after Olympia, Greece, the sacred mountain region in which the games were hosted. The Olympics were then held in late summer every four years, becoming so popular that ancient historians began to measure time by the 4-year-periods between Olympics. Ancient Greeks called that unit of time the "Olympiad."

At first, the games only had one event: the *stade*, a 200-yard footrace. Over time, other events were added, including boxing matches, chariot races, and longer footraces. The pentathlon—meaning "five contests"—included the *stade*, a long jump, discus and javelin throwing, and a wrestling match. At these ancient games, only men could compete. Women were not allowed to participate: married women couldn't even watch.

By 30 BCE, the Romans had conquered Greece. The games continued to occur, but began to decline in influence and popularity. Before, only amateur athletes could compete. But the Romans allowed professionals to take part in the games too, which made it difficult for common citizens to prevail in the events. Eventually, all Greek citizens were barred from participating. By the year 393 CE, the games themselves were outright banned, and after 12 centuries, the Olympics came to an end.

But the games couldn't stay gone forever. In 1896, a French nobleman named Pierre de Coubertin reestablished the games with the goal of promoting physical education. The first modern Olympics was held in Athens, Greece. A total of 14 nations and 241 athletes competed in 43 events, including footraces, gymnastics, swimming, tennis, wrestling, and shooting. By de Coubertin's final year organizing the games, 1924, the Olympics looked more like what we understand them as today. About 3,000 athletes—including over 100 women—from over 44 nations participated. The Winter Olympics began at this time, too. The winter events included bobsledding, ice hockey, and figure skating, alongside other cold weather sports. Eventually, organizers added a closing ceremony to both Winter and Summer Olympics where all the athletes were honored for their performances. Despite their rocky history, today's Olympics are a fitting way to honor the achievements of athletes throughout the world.

113. This passage is mostly about
   (A) ancient Greek cultures and customs.
   (B) the history of women in sports.
   (C) the evolution of an ancient event from when it first began to today.
   (D) the unfair treatment of Greeks during Roman rule.

114. According to the passage, the pentathlon included
   (A) biking and chariot-racing.
   (B) swimming and long jump.
   (C) discus throwing and wrestling.
   (D) tennis and gymnastics.

115. According to the passage, which of the following is true?
   (A) The Romans held the first Olympics in the 8th century.
   (B) The ancient Greek Olympics were a global event.
   (C) The modern Olympics do not allow female athletes to participate.
   (D) Olympiads were a way to mark periods in ancient history.

116. Which of the following can be inferred about the ancient Olympic games?
   (A) They were won by amateur competitors.
   (B) Both gods and mortals competed in the games.
   (C) They were not very popular.
   (D) They gave rise to the first calendar.

117. As it is used in the passage, the word "prevail" most nearly means
   (A) lose.
   (B) participate.
   (C) perform.
   (D) triumph.

118. Based on the passage, what can be inferred about ancient Greek society?
   (A) The Greeks did not value physical fitness.
   (B) The majority of Greeks were college educated.
   (C) Slavery was illegal.
   (D) Women were not treated equally to men.

119. As it is used in the passage, the word "inseparable" most nearly means
   (A) isolated.
   (B) indivisible.
   (C) separate.
   (D) single.

120. The author would most likely agree with which of the following statements?
   (A) It's an honor to participate in the Olympics.
   (B) The Romans allowing professional athletes to participate in the Olympics was a positive change for the games.
   (C) If the Romans had not conquered Greece, the Olympics would have continued uninterrupted until the present day.
   (D) The Olympic games are no longer relevant.

121. According to the passage, which of the following is a way in which the modern games differ from the ancient ones?
   (A) Summer sports have been added.
   (B) The Greeks no longer can participate.
   (C) A ceremony recognizing all participants closes the games.
   (D) The games include athletes from every country in the world.

122. What would be the most appropriate title for the passage?
   (A) The Evolution of an Ancient Athletic Event
   (B) The Greeks vs. the Romans
   (C) The Origins of Modern Sport
   (D) Olympic Winners, Past and Present

What does the word "green" make you think of? If you said nature, you're not alone. More than just a color, today being green means living an environmentally conscious life and treating the world around you with respect. Everything from carrying a reusable water bottle to growing your own vegetables is considered green living. Though many individuals and communities are trying to be more eco-friendly, recently, large cities struggle to stay green. Cities tend to have more residents and businesses than their smaller counterparts, meaning they usually have more concrete and steel than trees, as well as plenty of pollution-causing traffic. Still, some cities are doing a good job of encouraging their citizens to be more respectful toward the environment in their daily lives.

Four of the greenest cities in the world are in Europe. Vienna, Austria is ranked number one, partially because over half of its total <u>area</u> is made up of green spaces like parks and walking paths. Vienna also has a regularly-used public transportation system, which cuts down on the vehicle emissions that can cause pollution. Over 70% of residents in Vienne regularly use public transportation!

Two cities in Germany, Munich and Berlin, are also commonly considered some of the greenest cities in the world. In addition to being easily walkable, Munich has a rapid-transit system that is attractive to residents who like to get to their destinations quickly. This encourages the population to avoid driving, and because of this, Munich has cleaner air than many other cities. Berlin, Germany's capital, charges a high tax on things (like petroleum) that cause pollution. To avoid the tax, residents choose cleaner energy options like solar or wind to power their homes. Berlin also has a city-wide greywater recycling program, meaning the water used in dishwashers and washing machines is cleaned and reused in rooftop gardens.

Spain's capital of Madrid is another green city. In addition to the many trees planted among the city's buildings, Madrid is working to make 100% of the bulbs in its street lights energy-efficient. Even the city's pastimes are green—for residents and tourists looking for fun things to do in Madrid, the city offers are many walking, bike, and even solar-powered-boat tours.

Reducing pollution, using <u>sustainable</u> energy sources (like solar), and recycling and reusing as much as you can are all a big help to the environment and a key component to living green. Enjoying these green spaces, where trees clean the air we breathe, is a major benefit to our health. Green cities aren't just good for the Earth—they're good for us too!

123. This passage is mostly about
   (A) moving to an eco-friendly city.
   (B) the redefining of the word "green."
   (C) a current trend toward environmentalism in urban spaces.
   (D) why people should enjoy parks.

124. You would probably find this passage in
   (A) a lifestyle magazine.
   (B) an science journal.
   (C) an encyclopedia.
   (D) a travel diary.

125. According to the passage, being green can mean all of the following EXCEPT
   (A) walking instead of driving.
   (B) carrying a reusable water bottle.
   (C) taking mass transit.
   (D) using petroleum to cook your vegetables.

126. Which of the following can be inferred about most large cities?
   (A) They are becoming increasingly unpopular places to live.
   (B) They typically are bad for the environment.
   (C) Most large cities are in Europe.
   (D) They all prioritize eco-friendly living.

127. As it is used in the passage, the word "<u>area</u>" most nearly means
(A) land size.
(B) location.
(C) perimeter.
(D) place.

128. According to the passage, which city is moving toward using energy-efficient light bulbs?
(A) Berlin.
(B) Vienna.
(C) Madrid.
(D) Munich.

129. Based on the details of the passage, greywater
(A) is a dangerous pollutant.
(B) can be recycled for use in urban gardens.
(C) is being reused without being cleaned in Vienna.
(D) is only produced in one country.

130. The author of the passage would most likely agree with which of the following statements?
(A) Enough is being done to protect the Earth.
(B) It is important to study cities that have been successful at going "green."
(C) The only renewable energy resources are solar and wind.
(D) Traditional cities are a thing of the past.

131. As it is used in the passage, the word "<u>sustainable</u>" most nearly means
(A) conservative.
(B) renewable.
(C) resourceful.
(D) wasteful.

132. What would be the most appropriate title for the passage?
(A) Top Four Places to Live
(B) The Green City Phenomenon
(C) Ways to Reduce Your Home Energy Usage
(D) Nature and You: Perfect Together

Adam was psyched for Halloween. It had always been his favorite holiday, but this year was extra special. His brother would be home from school to hang with him. Adam had his costume ready weeks ago. Gray face paint and his dad's old, shredded work clothes would make him the perfect zombie. He couldn't wait to see what Dylan would wear—he was sure it would be extra creepy.

Walking home from school and thinking about how much fun they were going to have that night, Adam called Dylan.

"Dude! When are you getting here? I thought we could hang out a bit before going out to terrorize the neighborhood." Adam tried to keep it cool for his big brother. "You in?"

"Hey! Um…Yeah, about today...I'm really sorry, man, but I don't think I can make it. I've got a huge physics test this week, and my professor is holding a review session tonight. I'm not doing so great in this class, so I think I need to be there. I know we had plans..." Dylan waited for his brother to respond." Adam? You there?"

"Yeah, I'm here." Adam felt dejected, but he tried not to let it show. He could tell Dylan felt bad enough already, and he didn't want to make him feel worse; he understood that sometimes school had to come first. "I get it! You're in college now. The work is harder, you can't risk your GPA: that all makes sense. You're good, dude."

Adam swallowed the lump in his throat so Dylan couldn't tell he was upset. Dylan thanked him for being understanding. But after he got off the phone, Adam wasn't interested in putting on his costume or hanging out. He got home and saw that his mom had left out the big bowl of candy for the trick-or-treaters. He took it inside. Since he wouldn't be going out, he'd just answer the door for the little kids who'd come around with their moms later. It'd be fine.

Surprisingly, it was a busy afternoon. Even though the younger kids' costumes weren't scary, they were cute, and it was fun to see how excited the kids were to be dressed up. Adam gave nearly everyone extra candy; he couldn't help himself. After about an hour of answering the door, once the sun had set, he started to run out. His last two trick-or-treaters, a cowgirl and a scientist, were walking away down the sidewalk when Adam saw what looked like Frankenstein's Monster lurking in the shadows beyond the street light. As the monster began to approach, Adam was confused—the guy was way too tall to be a trick-or-treater, and he was lumbering toward him like the real deal. As soon as the light from porch hit the creature, though, Adam's spirits lifted.

"Dude, what a lame costume!" Dylan joked. He picked his little brother up in bear hug.

"Dylan!" Adam wanted to play it cool, but he was too excited. He punched Dylan's arm and ran inside to do his face paint and get the night started. Dylan had shown up after all! Of course they'd begin with a prank on their mom; it was only right! The night had just begin, and it was already shaping up to be the best Halloween ever.

133. This story is mostly about
   (A) a disagreement between brothers.
   (B) the reasons that one boy loves Halloween.
   (C) how one neighborhood celebrates a holiday.
   (D) an unexpected event that improves a boy's day.

134. It can be inferred that Adam "had his costume ready weeks ago" because
   (A) it was complicated and took a lot of effort to put together.
   (B) he was excited about Halloween.
   (C) he'd used the same costume before.
   (D) his mom had made him prepare it early.

135. According to the story, Dylan couldn't come home for Halloween because
   (A) he was failing physics.
   (B) he had a big test coming up.
   (C) he didn't really like Halloween.
   (D) he didn't care about spending time with Adam.

136. As it is used in the story, the word "dejected" most nearly means
   (A) annoyed.
   (B) downcast.
   (C) irate.
   (D) pathetic.

137. According to the story, Adam's revised plan for Halloween includes
   (A) helping younger kids go trick-or-treating.
   (B) hanging out with his friends.
   (C) handing out candy to trick-or-treaters.
   (D) watching a scary movie alone.

138. Based on his characterization in the passage, Dylan can best be described as
   (A) selfish and lazy.
   (B) hard-working and over-achieving.
   (C) fun-loving and family-oriented.
   (D) considerate but absentminded.

139. As it is used in the story, the word "lurking" most nearly means
   (A) announcing.
   (B) skulking.
   (C) stammering.
   (D) threatening.

140. From the story, it can be inferred that Adam
   (A) doesn't like candy.
   (B) looked forward to spending time with Dylan more than celebrating Halloween.
   (C) will be attending college next year.
   (D) is a better student than Dylan.

141. The author states that "Of course, they'd begin with a prank on their mom" to
   (A) emphasize the close and playful nature of the family.
   (B) suggest that the brothers are mad at their mother.
   (C) reveal a family Halloween tradition.
   (D) foreshadow an event that occurs later in the passage.

142. What would be the most appropriate title for this story?
   (A) The Costume Swap
   (B) Halloween: An Overrated Holiday
   (C) Feuding Brothers
   (D) A Halloween Surprise

Whether on class field trips or family outings, almost everyone has been to the zoo. Zoos are designed to entertain. While visitors may go to see the animals, they're ultimately dazzled by the elaborate gift shops, restaurants, and life-like duplications of the animals' natural habitats. Many of us grew up with zoos and have been raised to believe they're a healthy space for animals. However, it is critical that we take a closer look at how zoos treat their animals and whether they should exist anymore at all. We must ask whether zoos are designed for the benefit of animals or for the people who visit them.

Animals in captivity live very different lives than animals in the wild. In captivity, the animals live in much smaller enclosures than the places they would live in the wild. Because of this <u>confined</u> space, animals in zoos suffer from boredom, stress, and feelings of being trapped. Stress behaviors in animals can include pacing, swinging their heads back and forth, and performing other repetitive movements that many visitors assume are the animals' typical behavior, whether in the wild or in captivity. Since zoos buy and sell animals between themselves, they often separate animals from their families, which can cause increased stress and confusion for the animals. Many zoos also breed animals in captivity because baby animals attract visitors. Every new baby born in a zoo is another animal that will spend its whole life in captivity, never knowing the freedom of the wild. Most animals born in zoos stay there until they die. It is very rare for zoos to release any of their animals into the wild. Zoos also carry risk, such as the possibility of animals escaping or a child falling into an enclosure. In these instances, the animals can be killed to protect the safety of visitors. Is it fair for animals to die when they've done nothing wrong?

If people want to see wild animals, there are better choices than zoos. Visiting an animal safely and from a distance in its natural habitat is the best way to see animals. Wildlife sanctuaries are also a good choice. A sanctuary does not buy, sell, or breed animals like a zoo does, but rather protects animals who can no longer survive in the wild. Sanctuaries are far larger than zoo enclosures as well, giving the animals the space to roam and live similarly to how they'd live in the wild, putting the <u>wellbeing</u> of the animals before the entertainment of the guests. The best way to look out for the best interests of wild animals is to help protect their natural habitats, where animals are happier, healthier, and freer than they'd ever be in a zoo. Ultimately, zoos are an outdated tool of animal conservation, and it's time for society to leave them behind.

143. This passage is mostly about
   (A) how zoos raise money.
   (B) why zoos should no longer exist.
   (C) how to protect endangered species.
   (D) conservation efforts in North America.

144. What would be the most appropriate title for this passage?
   (A) Baby Animals
   (B) Time for Zoos to Go Extinct
   (C) Zoos: The Great American Pastime
   (D) The Cleveland Metroparks Zoo

145. According to the facts of the passage
   (A) zookeepers bond with the animals they care for.
   (B) animals in zoos live longer than those in the wild.
   (C) animals have similar lives in zoos as they'd have in the wild.
   (D) family groups get broken up when animals are traded between zoos.

146. The author says that wildlife sanctuaries
  (A) are similar to circuses.
  (B) are zoos' biggest competition.
  (C) are a healthier and more thoughtful alternative to zoos.
  (D) breed far more animals than zoos do.

147. According to the facts of the passage, which of the following is true?
  (A) Baby animals are rarely born in zoos.
  (B) Animals in zoos are happier than animals in the wild.
  (C) Most animals born in zoos are released into the wild once they reach a certain age.
  (D) Most animals born in zoos stay in captivity until they die.

148. It can be inferred from the passage that
  (A) many visitors do not recognize the stress-induced behaviors of animals when they see them.
  (B) though zoos have their problems, they're still the best way to support animal conservation efforts.
  (C) zoos always put animal welfare above guest entertainment.
  (D) zoos spend more money on conservation than anyone else.

149. The author would most likely agree with which of the following statements?
  (A) Zoos are a lovely place to visit while on vacation.
  (B) A trip to the zoo makes a great class field trip.
  (C) Wildlife should not be exploited for the entertainment of humans.
  (D) Animal exhibits at zoos are just as nice as an animal's natural habitat.

150. Which of the following can be inferred from the passage?
  (A) Animals in sanctuaries are less stressed than animals in zoos.
  (B) Animals are at their happiest in captivity.
  (C) Animals in zoos enjoy seeing the visitors.
  (D) The risk of animal escape from zoos is a major threat to nearby cities.

151. As it is used in the passage, the word "<u>confined</u>" most nearly means
  (A) expansive.
  (B) freezing.
  (C) large.
  (D) limited.

152. As it is used in the passage, the word "<u>wellbeing</u>" most nearly means
  (A) best interests.
  (B) emotions.
  (C) illness.
  (D) tempers.

Vocabulary

153. A <u>respected</u> leader
    (A) admired
    (B) cowardly
    (C) demure
    (D) unassuming

154. A <u>verdant</u> pasture
    (A) actual
    (B) lush
    (C) mysterious
    (D) watery

155. An <u>incalculable</u> value
    (A) faulty
    (B) literal
    (C) nimble
    (D) priceless

156. Held her idol in <u>esteem</u>
    (A) disdain
    (B) ignorance
    (C) regard
    (D) scorn

157. His <u>generous</u> favor
    (A) belittled
    (B) kind
    (C) selfish
    (D) vibrant

158. The requests of a <u>demanding</u> boss
    (A) careful
    (B) mental
    (C) taxing
    (D) useless

159. A <u>failing</u> company's downfall
    (A) celebrated
    (B) flawed
    (C) perfect
    (D) remarkable

160. The <u>stubborn</u> leader's refusal
    (A) accepting
    (B) compliant
    (C) flexible
    (D) willful

161. Made a <u>selfish</u> decision for himself
    (A) altruistic
    (B) egotistical
    (C) obsessive
    (D) refreshing

162. An <u>incompetent</u> manager
    (A) complacent
    (B) bored
    (C) incapable
    (D) secretive

163. The <u>mutinous</u> crew members
    (A) avid
    (B) minimal
    (C) opulent
    (D) revolutionary

164. A <u>riotous</u> joke
    (A) bland
    (B) hysterical
    (C) miniscule
    (D) sordid

165. A <u>despicable</u> narcissist
    (A) disgusted
    (B) estranged
    (C) ethical
    (D) wretched

166. They <u>despised</u> their boss
    (A) changed
    (B) doubled
    (C) hated
    (D) simulated

167. The business that would <u>inevitably</u> fail
    (A) belatedly
    (B) magically
    (C) successfully
    (D) unavoidably

168. The <u>desperate</u> beggar
    (A) elated
    (B) grateful
    (C) hopeless
    (D) perky

169. He was terribly <u>lonely</u>
    (A) friendly
    (B) pleased
    (C) solitary
    (D) unusual

170. <u>Incapable</u> of making friends
    (A) cruel
    (B) inept
    (C) rude
    (D) unfriendly

171. She <u>regretted</u> her arrival
    (A) finished
    (B) befriended
    (C) rued
    (D) selected

172. They <u>conspired</u> against him
    (A) behaved
    (B) celebrated
    (C) decorated
    (D) schemed

173. A <u>foolish</u> mistake
    (A) brave
    (B) clever
    (C) nonsensical
    (D) sensible

174. A <u>supportive</u> ally
    (A) destructive
    (B) disproving
    (C) helpful
    (D) opposing

Mathematics

Questions 175-238, 45 Minutes

175. James is plotting a road trip on a map. Which unit would be most appropriate for calculating the distance he will travel?
    (A) centimeters
    (B) lightyears
    (C) miles
    (D) yards

176. What is the radius, in meters, of a circle whose diameter is 50 km?
    (A) 25 m
    (B) 50 m
    (C) 25,000 m
    (D) 50,000 m

177. If all of the angles within a triangle are 60°, what kind of triangle is it?
    (A) equilateral
    (B) isosceles
    (C) scalene
    (D) None of the above

178. The circumference of a pizza pie 12π inches. If the pizza pie is split into 4 equal pieces, what is the area of each of the slices?
    (A) 6π sq. in.
    (B) 9π sq. in.
    (C) 12π sq. in.
    (D) 24π sq. in.

179. If the LCM of 3, 5, and 25 can be represented as 3^a5^b, then which of the following is equivalent to ab?
    (A) 2
    (B) 27
    (C) 75
    (D) 125

180. Which of the following is equivalent to 902.4?
    (A) $(9 \times 10^1) + (2 \times 10^0) + (4 \times 10^{-2})$
    (B) $(9 \times 10^1) + (2 \times 10^0) + (4 \times 10^{-1})$
    (C) $(9 \times 10^2) + (2 \times 10^0) + (4 \times 10^{-1})$
    (D) $(9 \times 10^2) + (2 \times 10^1) + (4 \times 10^{-1})$

181. What is equivalent to $2^3 \times 2^1$?
    (A) 2^3
    (B) 2^5
    (C) 4^2
    (D) 4^4

182. The surface area of a sphere is given by $SA = 4\pi r^2$, where r represents the radius. What is the surface area of this sphere?

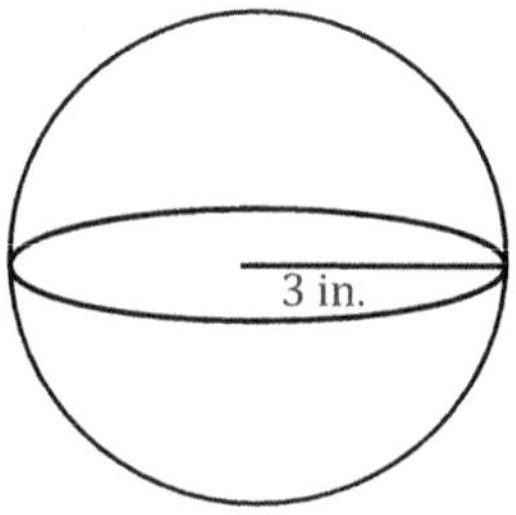
3 in.

    (A) 9 in^2
    (B) 24π in^2
    (C) 36π in^2
    (D) 144π in^2

183. Which of the following is equivalent to 81,050?
    (A) $(8 \times 10^3) + (1 \times 10^2) + 5$
    (B) $(8 \times 10^4) + (1 \times 10^2) + (5 \times 10^1)$
    (C) $(8 \times 10^4) + (1 \times 10^3) + (5 \times 10^1)$
    (D) $(8 \times 10^4) + (1 \times 10^3) + (5 \times 10^2)$

184. The area of Triangle A is 36 square inches. If you double the height and cut the base in half, what is the new area of the triangle?
    (A) 6 square inches
    (B) 18 square inches
    (C) 36 square inches
    (D) 72 square inches

185. What is the prime factorization of 50?
(A) 2×5^2
(B) 5^2
(C) 2×25
(D) $2 \times 2 \times 5$

186. What is equivalent to $(y^2z^3) \times (y^3z)$?
(A) y^5z^3
(B) y^5z^4
(C) y^6z^3
(D) y^6z^4

187. A cube has a side length of 5 feet. What is its volume?
(A) 25 ft^3
(B) 125 ft^3
(C) 150 ft^3
(D) 625 ft^3

188. Express 6% as a decimal.
(A) 0.006
(B) 0.06
(C) 0.16
(D) 0.6

189. Express 0.013 as a percent.
(A) 0.00013%
(B) 1.3%
(C) 13%
(D) 130%

190. Which of the following numbers is evenly divisible by 15?
(A) 220
(B) 230
(C) 320
(D) 330

191. A square has a perimeter of 8 inches. The length and width of the square are both increased by 1 inch, as shown. What is the area of the final, larger square?

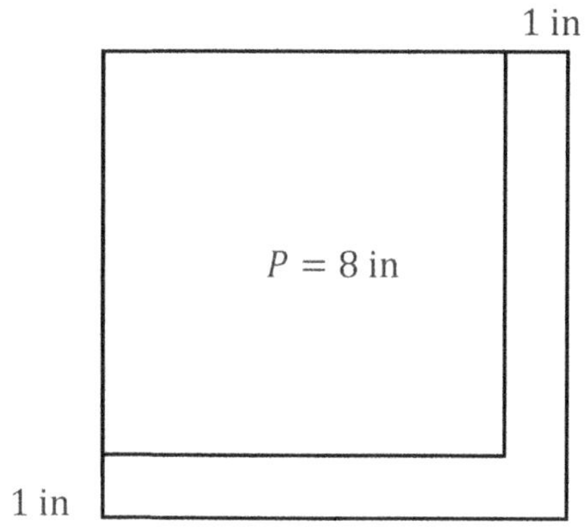
1 in
$P = 8$ in
1 in

(A) 3
(B) 4
(C) 9
(D) 10

192. Which fraction is largest?
(A) $\frac{2}{8}$
(B) $\frac{1}{3}$
(C) $\frac{1}{4}$
(D) $\frac{4}{6}$

193. Which two values have $13x^2y^2z$ as their GCF?
(A) $13x^3y^2z^2$ and $13x^3y^2z$
(B) $13x^2y^2$ and $26xyz$
(C) $13x^3y^2$ and $20x^2y^2z^4$
(D) $13x^2y^3z^4$ and $169x^4y^2z$

194. Which of the following fractions is closest in value to 1?
(A) $\frac{3}{4}$
(B) $\frac{5}{6}$
(C) $\frac{6}{7}$
(D) $\frac{7}{8}$

195. Solve: $\frac{3}{8}y - \frac{1}{4} > \frac{7}{16}$.
(A) $y > \frac{64}{60}$
(B) $y < \frac{64}{60}$
(C) $y > \frac{11}{6}$
(D) $y < \frac{11}{6}$

196. What is the most appropriate unit for measuring the volume of a liquid?
(A) kilograms
(B) milliliters
(C) square centimeters
(D) tons

197. What is the sum of the angles in a quadrilateral?
(A) 180°
(B) 360°
(C) 540°
(D) 720°

198. What is the measure of $\angle A$?

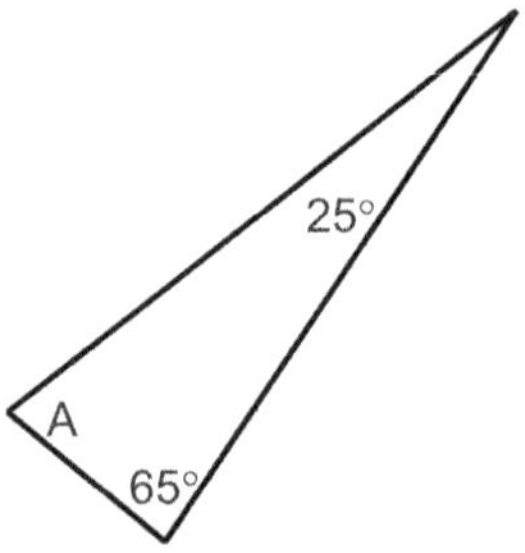
25°
A
65°

Note: Figure not drawn to scale

(A) 65°
(B) 90°
(C) 115°
(D) 155°

199. What is the LCM of $3a^2bc$ and $5ab^2c$ if a, b, and c are prime numbers?
(A) $15abc$
(B) $15ab^2c$
(C) $15a^2b^2c$
(D) $15a^2b^2c^2$

200. Solve: $-\frac{5}{4}y \leq 2$
(A) $y \geq \frac{8}{5}$
(B) $y \leq \frac{8}{5}$
(C) $y \geq -\frac{8}{5}$
(D) $y \leq -\frac{8}{5}$

201. What is the slope of a line parallel to the line $-3x - y = 5$?
(A) -3
(B) $-\frac{1}{3}$
(C) $\frac{1}{3}$
(D) 3

202. What is the slope of the line shown in the graph?

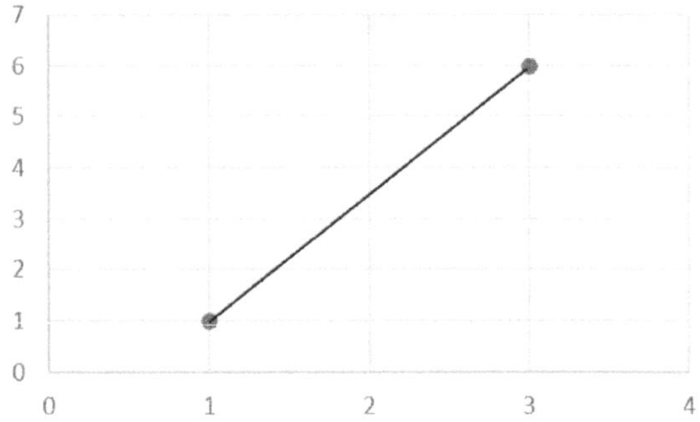
7
6
5
4
3
2
1
0
0
1
2
3
4

(A) $-\frac{5}{2}$
(B) $-\frac{2}{5}$
(C) $\frac{2}{5}$
(D) $\frac{5}{2}$

Problem Solving

203. Solve: $(-16) \div (-8) \times (-2) =$
(A) -4
(B) -1
(C) 1
(D) 4

204. Timothy started eating a jar of peanuts on Monday. Each day, he eats 20% of the peanuts in the jar. What percent of the peanuts remain in the jar on Tuesday?
(A) 49%
(B) 51%
(C) 64%
(D) 72%

205. Which of the following would equal 7.52 when rounded to the hundredths place?
(A) $1.873 + 5.643$
(B) $2.907 + 6.132$
(C) $4.604 + 0.839$
(D) $3.581 + 3.945$

206. What is the difference of 0.8765 and 0.1586 rounded to the nearest thousandth?
(A) 0.7
(B) 0.7179
(C) 0.718
(D) 0.72

207. In the zoo, there are five more giraffes than there are lions, and there are four times as many zebras as there are lions. If the difference of zebras and lions is equal to one more than the number of giraffes, how many lions are there?
(A) 3
(B) 6
(C) 9
(D) 12

208. Linda can clean $\frac{4}{9}$ of her bedroom in one hour. How long will it take her to clean her entire bedroom?
(A) 26 minutes
(B) 1 hour 15 minutes
(C) 2 hours 15 minutes
(D) 4 hours

209. What is the value of $\sqrt{9 + 25}$?
(A) 6
(B) 8
(C) $\sqrt{34}$
(D) 34

210. A rhombus has how many more sides than a trapezoid?
(A) 0
(B) 1
(C) 2
(D) 3

211. Kathleen is making a bouquet of flowers. She paid $18 for carnations and three times as much for roses. How much did she pay for all the flowers in total?
(A) $24.00
(B) $54.00
(C) $72.00
(D) $78.00

212. Jerry runs 5 miles in 40 minutes. How fast is he running?
(A) 6 miles per hour
(B) 7.5 miles per hour
(C) 9 miles per hour
(D) 9.5 miles per hour

213. When a number is increased by 50% of itself, the result is 300. What is the number?
(A) 100
(B) 200
(C) 300
(D) 450

214. If the average of 3, 6, 7, and x is equal to the average of 2 and x, what is the value of x?
(A) 8
(B) 10
(C) 12
(D) 14

215. In a pet store, the ratio of dogs to cats to fish is 2:3:20. If there are 12 cats in a pet store, how many fish are there?
(A) 8
(B) 18
(C) 80
(D) 120

216. Which of the following statements is true?
(A) A square is a type of rhombus.
(B) A rhombus is a type of square.
(C) A rhombus and square have no relation at all.
(D) A rhombus and a square are both types of rectangles.

217. A group of middle school students are surveyed about whether they spend their Saturdays reading for pleasure, playing video games, or doing both. Of the 145 students surveyed, 27 said that they do neither, 67 said that they read for pleasure, and 81 said that they play video games. How many students read for pleasure but never play video games?
(A) 14
(B) 30
(C) 37
(D) 50

218. Charlie went shopping at the grocery store. She bought 2 loaves of bread for $5.60 each, a peach pie for $12.50, a 3-lb bag of fruit for $4.80, and a dozen eggs for $3.15. If she had $40 to spend, how much money does she have at the end of her shopping trip?
(A) $8.35
(B) $9.35
(C) $13.95
(D) $14.95

219. Racecars can reach an average top speed of 200 miles per hour. At this rate, how many miles could be driven in a racecar over 7.5 minutes?
(A) 15 miles
(B) 25 miles
(C) 45 miles
(D) 50 miles

220. Solve for m: $12 + 3m = -m + 6$
(A) $-\frac{3}{2}$
(B) -1
(C) $\frac{3}{2}$
(D) 3

221. What is 1% of 320?
(A) 3.2
(B) 32
(C) 3200
(D) $\frac{1}{320}$

222. How many yards are in 441 inches?
(A) 4.41 yards
(B) 12.25 yards
(C) 15.5 yards
(D) 44.1 yards

223. Grace has 3 blue shirts, 8 white shirts, 5 black shirts, and 2 gray shirts. If she picks a shirt at random to wear tomorrow, what is the probability she will choose a white shirt?
(A) $\frac{5}{18}$
(B) $\frac{1}{3}$
(C) $\frac{4}{9}$
(D) $\frac{1}{2}$

224. The numbers in the following Venn diagram represent how many students can play a particular instrument or instruments. If there are 34 students in the class, how many students cannot play the flute, piano, or violin?

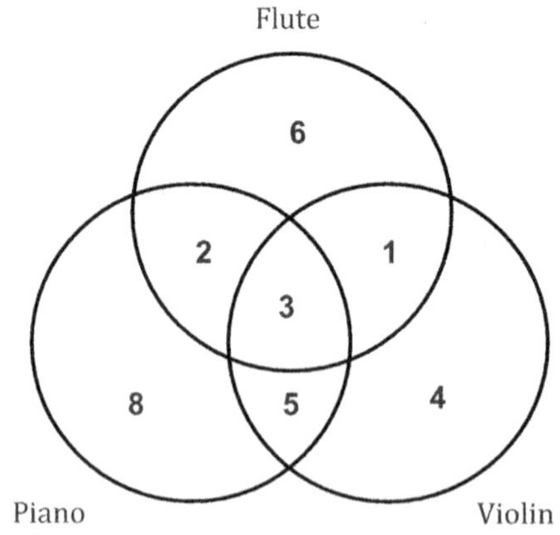
Flute
6
2
1
3
8
5
4
Piano
Violin

(A) 2
(B) 3
(C) 4
(D) 5

225. Solve: $2.1 - 1.093 =$
(A) 0.07
(B) 1.003
(C) 1.007
(D) 1.07

226. 150 centimeters equals:
(A) .015 meters
(B) .15 meters
(C) 1.5 meters
(D) 15 meters

227. Solve: $\frac{3}{5} - \frac{1}{3} =$
(A) $\frac{1}{5}$
(B) $\frac{2}{5}$
(C) $\frac{4}{15}$
(D) $\frac{14}{15}$

228. Danielle, Isabella, and Courtney keep track of how many points they each score in each basketball game. The following table reflects their points through the first three games. What is Isabella's average points per game?

	Game 1	Game 2	Game 3	Total
Courtney	10	2	6	18
Danielle	8	9	7	24
Isabella	11	5	14	30
Total	29	16	27	72

(A) 6
(B) 8
(C) 10
(D) 12

229. If $10^x = 10{,}000$, then $x =$?
(A) 2
(B) 3
(C) 4
(D) 5

230. If the prime factorization of 500 is $2^x \times 5^y$, then what does xy equal?
(A) 3
(B) 4
(C) 5
(D) 6

231. Solve: $6{,}036 \div 12 =$
(A) 50
(B) 53
(C) 503
(D) 5003

232. How much money does Dana need to buy 18 donuts for her party?

Use the following chart for questions 232 and 233.

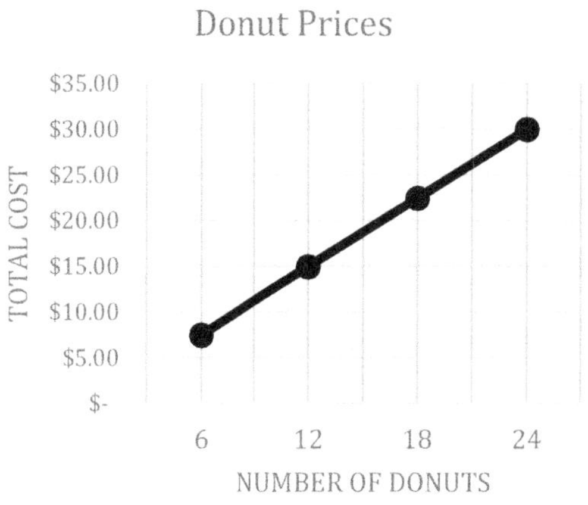
Donut Prices
$35.00
$30.00
$25.00
$20.00
$15.00
$10.00
$5.00
$-
TOTAL COST
6
12
18
24
NUMBER OF DONUTS

(A) $7.50
(B) $15.00
(C) $22.50
(D) $30.00

233. Louise wants to buy 32 donuts. Based on the relationship shown, how much money does she need? [See fig for q. 232]
(A) $32
(B) $36
(C) $40
(D) $48

234. The tax on a \$320 coat was \$16. What was the tax rate, in percent, on the coat?
(A) 0.05%
(B) 0.5%
(C) 5%
(D) 5.5%

235. David and Josie are playing a game that involves choosing differently colored ribbons at random. At the beginning of the game, there are 5 yellow ribbons, 4 blue ribbons, and 2 red ribbons. David goes first and randomly selects a yellow ribbon, which he keeps. If Josie goes next, what is the probability that she will select a yellow ribbon?
(A) $\frac{4}{11}$
(B) $\frac{2}{5}$
(C) $\frac{5}{11}$
(D) $\frac{1}{2}$

236. Solve for x: $\frac{1.25}{5} = (2x)(0.25)$
(A) 0.05
(B) 0.25
(C) 0.5
(D) 1.25

237. What is the value of $\sqrt{64x} - \sqrt{25x}$?
(A) x
(B) 3
(C) $3\sqrt{x}$
(D) $3x$

238. A park has x pairs of ducks. If each pair of ducks had eight ducklings, what algebraic expression would express the total number of ducks and ducklings?
(A) $8x$
(B) $10x$
(C) $x + 8$
(D) $2x + 8$

Language Skills

Questions 239-298, 25 Minutes

88.1

For questions 239-278, choose the sentence that contains an error in punctuation, capitalization, or usage. If there is no error, select choice (D).

239. (A) Told me to get a job.
 (B) She kept passing her house.
 (C) He lost his keys.
 (D) No mistake.

240. (A) Henry added nuts to the sundae after his sister requests them.
 (B) They waited in line for three hours before the store opened.
 (C) She knows she has to study if she wants to pass the class.
 (D) No mistake.

241. (A) Children usually look forward to Recess.
 (B) The mail carrier usually received tips around the holidays.
 (C) The first of July was Mariah's birthday.
 (D) No mistake.

242. (A) She was brave and smart.
 (B) The dog jumped up and barked out the window.
 (C) They had vacationed in Australia, in China, and South Africa.
 (D) No mistake.

243. (A) Melissa threw out the pencil Mark gifted her.
 (B) The story who Mark told was sad.
 (C) They realized that the art supplies weren't theirs.
 (D) No mistake.

244. (A) His office was located in downtown Manhattan.
 (B) The case went all the way to the Supreme Court.
 (C) The astronomer hoped to explore the entire Universe.
 (D) No mistake.

245. (A) They cooked dinner and baked a cake.
 (B) Clarissa hurried home to play video games.
 (C) She wanted to go home, to make her bed, and eat dinner.
 (D) No mistake.

246. (A) Mindy's cousin was accused of breaking the law.
 (B) "I'm sorry" said Beth.
 (C) The area of the house's front yard was too small.
 (D) No mistake.

247. (A) His birthday happened only every four years, on leap years.
 (B) The soldier received an award for bravery.
 (C) Erin had read every single book in the School Library.
 (D) No mistake.

248. (A) Many students forgot that they had to turn in a project.
 (B) Each person gets a balloon as soon as they walk through the door.
 (C) After the bell rang, the students are leaping out of their seats.
 (D) No mistake.

249. (A) She's not the only one here.
 (B) Marisa's brother's dog is lost.
 (C) The childrens books are ruined.
 (D) No mistake.

250. (A) That college is very prestigious.
(B) He slowly read each page of the book.
(C) She ensured the essay was accurately.
(D) No mistake.

251. (A) Her computer was glitchy.
(B) The bouquet of flowers is vibrant.
(C) Amber walked slow.
(D) No mistake.

252. (A) Marcy is more happier than Josh.
(B) Her house is the largest in the neighborhood.
(C) Their school is bigger than ours.
(D) No mistake.

253. (A) The first person was the winner.
(B) Maude ate ravenous.
(C) The city was crowded.
(D) No mistake.

254. (A) Elise confided her secret to her best friend.
(B) Petra longed to travel to Paris someday to see the Eiffel Tower.
(C) Louis knew he was a Taurus because he was born in may.
(D) No mistake.

255. (A) He vowed to never give up.
(B) She wished she could understand him.
(C) Daisy swears she hasn't got none.
(D) No mistake.

256. (A) Christine ordered a salad for lunch on Tuesday.
(B) What time is it? Keshia asked.
(C) We toured the Metropolitan Museum of Art on a field trip.
(D) No mistake.

257. (A) In addition to financial success, many partners also have success in the arts.
(B) Every person on the team is an excellent runner.
(C) Her professor can't believe she got the question right.
(D) No mistake.

258. (A) Thomas is taller than his uncle.
(B) Raj was more faster than the other runners.
(C) Selena was the bravest kid in her class.
(D) No mistake.

259. (A) Benjamin couldn't stop working.
(B) She can't hardly be held accountable.
(C) The music was not too bad.
(D) No mistake.

260. (A) "Whats this?" asked Matt.
(B) She disposed of all her childhood diaries.
(C) Linda's keys were stuck in the lock.
(D) No mistake.

261. (A) You're not going to get away with this.
(B) Her friend's lie was believed by everyone.
(C) Other peoples opinions are not important.
(D) No mistake.

262. (A) The library book's were ruined in the flood.
(B) Each cat's claws had to be carefully trimmed.
(C) The professor's glasses were broken.
(D) No mistake.

263. (A) Her german ancestors had lived in Berlin.
(B) She knew how to speak Italian fluently.
(C) Only Clarissa knew that she wasn't British.
(D) No mistake.

264. (A) Each painting was more beautiful than the last.
(B) She was a very graceful dancer.
(C) He mistakenly called her by the wrong name.
(D) No mistake.

265. (A) The first of February was a holiday in her country.
(B) Her entire family was Italian.
(C) The largest country in South America is Brazil.
(D) No mistake.

266. (A) The ship wrecked violently.
(B) Each student finished the test.
(C) She was too impatient to wait.
(D) No mistake.

267. (A) Neither she nor her sister took the money.
(B) The flowers never didn't bloom.
(C) They couldn't believe this was happening.
(D) No mistake.

268. (A) Her house was bigger than his.
(B) She played better than he did.
(C) He fought the most hardest.
(D) No mistake.

269. (A) Erica playing soccer.
(B) Beth ran.
(C) Veronica had three bikes.
(D) No mistake.

270. (A) Every son's house had a fireplace.
(B) He cried backstage, then he went out and performed.
(C) "What do they have in common," asked Jonathan.
(D) No mistake.

271. (A) The clerk was rude and mean.
(B) She was imaginative yet she isn't clever.
(C) Kacey loved pie but hated cake.
(D) No mistake.

272. (A) Dan's phone was on silent.
(B) Where is she? asked Jenny.
(C) Josiah's house's chimney was dirty.
(D) No mistake.

273. (A) The dogs across the street barks loudly.
(B) Her cat is quickly running around the house.
(C) My friends are going to the movies this weekend.
(D) No mistake.

274. (A) The Great Wall of China stretches for thousands of miles.
(B) The tour group was excited to see big ben in London.
(C) A famous attraction in Egypt is the Great Pyramid of Giza.
(D) No mistake.

275. (A) The grocery store was freezing.
(B) She wrote too sloppy.
(C) Her teddy bear was so soft.
(D) No mistake.

276. (A) The desert used to be a less pleasant place to live.
(B) Their parents are going to build a new house in a few years.
(C) If Josh gets another parking ticket, his parents revoked his driving privileges.
(D) No mistake.

277. (A) She hoped to graduate top of her class.
(B) The lightbulb was broken.
(C) His brother too annoying.
(D) No mistake.

278. (A) When she goes to college in the fall, her major will be philosophy.
(B) Everyone made it to the beach in time to watch the fireworks.
(C) She will not believe she has wasted another day.
(D) No mistake.

Spelling

For questions 279-288, choose the sentence that contains an error in spelling. If there is no error, select choice (D).

279. (A) He thought he had heard something behind him.
(B) The students forgot there homework on Monday.
(C) She was dedicated to her creative pursuits.
(D) No mistake.

280. (A) She whistled cheerfully during her long commute.
(B) Mariska's favorite genre of music was jazz.
(C) She wondered weather she should choose green or blue.
(D) No mistake.

281. (A) He took a different path than his friends expected.
(B) She wondered wich way her sister had run.
(C) The building was too tall to miss.
(D) No mistake.

282. (A) There was once a woman who was very cheerful.
(B) The pot was full of gold coins.
(C) She became tired of dragging such a heavy wait.
(D) No mistake.

283. (A) Indeed, the exam was terribly challenging.
(B) All of a sudden, the boulder was falling from the cliff.
(C) The professor couldn't chose which day to hold the exam.
(D) No mistake.

284. (A) The old woman stared after it till it was fairly out of sight.
(B) The manager was feared for his viscious temper.
(C) The old woman seized her sweeping broom.
(D) No mistake.

285. (A) She crept into the house as quietly as a mouse.
(B) He delivered the package promptly.
(C) Only her great ant could give her compliments.
(D) No mistake.

286. (A) She was so proud of her daughter's achievements.
(B) He was quiet tired after the long journey.
(C) He sped down the highway with urgency.
(D) No mistake.

287. (A) The kittens were playfully fighting in the pen.
(B) They were rather upset at the disagreement.
(C) She thought they wanted to frolic outside.
(D) No mistake.

288. (A) The celebration was scheduled for the end of the month.
(B) The old woman told them to never fight again
(C) He was frightened by her ghastly appearence.
(D) No mistake.

Composition

289. Choose the group of words that best completes this sentence.

After a cold day shoveling snow, ____________.

(A) Peter warmed up by the fire.
(B) warm up by the fire was what Peter did.
(C) afterward, Peter warmed up by the fire.
(D) warming up by the fire is what Peter wanted to do.

290. Choose the group of words that best completes this sentence.

When his team won their soccer tournament, ____________.

(A) joy is what Marco was feeling.
(B) Marco was overjoyed.
(C) joyful was Marco.
(D) Marco was feeling joy.

291. Which of these best fits under the topic "Keeping Reptiles as Pets"?

(A) Reptiles live on every continent except Antarctica.
(B) Reptiles require special care when kept indoors.
(C) Reptiles may travel a far distance to find food.
(D) none of these

292. Which of these sentences would best fit at the end of the paragraph?

(1) Perhaps the most basic form of exercise, walking is still one of the best ways to stay in shape. (2) Nearly everyone has access to a place outside where they can walk, whether it be in their own neighborhood or a nearby park. (3) Some people choose to walk inside, such as on a treadmill or at a large indoor place like a mall.

(A) Malls have many different stores to shop in.
(B) A pair of sneakers is all you need to start your walking exercise.
(C) Treadmills are expensive pieces of exercise equipment.
(D) Running is also great exercise.

293. Which of these best fits under the topic "The History of Flight"?

(A) The first successful helicopter flight happened in 1939.
(B) Airplanes are a convenient way to travel.
(C) Many people prefer driving to flying.
(D) none of these

294. Choose the best word or words to join the thoughts together.

David loved to study astronomy; ____________ his sister Amelia wanted to become an astronaut.

(A) carefully,
(B) similarly,
(C) obviously,
(D) none of these

295. Which of these expresses the idea most clearly?

(A) In order to avoid a sunburn, applying sunscreen is what Sarah did.
(B) Sarah applied, in order to avoid a sunburn, sunscreen.
(C) Sarah wanted to avoid a sunburn, so she applied sunscreen.
(D) Sarah applied sunscreen to avoid a sunburn.

296. Which sentence does *not* belong in the paragraph?

(1) Carrots are a common vegetable. (2) They are easily recognized by their bright orange color and long, cylindrical shape. (3) Carrots are very nutritious and there are many ways to cook them. (4) Green beans are one of the easiest vegetables to grow.

(A) Sentence 1
(B) Sentence 2
(C) Sentence 3
(D) Sentence 4

297. Which sentence does *not* belong in the paragraph?

(1) The volleyball team practiced long and hard for their upcoming tournament. (2) Each team member felt confident. (3) Some of the girls were left-handed. (4) They were prepared and ready to play.

(A) Sentence 1
(B) Sentence 2
(C) Sentence 3
(D) Sentence 4

298. Choose the group of words that best completes this sentence.

Most doctors recommend ____________________.

(A) to exercise daily
(B) exercising daily is something you should do
(C) daily exercise
(D) for exercising daily

298 - 239

7

Scoring Practice Test 1

Using your answer sheet and referring to the answer key at the back of the book, calculate the percentage of questions you answered correctly in each section by taking the number of questions you answered correctly in that section and dividing it by the number of questions in that section. Multiply this number by 100 to determine your percentage score. The higher the percentage, the stronger your performance in that section. The lower the percentage, the more time you should spend practicing that section.

Note that the actual test will not evaluate your score based on percentage correct or incorrect. Instead, it will evaluate your performance relative to all other students in your grade who took the test.

Record your results here:

Section	**Questions Correct**	**Total Questions**	**Percent Questions Correct**
Verbal Skills	____	60	____%
Quantitative Skills	____	52	____%
Reading Comprehension	____	62	____%
Mathematics Achievement	____	64	____%
Language	____	60	____%

Remember that, depending on the curriculum at your school, there may be material on this test that you have not yet been taught. If this is the case, and you would like to improve your score beyond what is expected of your grade, consider outside help from an adult—such as a tutor or teacher—who can help you learn more about the topics that are new to you.

Answer Key

The keys are organized by section, and each question has an answer associated with it. Remember: there are detailed answer explanations available online at www.thetutorverse.com/books. Be sure to obtain permission before going online.

Practice Test 2

Overview

The practice test is designed to assess your understanding of key skills and concepts. It is important to take the final practice test after completing the diagnostic tests and after you have spent time studying and practicing.

The main difference between the practice tests and the actual test is that the practice tests are scored differently from how the actual exam is scored. On the actual exam, your score will be determined by how well you did compared to other students in your grade. On the practice tests, however, we will score every question in order to gauge your mastery over skills and concepts.

Format

The format of the practice test is similar to that of the actual test. The number of questions included in each section mirror those of the actual test. This is done by design, in order to help familiarize you with the actual length of the test.

In addition to the reading, verbal, and language concepts reviewed in this workbook, this practice test also includes mathematics and quantitative reasoning material, similar to what will be on the actual exam. If you feel you need more practice on the math concepts covered in this test, consider consulting our other book, "HSPT Mathematics and Quantitative Reasoning: 1,300+ Practice Problems," which is available for purchase at www.thetutorverse.com/books.

The practice test includes the following sections:

Diagnostic Test Section	**Questions**	**Time Limit**
Verbal Skills	60	16 minutes
Quantitative Skills	52	30 minutes
Reading Comprehension	62	25 minutes
Mathematics	64	45 minutes
Language	60	25 minutes
Total	**298**	**2h 21 minutes**

Generally, 2 brief breaks are given between sections of the test; however, the timing and duration of the breaks are determined by the individual school that is administering the exam.

Calculators

Students are not permitted to use calculators on the HSPT. **To ensure the results of the practice test are as accurate as possible, do not use a calculator on this exam.** If you have a diagnosed learning disability which requires the use of a calculator, contact your testing site to organize special accommodations and continue to practice with a calculator as needed.

Answering

Use the answer sheet provided on the next several pages to record your answers. You may wish to tear these pages out of the workbook.

Practice Test Answer Sheet

[Carefully tear or cut out this page.]

Section 1: Verbal Skills

1 ⒶⒷⒸⒹ	13 ⒶⒷⒸⒹ	25 ⒶⒷⒸⒹ	37 ⒶⒷⒸⒹ	49 ⒶⒷⒸⒹ
2 ⒶⒷⒸⒹ	14 ⒶⒷⒸⒹ	26 ⒶⒷⒸ	38 ⒶⒷⒸ	50 ⒶⒷⒸ
3 ⒶⒷⒸⒹ	15 ⒶⒷⒸⒹ	27 ⒶⒷⒸⒹ	39 ⒶⒷⒸⒹ	51 ⒶⒷⒸⒹ
4 ⒶⒷⒸⒹ	16 ⒶⒷⒸⒹ	28 ⒶⒷⒸⒹ	40 ⒶⒷⒸⒹ	52 ⒶⒷⒸⒹ
5 ⒶⒷⒸⒹ	17 ⒶⒷⒸⒹ	29 ⒶⒷⒸⒹ	41 ⒶⒷⒸⒹ	53 ⒶⒷⒸⒹ
6 ⒶⒷⒸⒹ	18 ⒶⒷⒸ	30 ⒶⒷⒸⒹ	42 ⒶⒷⒸⒹ	54 ⒶⒷⒸⒹ
7 ⒶⒷⒸⒹ	19 ⒶⒷⒸⒹ	31 ⒶⒷⒸ	43 ⒶⒷⒸⒹ	55 ⒶⒷⒸⒹ
8 ⒶⒷⒸⒹ	20 ⒶⒷⒸⒹ	32 ⒶⒷⒸⒹ	44 ⒶⒷⒸⒹ	56 ⒶⒷⒸⒹ
9 ⒶⒷⒸⒹ	21 ⒶⒷⒸⒹ	33 ⒶⒷⒸⒹ	45 ⒶⒷⒸⒹ	57 ⒶⒷⒸⒹ
10 ⒶⒷⒸ	22 ⒶⒷⒸⒹ	34 ⒶⒷⒸⒹ	46 ⒶⒷⒸⒹ	58 ⒶⒷⒸ
11 ⒶⒷⒸⒹ	23 ⒶⒷⒸ	35 ⒶⒷⒸ	47 ⒶⒷⒸ	59 ⒶⒷⒸⒹ
12 ⒶⒷⒸⒹ	24 ⒶⒷⒸⒹ	36 ⒶⒷⒸⒹ	48 ⒶⒷⒸⒹ	60 ⒶⒷⒸⒹ

Section 2: Quantitative Skills

61 ⒶⒷⒸⒹ	72 ⒶⒷⒸⒹ	83 ⒶⒷⒸⒹ	94 ⒶⒷⒸⒹ	105 ⒶⒷⒸⒹ
62 ⒶⒷⒸⒹ	73 ⒶⒷⒸⒹ	84 ⒶⒷⒸⒹ	95 ⒶⒷⒸⒹ	106 ⒶⒷⒸⒹ
63 ⒶⒷⒸⒹ	74 ⒶⒷⒸⒹ	85 ⒶⒷⒸⒹ	96 ⒶⒷⒸⒹ	107 ⒶⒷⒸⒹ
64 ⒶⒷⒸⒹ	75 ⒶⒷⒸⒹ	86 ⒶⒷⒸⒹ	97 ⒶⒷⒸⒹ	108 ⒶⒷⒸⒹ
65 ⒶⒷⒸⒹ	76 ⒶⒷⒸⒹ	87 ⒶⒷⒸⒹ	98 ⒶⒷⒸⒹ	109 ⒶⒷⒸⒹ
66 ⒶⒷⒸⒹ	77 ⒶⒷⒸⒹ	88 ⒶⒷⒸⒹ	99 ⒶⒷⒸⒹ	110 ⒶⒷⒸⒹ
67 ⒶⒷⒸⒹ	78 ⒶⒷⒸⒹ	89 ⒶⒷⒸⒹ	100 ⒶⒷⒸⒹ	111 ⒶⒷⒸⒹ
68 ⒶⒷⒸⒹ	79 ⒶⒷⒸⒹ	90 ⒶⒷⒸⒹ	101 ⒶⒷⒸⒹ	112 ⒶⒷⒸⒹ
69 ⒶⒷⒸⒹ	80 ⒶⒷⒸⒹ	91 ⒶⒷⒸⒹ	102 ⒶⒷⒸⒹ	
70 ⒶⒷⒸⒹ	81 ⒶⒷⒸⒹ	92 ⒶⒷⒸⒹ	103 ⒶⒷⒸⒹ	
71 ⒶⒷⒸⒹ	82 ⒶⒷⒸⒹ	93 ⒶⒷⒸⒹ	104 ⒶⒷⒸⒹ	

Section 3: Reading

113 ⒶⒷⒸⒹ	121 ⒶⒷⒸⒹ	129 ⒶⒷⒸⒹ	137 ⒶⒷⒸⒹ	145 ⒶⒷⒸⒹ
114 ⒶⒷⒸⒹ	122 ⒶⒷⒸⒹ	130 ⒶⒷⒸⒹ	138 ⒶⒷⒸⒹ	146 ⒶⒷⒸⒹ
115 ⒶⒷⒸⒹ	123 ⒶⒷⒸⒹ	131 ⒶⒷⒸⒹ	139 ⒶⒷⒸⒹ	147 ⒶⒷⒸⒹ
116 ⒶⒷⒸⒹ	124 ⒶⒷⒸⒹ	132 ⒶⒷⒸⒹ	140 ⒶⒷⒸⒹ	148 ⒶⒷⒸⒹ
117 ⒶⒷⒸⒹ	125 ⒶⒷⒸⒹ	133 ⒶⒷⒸⒹ	141 ⒶⒷⒸⒹ	149 ⒶⒷⒸⒹ
118 ⒶⒷⒸⒹ	126 ⒶⒷⒸⒹ	134 ⒶⒷⒸⒹ	142 ⒶⒷⒸⒹ	150 ⒶⒷⒸⒹ
119 ⒶⒷⒸⒹ	127 ⒶⒷⒸⒹ	135 ⒶⒷⒸⒹ	143 ⒶⒷⒸⒹ	151 ⒶⒷⒸⒹ
120 ⒶⒷⒸⒹ	128 ⒶⒷⒸⒹ	136 ⒶⒷⒸⒹ	144 ⒶⒷⒸⒹ	152 ⒶⒷⒸⒹ

(Section 3: Reading continued on reverse)

153 ⒶⒷⒸⒹ	158 ⒶⒷⒸⒹ	163 ⒶⒷⒸⒹ	168 ⒶⒷⒸⒹ	173 ⒶⒷⒸⒹ
154 ⒶⒷⒸⒹ	159 ⒶⒷⒸⒹ	164 ⒶⒷⒸⒹ	169 ⒶⒷⒸⒹ	174 ⒶⒷⒸⒹ
155 ⒶⒷⒸⒹ	160 ⒶⒷⒸⒹ	165 ⒶⒷⒸⒹ	170 ⒶⒷⒸⒹ	
156 ⒶⒷⒸⒹ	161 ⒶⒷⒸⒹ	166 ⒶⒷⒸⒹ	171 ⒶⒷⒸⒹ	
157 ⒶⒷⒸⒹ	162 ⒶⒷⒸⒹ	167 ⒶⒷⒸⒹ	172 ⒶⒷⒸⒹ	

Section 4: Mathematics

175 ⒶⒷⒸⒹ	188 ⒶⒷⒸⒹ	201 ⒶⒷⒸⒹ	214 ⒶⒷⒸⒹ	227 ⒶⒷⒸⒹ
176 ⒶⒷⒸⒹ	189 ⒶⒷⒸⒹ	202 ⒶⒷⒸⒹ	215 ⒶⒷⒸⒹ	228 ⒶⒷⒸⒹ
177 ⒶⒷⒸⒹ	190 ⒶⒷⒸⒹ	203 ⒶⒷⒸⒹ	216 ⒶⒷⒸⒹ	229 ⒶⒷⒸⒹ
178 ⒶⒷⒸⒹ	191 ⒶⒷⒸⒹ	204 ⒶⒷⒸⒹ	217 ⒶⒷⒸⒹ	230 ⒶⒷⒸⒹ
179 ⒶⒷⒸⒹ	192 ⒶⒷⒸⒹ	205 ⒶⒷⒸⒹ	218 ⒶⒷⒸⒹ	231 ⒶⒷⒸⒹ
180 ⒶⒷⒸⒹ	193 ⒶⒷⒸⒹ	206 ⒶⒷⒸⒹ	219 ⒶⒷⒸⒹ	232 ⒶⒷⒸⒹ
181 ⒶⒷⒸⒹ	194 ⒶⒷⒸⒹ	207 ⒶⒷⒸⒹ	220 ⒶⒷⒸⒹ	233 ⒶⒷⒸⒹ
182 ⒶⒷⒸⒹ	195 ⒶⒷⒸⒹ	208 ⒶⒷⒸⒹ	221 ⒶⒷⒸⒹ	234 ⒶⒷⒸⒹ
183 ⒶⒷⒸⒹ	196 ⒶⒷⒸⒹ	209 ⒶⒷⒸⒹ	222 ⒶⒷⒸⒹ	235 ⒶⒷⒸⒹ
184 ⒶⒷⒸⒹ	197 ⒶⒷⒸⒹ	210 ⒶⒷⒸⒹ	223 ⒶⒷⒸⒹ	236 ⒶⒷⒸⒹ
185 ⒶⒷⒸⒹ	198 ⒶⒷⒸⒹ	211 ⒶⒷⒸⒹ	224 ⒶⒷⒸⒹ	237 ⒶⒷⒸⒹ
186 ⒶⒷⒸⒹ	199 ⒶⒷⒸⒹ	212 ⒶⒷⒸⒹ	225 ⒶⒷⒸⒹ	238 ⒶⒷⒸⒹ
187 ⒶⒷⒸⒹ	200 ⒶⒷⒸⒹ	213 ⒶⒷⒸⒹ	226 ⒶⒷⒸⒹ	

Section 5: Language Skills

239 ⒶⒷⒸⒹ	251 ⒶⒷⒸⒹ	263 ⒶⒷⒸⒹ	275 ⒶⒷⒸⒹ	287 ⒶⒷⒸⒹ
240 ⒶⒷⒸⒹ	252 ⒶⒷⒸⒹ	264 ⒶⒷⒸⒹ	276 ⒶⒷⒸⒹ	288 ⒶⒷⒸⒹ
241 ⒶⒷⒸⒹ	253 ⒶⒷⒸⒹ	265 ⒶⒷⒸⒹ	277 ⒶⒷⒸⒹ	289 ⒶⒷⒸⒹ
242 ⒶⒷⒸⒹ	254 ⒶⒷⒸⒹ	266 ⒶⒷⒸⒹ	278 ⒶⒷⒸⒹ	290 ⒶⒷⒸⒹ
243 ⒶⒷⒸⒹ	255 ⒶⒷⒸⒹ	267 ⒶⒷⒸⒹ	279 ⒶⒷⒸⒹ	291 ⒶⒷⒸⒹ
244 ⒶⒷⒸⒹ	256 ⒶⒷⒸⒹ	268 ⒶⒷⒸⒹ	280 ⒶⒷⒸⒹ	292 ⒶⒷⒸⒹ
245 ⒶⒷⒸⒹ	257 ⒶⒷⒸⒹ	269 ⒶⒷⒸⒹ	281 ⒶⒷⒸⒹ	293 ⒶⒷⒸⒹ
246 ⒶⒷⒸⒹ	258 ⒶⒷⒸⒹ	270 ⒶⒷⒸⒹ	282 ⒶⒷⒸⒹ	294 ⒶⒷⒸⒹ
247 ⒶⒷⒸⒹ	259 ⒶⒷⒸⒹ	271 ⒶⒷⒸⒹ	283 ⒶⒷⒸⒹ	295 ⒶⒷⒸⒹ
248 ⒶⒷⒸⒹ	260 ⒶⒷⒸⒹ	272 ⒶⒷⒸⒹ	284 ⒶⒷⒸⒹ	296 ⒶⒷⒸⒹ
249 ⒶⒷⒸⒹ	261 ⒶⒷⒸⒹ	273 ⒶⒷⒸⒹ	285 ⒶⒷⒸⒹ	297 ⒶⒷⒸⒹ
250 ⒶⒷⒸⒹ	262 ⒶⒷⒸⒹ	274 ⒶⒷⒸⒹ	286 ⒶⒷⒸⒹ	298 ⒶⒷⒸⒹ

Verbal Skills

Questions 1-60, 16 Minutes

1. Which word does *not* belong with the others?
   (A) embrace
   (B) greet
   (C) ignore
   (D) welcome

2. Devious most nearly means
   (A) anxious
   (B) deceitful
   (C) helpful
   (D) intelligent

3. Which word does *not* belong with the others?
   (A) prohibit
   (B) ban
   (C) encourage
   (D) forbid

4. Pig is to farm as dolphin is to
   (A) aquarium
   (B) fish
   (C) mammal
   (D) wild

5. Encourage most nearly means
   (A) challenge
   (B) complain
   (C) fight
   (D) motivate

6. Which word does *not* belong with the others?
   (A) bracelet
   (B) necklace
   (C) ring
   (D) shoe

7. Trial is to jury as competition is to
   (A) athletes
   (B) judges
   (C) score
   (D) sports

8. Specific means the opposite of
   (A) changing
   (B) complicated
   (C) exact
   (D) general

9. Relinquish most nearly means
   (A) contain
   (B) crush
   (C) keep
   (D) surrender

10. Marty does not eat meat. Burgers contain meat. Marty does not eat burgers. If the first two statements are true, then the third is
    (A) True
    (B) False
    (C) Uncertain

11. Which word does *not* belong with the others?
    (A) passport
    (B) suitcase
    (C) ticket
    (D) vacation

12. Literal means the opposite of
    (A) bewitched
    (B) figurative
    (C) general
    (D) scientific

13. Compromise most nearly means
    (A) agreement
    (B) argument
    (C) challenge
    (D) solution

14. Proficient means the opposite of
    (A) accomplished
    (B) complete
    (C) incapable
    (D) disastrous

15. Float is to sink as climb is to
    (A) fall
    (B) mountain
    (C) sports
    (D) succeed

16. Which word does *not* belong with the others?
    (A) give
    (B) loan
    (C) share
    (D) take

17. Authentic most nearly means
    (A) phony
    (B) powerful
    (C) true
    (D) unreal

18. Purple is Juan's favorite color. Lilacs are flowers that are purple. Juan likes lilacs. If the first two statements are true, then the third is
    (A) True
    (B) False
    (C) Uncertain

19. Brief is to lengthy as simple is to
    (A) complex
    (B) easy
    (C) quick
    (D) task

20. Gruesome most nearly means
    (A) comforting
    (B) dreadful
    (C) soothing
    (D) worrisome

21. Which word does *not* belong with the others?
    (A) condiments
    (B) ketchup
    (C) mayonnaise
    (D) mustard

22. Detect means the opposite of
    (A) arrive
    (B) ignore
    (C) notice
    (D) observe

23. Mammals breastfeed their young. Monkeys are mammals. All monkeys breastfeed their young. If the first two statements are true, then the third is
    (A) True
    (B) False
    (C) Uncertain

24. Obvious is to subtle as chaotic is to
    (A) blatant
    (B) confused
    (C) disorderly
    (D) peaceful

25. Capture means the opposite of
    (A) delete
    (B) hold
    (C) release
    (D) trap

26. Felines have whiskers. All cats are felines. All cats have whiskers. If the first two statements are true, then the third is
    (A) True
    (B) False
    (C) Uncertain

27. Annoy most nearly means
    (A) comfort
    (B) contact
    (C) irritate
    (D) regulate

28. Alert is to aware as obnoxious is to
    (A) annoying
    (B) loud
    (C) pleasant
    (D) unaware

29. Which word does *not* belong with the others?
    (A) class
    (B) history
    (C) math
    (D) science

30. Sparse means the opposite of
    (A) abundant
    (B) meager
    (C) mediocre
    (D) slight

31. The United Kingdom is in Europe. Scotland is part of the United Kingdom. Scotland is in Europe. If the first two statements are true, then the third is
    (A) True
    (B) False
    (C) Uncertain

32. Perform most nearly means
    (A) act
    (B) design
    (C) fail
    (D) organize

33. Which word does *not* belong with the others?
    (A) fable
    (B) lie
    (C) story
    (D) tale

34. Prove is to theory as solve is to
    (A) answer
    (B) discover
    (C) experiment
    (D) issue

35. Rupert is a black cat. Rupert has a pink nose. All black cats have pink noses. If the first two statements are true, then the third is
    (A) True
    (B) False
    (C) Uncertain

36. Which word does *not* belong with the others?
    (A) dentist
    (B) doctor
    (C) nurse
    (D) profession

37. Which word does *not* belong with the others?
    (A) auburn
    (B) blonde
    (C) brunette
    (D) curly

38. Some movies are musicals. Some musicals are sad. Movies that are musicals are always sad. If the first two statements are true, then the third is
    (A) True
    (B) False
    (C) Uncertain

39. Mountain is to range as hill is to
    (A) grassy
    (B) nature
    (C) sledding
    (D) valley

40. Amplify means the opposite of
    (A) behave
    (B) diminish
    (C) increase
    (D) turn

41. Splendor most nearly means
    (A) discount
    (B) expense
    (C) glory
    (D) horror

42. Which word does *not* belong with the others?
    (A) dictionary
    (B) encyclopedia
    (C) novel
    (D) thesaurus

43. Insignificant means the opposite of
    (A) attractive
    (B) complicated
    (C) important
    (D) irrelevant

44. Watch is to clock as tablet is to
    (A) computer
    (B) device
    (C) drawing
    (D) electronics

45. Innocent most nearly means
    (A) free
    (B) guilty
    (C) healthy
    (D) honest

46. Which word does *not* belong with the others?
    (A) emulate
    (B) generate
    (C) imitate
    (D) mimic

47. The silver snake is longer than the black snake. The yellow snake is longer than the black snake. The yellow snake is longer than the silver snake. If the first two statements are true, then the third is
    (A) True
    (B) False
    (C) Uncertain

48. Voracious most nearly means
    (A) inconsistent
    (B) ravenous
    (C) shocking
    (D) unstable

49. Which word does *not* belong with the others?
    (A) glass
    (B) steel
    (C) tool
    (D) wood

50. People need water to live. Water can be found in rivers. People always live near rivers. If the first two statements are true, then the third is
    (A) True
    (B) False
    (C) Uncertain

51. Repulse most nearly means
    (A) admire
    (B) beat
    (C) disgust
    (D) welcome

52. Which word does *not* belong with the others?
    (A) free
    (B) control
    (C) limit
    (D) restrict

53. Tirade means the opposite of
    (A) attack
    (B) condemnation
    (C) endorsement
    (D) rant

54. Palatial most nearly means
    (A) glacial
    (B) luxurious
    (C) tedious
    (D) thrifty

55. Waves is to ocean as gusts is to
    (A) fire
    (B) storm
    (C) water
    (D) wind

56. Possess most nearly means
    (A) discard
    (B) own
    (C) release
    (D) scare

57. Which word does *not* belong with the others?
 (A) breakfast
 (B) eggs
 (C) pancakes
 (D) waffles

58. Waynesville is a larger town than Riverdale. Ventura is a larger town than Riverdale. Ventura is a larger town than Waynesville. If the first two statements are true, then the third is
 (A) True
 (B) False
 (C) Uncertain

59. Which word does *not* belong with the others?
 (A) alligator
 (B) crab
 (C) lizard
 (D) turtle

60. Explicit most nearly means
 (A) dangerous
 (B) inappropriate
 (C) specific
 (D) unnecessary

Quantitative Skills

Questions 61-112, 30 Minutes

61. Fill in the blank in this series: 9, ___, 36, 72...
    (A) 12
    (B) 18
    (C) 27
    (D) 144

62. What number subtracted from the sum of 8 and 6 makes 3 more than 9?
    (A) 2
    (B) 3
    (C) 9
    (D) 10

63. Examine I, II, and III and find the *best* answer:

I. 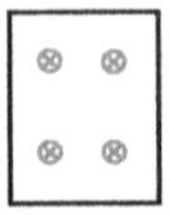

II. 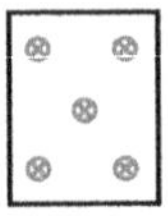

III. 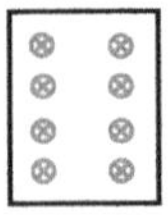

    (A) The sum of I and II is less than III
    (B) III is greater than I which is greater than II
    (C) The difference of III and I is less than II
    (D) The difference of III and II is greater than I

64. What number is 30% of the sum of 5^2 and 5?
    (A) 3
    (B) 8.5
    (C) 9
    (D) 10

65. Examine I, II, and III, and find the *best* answer.

    I. 65%
    II. 0.067
    III. $\frac{7}{10}$

    (A) II < I < III
    (B) II = III < I
    (C) I > III > II
    (D) III < II < I

66. Examine the angles below and find the *best* answer.

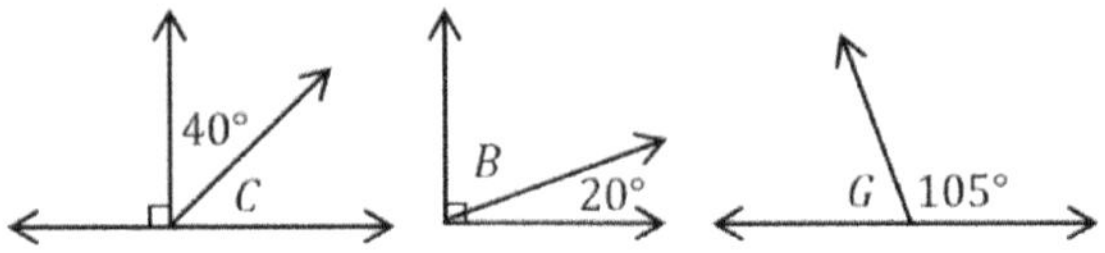
40°
C
B
20°
G
105°

    (A) $\angle G = \angle B > \angle C$
    (B) $\angle G > \angle B > \angle C$
    (C) $\angle B + \angle C = \angle G$
    (D) $\angle B < \angle C$

67. Examine I, II, and III and find the *best* answer.

    I. 32 oz.
    II. 24 oz.
    III. 12 oz.

    (A) The sum of II and III is less than I
    (B) The difference of I and III is greater than II
    (C) The difference of II and III is equal to I
    (D) The difference of I and II is less than III

68. In the sequence 58, 49, 38, 29..., what number should come next?
    (A) 17
    (B) 18
    (C) 19
    (D) 28

69. Without measuring the following segments, examine the following and find the best answer.

    I. The length of PR, where Q is the center of the circle
    II. The length of QT, where Q is the center of the circle
    III. The length of SU, a chord of circle Q

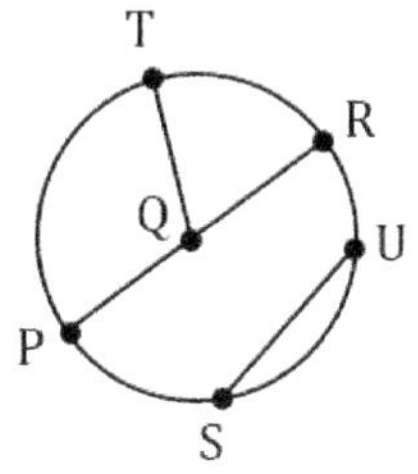

T
R
Q
U
P
S

(A) II < III
(B) III < II
(C) I > III
(D) I = II

70. Examine I, II, and III and find the *best* answer when *x* and *y* are both positive.

    I. $-x + y + 2x$
    II. $-x - (-y)$
    III. $2(x + y) - y$

(A) III > I > II
(B) II > I
(C) I = II = III
(D) I > II = III

71. Fill in the blank in this series: 5, ___, 45, −135 ...
(A) −30
(B) −15
(C) 15
(D) 30

72. What number is 4 less than the sum of 10% of 90 and $\frac{1}{2}$ of 28?
(A) 17
(B) 19
(C) 25
(D) 27

73. What number is $\frac{2}{5}$ of the product of 4, 5, and 6?
(A) 10
(B) 24
(C) 36
(D) 48

74. Examine the following and find the best answer:

    I. $58{,}000 \div 100$
    II. 58×10^2
    III. 580×10^{-1}

(A) I and III are equal
(B) II and III are equal
(C) I is smaller than II
(D) II is smaller than III

75. What number should fill in the blank in this series: 60, ____, 30, 10, 0?
(A) 35
(B) 36
(C) 40
(D) 50

76. The following graph shows how many electoral votes certain states will have. Find the *best* answer.

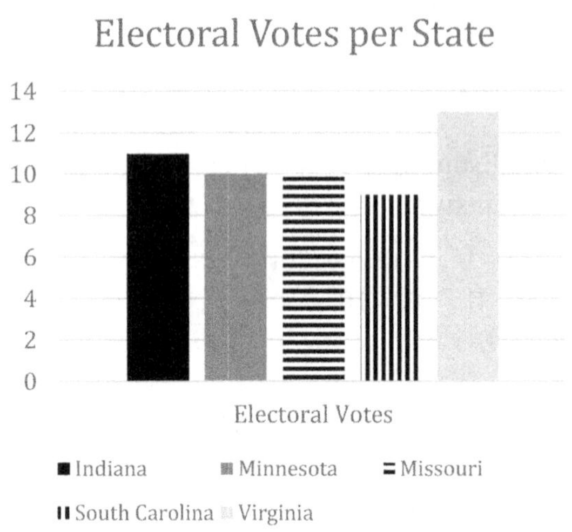
Electoral Votes per State
14
12
10
8
6
4
2
0
Electoral Votes
Indiana
Minnesota
Missouri
South Carolina
Virginia

(A) Indiana has the greatest number of electoral votes
(B) The sum of Indiana and Minnesota is greater than the sum of Missouri and South Carolina
(C) The sum of Virginia and South Carolina is less than the sum of Minnesota and Missouri
(D) Minnesota has the least number of electoral votes

77. What number is $\frac{1}{3}$ of the difference of 6^2 and 6?
(A) 10
(B) 12
(C) 16
(D) 20

78. What number when subtracted from 54 makes twice as much as $\frac{5}{6}$ of 30?
(A) 4
(B) 29
(C) 79
(D) 104

79. Examine I, II, and III and find the best answer.

I. the y-intercept of $y = -2x - 6$
II. the y-intercept of $6x + 3y = 1$
III. the y-intercept of the line shown

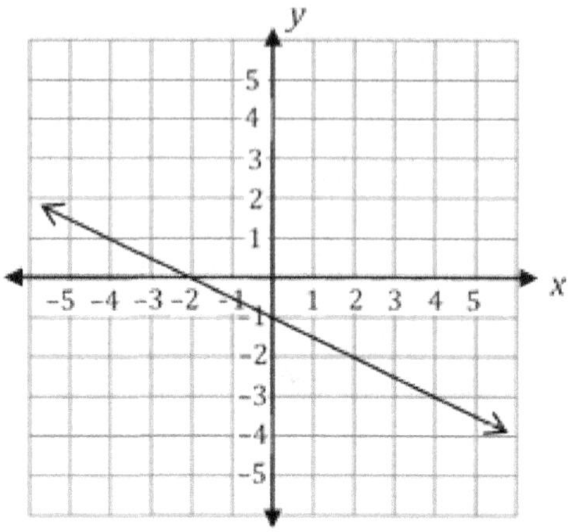
y
x
5
4
3
2
1
-1
-2
-3
-4
-5
-5 -4 -3 -2 -1
1 2 3 4 5

(A) I > II
(B) II < III
(C) I < III
(D) I = III

80. What number subtracted from the sum of 5 and 8 makes the difference of 12 and 4?
(A) 3
(B) 5
(C) 7
(D) 9

81. Examine the following and find the best answer:

I. 60,293
II. 6.02×10^4
III. 0.060293×10^6

(A) I and III are equal
(B) I, II, and III are equal
(C) I is smaller than II
(D) II is greater than III

82. Examine the following circle with center O and find the best answer.

I. The length of OR
II. The length of RS
III. The sum of the lengths of MO and OS

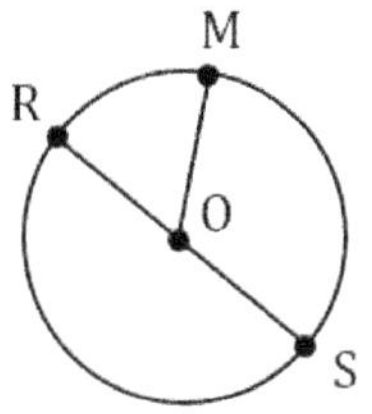
M
R
O
S

(A) I < II < III
(B) I > II
(C) I < II = III
(D) III < I

83. In the sequence 1,000, 200, 100,____,10, what number should fill in the blank?
(A) 5
(B) 20
(C) 50
(D) 90

84. What number subtracted from the product of 7 and 4 makes 10 less than 19?
(A) 1
(B) 15
(C) 18
(D) 19

85. Examine I, II, and III, and find the *best* answer.

III. $\frac{1}{2}$ of 23
II. $\frac{1}{3}$ of 23
III. $\frac{1}{5}$ of 23

(A) I < II < III
(B) I < III < II
(C) II < III < I
(D) III < II < I

86. Examine I, II, and III and find the *best* answer when x and y are both positive.

I. $4(x+y)$
II. $2(2x+y)$
III. $3x+x+y$

(A) I < II < III
(B) I = II
(C) III > I
(D) III < II < I

87. Examine I, II, and III and find the *best* answer:

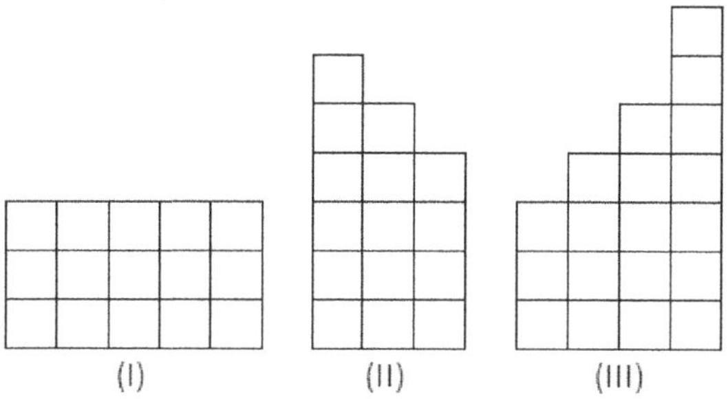
(I)
(II)
(III)

(A) I = II = III
(B) I < II < III
(C) III > I = II
(D) II > III > I

88. In the sequence 217, 219, 221..., what number should come next?
(A) 222
(B) 223
(C) 225
(D) 232

89. Examine I, II, and III and find the *best* answer when x and y are both positive.

I. $x+y$
II. $x+3y-y$
III. $\frac{4x+2y}{2}$

(A) I = II
(B) I > II
(C) III > I
(D) II = III

90. Examine I, II, and III, and find the *best* answer.

I. $\frac{1}{6}$ of 9
II. 1.4
III. $\sqrt{4}$

(A) II > I > III
(B) I > II > III
(C) II > III > I
(D) III > I > II

91. Examine the following and find the best answer.

I. The length of OB, where O is the center of the circle
II. The length of OC, where O is the center of the circle
III. The length of BD, the diameter of circle O

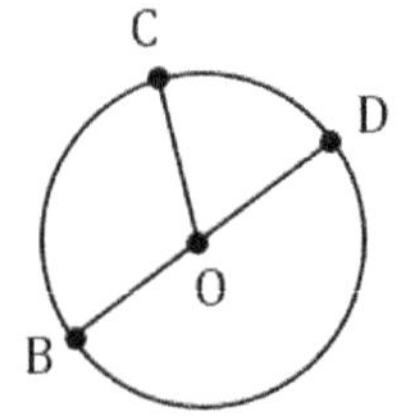
C
D
O
B

(A) I = II > III
(B) I = II = III
(C) III > I > II
(D) III > I = II

92. Fill in the blank in this series:
$\frac{1}{4}, -\frac{1}{2}, \_\_, -2 \ldots$
(A) $\frac{1}{2}$
(B) 1
(C) −1
(D) −2

93. Examine I, II, and III and find the *best* answer:

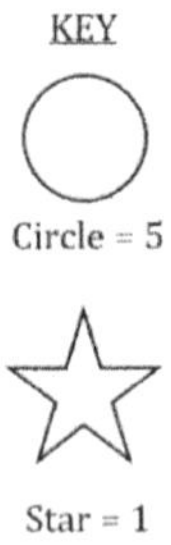
KEY
Circle = 5
Star = 1

I. 

II. 

III. 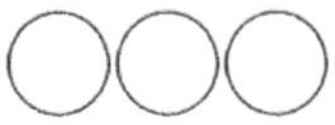

(A) I and III are equal, and both are greater than II
(B) I and III are equal, and both are less than II
(C) III is greater than I which is greater than II
(D) II is greater than I which is greater than III

94. In the sequence 33, 36, 40, 44, 48..., one number is *wrong*. That number should be:
(A) 32
(B) 34
(C) 39
(D) 45

95. Examine the following and find the best answer:

I. $4 \times \frac{1}{2^2}$
II. $2 + 2^2$
III. $4 \div 2^1$

(A) I, II, and III are equal
(B) I is greater than II
(C) I is smaller than III
(D) III is greater than II

96. In the sequence 20.5, 21, 21.5, 22..., what number should come next?
(A) 22.1
(B) 22.5
(C) 23
(D) 23.5

97. Examine I, II, and III and find the *best* answer:

KEY

Large House = 10 houses

Small House = 1 house

I.
II.
III.

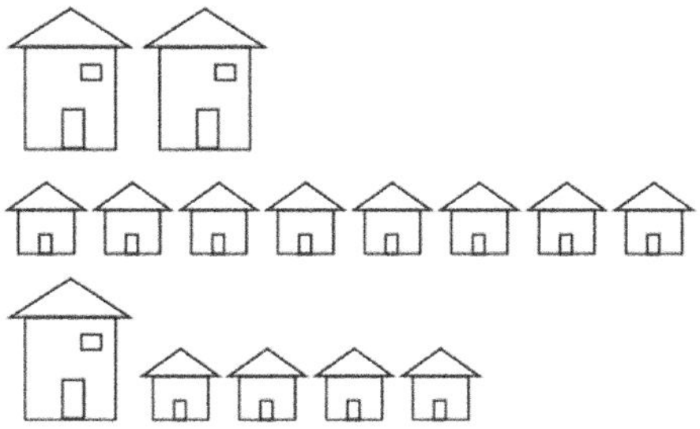

(A) II > III > I
(B) I > III > II
(C) II + III < I
(D) I > II > III

98. What element should come next in this series: 1, 6, 12, 17,___?
(A) 21
(B) 22
(C) 23
(D) 24

99. What number subtracted from 45 is equal to the median of 42, 15, and 33?
(A) 3
(B) 10
(C) 12
(D) 30

100. Examine I, II, and III and find the *best* answer.

I. 3 weeks
II. 21 days
III. 2 weeks

(A) III = II < I
(B) III < I < II
(C) I = II < III
(D) III < I = II

101. In the sequence 102, 34, $\frac{34}{3}$, $\frac{34}{9}$..., what number should come next?
(A) $\frac{34}{27}$
(B) $\frac{34}{18}$
(C) $\frac{34}{15}$
(D) $\frac{34}{12}$

102. Examine I, II, and III and find the best answer.

I. the y-intercept of the line shown
II. the y-intercept of $2x + 4y = 4$
III. the y-intercept of $y = 2x - 4$

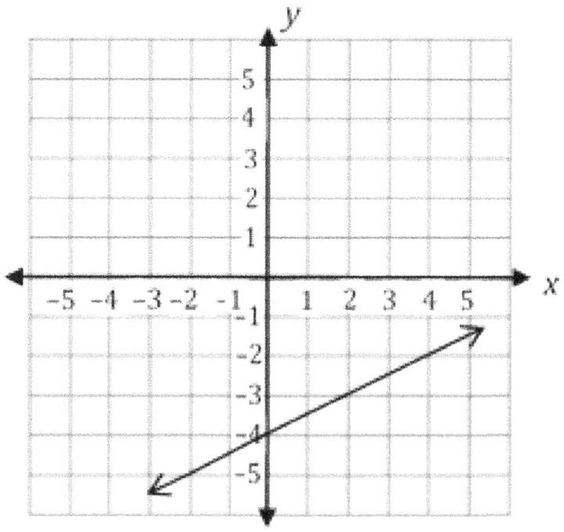
y
x
5
4
3
2
1
-5 -4 -3 -2 -1
1 2 3 4 5
-1
-2
-3
-4
-5

(A) I > II
(B) I = III
(C) I > III
(D) II < III

103. Examine I, II, and III, and find the *best* answer.

I. $\frac{3}{4}$ of 16
II. $\frac{2}{3}$ of 21
III. $\frac{1}{2}$ of 30

(A) I < II < III
(B) I > II > III
(C) II = I > III
(D) III = I > II

104. Examine angles *A, B, C, D, E, F, G,* and *H* and find the best answer.

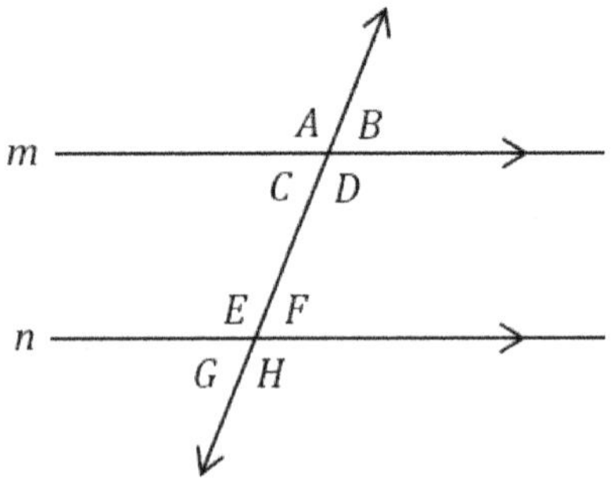
m
n
A
B
C
D
E
F
G
H

(A) $\angle A + \angle D = \angle E + \angle G$
(B) $\angle D + \angle B = \angle F + \angle H$
(C) $\angle B + \angle C = \angle F + \angle H$
(D) $\angle A + \angle C = \angle D + \angle E$

105. Examine the line graph and find the *best* answer.

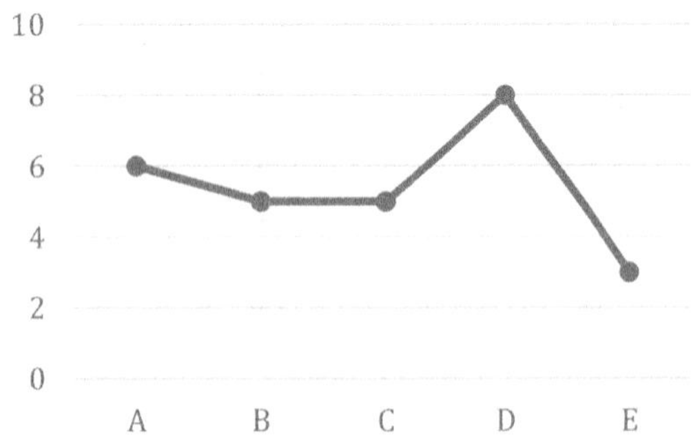
10
8
6
4
2
0
A
B
C
D
E

(A) A, B, and C are equal
(B) B plus C is less than A plus E
(C) A plus C equals D plus E
(D) D plus E is less than B plus C

106. Examine I, II, and III and find the *best* answer when *x* and *y* are both positive.

I. $3(x - y)$
II. $2x - y + x$
III. $x + 2x$

(A) III > I > II
(B) III > II > I
(C) I = II
(D) I > II

107. The following graph records how many points Jasmine and Isabella scored in their first through fifth basketball games of the season. Find the *best* answer.

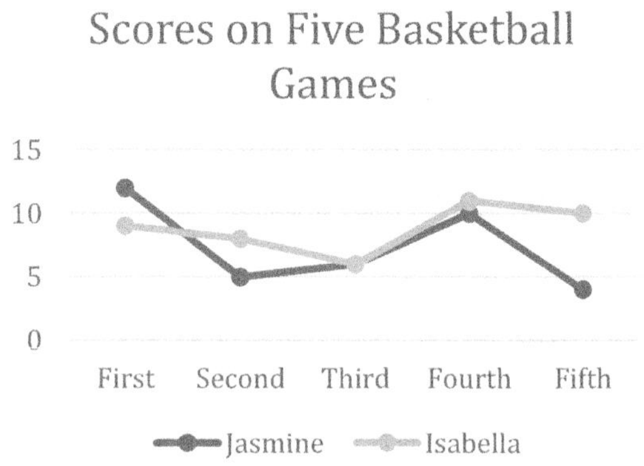
Scores on Five Basketball Games
15
10
5
0
First
Second
Third
Fourth
Fifth
Jasmine
Isabella

(A) Jasmine and Isabella scored the same number of points in the fourth game
(B) Isabella scored fewer points in the fifth game
(C) Jasmine scored fewer points in the first game
(D) Jasmine and Isabella scored the same number of points in the third game

108. Examine I, II, and III and find the *best* answer.

I. 12 oz.
II. 9 oz.
III. 6 oz.

(A) I - II > III
(B) II < I - III
(C) II = I - III
(D) I + III = II + II

109. Examine the angles and find the *best* answer.

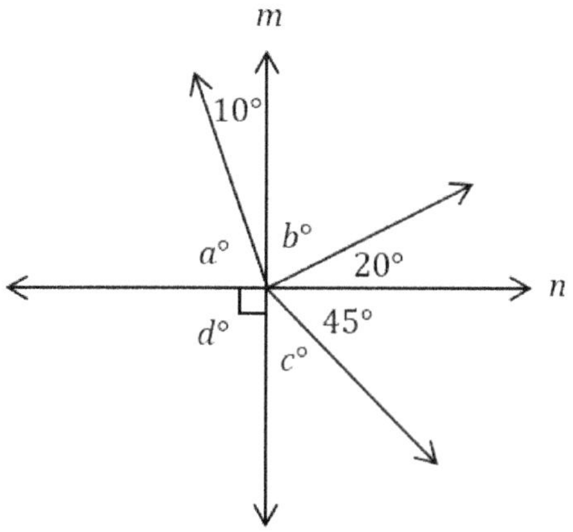
m
10°
a°
b°
20°
n
d°
45°
c°

(A) $a = c$
(B) $a + d = b + c$
(C) $c < a < b < d$
(D) $d > a > b > c$

110. In the sequence 12, 10, 6, 3, 0..., one number is *wrong*. That number should be:
(A) 7
(B) 8
(C) 9
(D) 13

111. What number subtracted from 72 is equal to the average of 13, 18, and 20?
(A) 21
(B) 41
(C) 54
(D) 55

112. Examine I, II, and III and find the best answer.

I. the y-intercept of $4x + y = 4$
II. the y-intercept of the line shown
III. the y-intercept of $y = 4x$

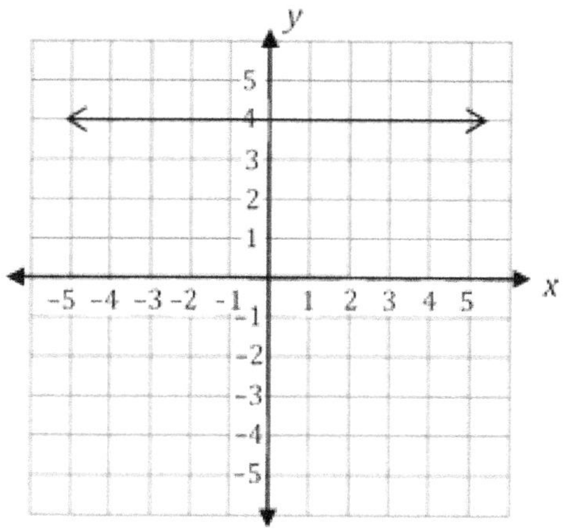
y
x
5
4
3
2
1
-1
-2
-3
-4
-5
-5 -4 -3 -2 -1
1 2 3 4 5

(A) I < II = III
(B) I = II > III
(C) III > II = I
(D) I = II = III

Reading

Questions 113-174, 25 Minutes

Though animals' teeth generally reflect their diet (with carnivores having sharp teeth for ripping into meat and herbivores having flat teeth for chewing plants) the teeth of one animal, called the tufted deer, are an exception. The tufted deer is general known for one unusual trait: being an herbivore with fangs! Their fangs, which curl down from their top row of teeth, have earned the deer comparisons to saber-tooth tigers and vampires; the only difference is that, instead of blood or meat, tufted deer feed on leaves, fruit, grass, and twigs. Their fangs mostly serve defensive purposes—for chewing their food, they use flat teeth in the back of their mouths.

Besides their unusual front teeth, tufted deer look similar to other species of deer. They are medium sized with brown or gray fur. Though their fangs may be their most notable feature, their name comes from the distinctive tufts of hair on their foreheads. Like other deer, males of the species usually grow antlers, which are often short enough to be hidden by their hair. Tufted deer bark to communicate with each other, often when alarmed or alerting other deer of nearby danger. During the mating season, males will also bark to attract mates. Female deer of the species have one to two babies at a time, and care for them until the children are old enough to survive on their own. The babies, called "fawns," are born with white spots on their backs, spots that vanish as the young deer grows. Though tufted deer sometimes live in pairs, they're more often solitary and territorial, not traveling far from their homes.

Tufted deer prefer to live in high altitude rainforests with a water source nearby, and are most commonly found around Burma and China. Tufted deer are considered near threatened, which means their population numbers are decreasing in the wild. Humans are considered the biggest threat to the tufted deer, as we are to many other animal populations. Thousands of tufted deer are hunted each year from their fur meat and fur. Their habitats are being destroyed through logging and deforestation. Tufted deer are a unique species that could face extinction if humans continue to hunt them and destroy their homes.

113. This passage is mostly about
   (A) animal dentistry.
   (B) the most endangered animal.
   (C) a unique species of deer.
   (D) the differences between herbivores and carnivores.

114. What would be the most appropriate title for this passage?
   (A) Antlered Deer
   (B) Deer of Asia
   (C) The Fanged Deer of Asia
   (D) Rainforest Animals

115. The author states that tufted deer
   (A) are related to saber-tooth tigers, as indicated by their sharp fangs.
   (B) are carnivores who hunt small mammals.
   (C) only eat in the summer months and hibernate all winter.
   (D) eat plants like fruit, grass, leaves, and twigs.

116. Tufted deer
   (A) all have hidden antlers.
   (B) take care of their young until they're able to survive on their own.
   (C) are the smallest deer species.
   (D) do not look anything like other species of deer.

117. According to the facts in the passage, tufted deer live in
   (A) cold-weather forests.
   (B) dry, desert climates.
   (C) high-altitude rainforests.
   (D) coastal habitats.

118. Which of the following can be inferred from the passage?
   (A) Tufted deer are thriving and increasing in population each year.
   (B) Destroying an animal's habitat makes that animal more likely to go extinct.
   (C) To slow their extinction, tufted deer should be raised in zoos.
   (D) Tufted deer live in large communities with other numbers from their species.

119. It can be inferred from the passage that tufted deer
   (A) use their fangs to protect themselves or their territory.
   (B) feed primarily on the blood of other animals.
   (C) have never been officially studied by scientists.
   (D) would survive better if they lived at lower altitudes.

120. The author would most likely agree with which of the following statements?
   (A) Tufted deer are only interesting to scientists.
   (B) The hunting of tufted deer should be regulated.
   (C) The most well-known animals are the most interesting.
   (D) Tufted deer are the most unique animal there is.

121. As it is used in the passage, the word "distinctive" most nearly means
   (A) messy.
   (B) ruffled.
   (C) similar.
   (D) unique.

122. As it is used in the passage, the word "vanish" most nearly means
   (A) disappear.
   (B) grow.
   (C) molt.
   (D) stay.

Alligators and crocodiles; sawgrass and cypress trees; these are just some residents of the Florida Everglades. Though the Everglades may have a reputation as being a giant swamp, it's actually a massive slow-moving river covering more than 1.5 million acres of land in southern Florida. The Everglades is classified as a National Park, the third largest in the continental United States. There are only two seasons in the Everglades: wet and dry. Still, all-year-round, people who visit the Everglades can appreciate the area's natural beauty and abundant wildlife.

Though the Everglades is famous for its alligators, many other animals call the area home as well. Over 600 unique species of birds and fish live in the Everglades, in addition to over 100 species of mammals, reptiles, and amphibians. Thirty-six of these species are threatened or endangered, including the leatherback turtle, West Indian Manatee, Florida panther, and American crocodile. The Everglades is also unique for being the only place in the world where alligators and crocodiles coexist; typically, the live in different regions and do not interact.

Plants are another prominent feature of the Everglades, with sawgrass plants being the most common. Sawgrass plants are named after their sharp blades, which have been known to rip through clothing on contact! These plants grow in the water and can reach up to 6 feet tall. Fortunately, boats in the Everglades can cruise right over sawgrass plants, keeping passengers from getting injured by the dangerous plants.

For many in Florida, the Everglades is more than just a beautiful nature preserve, but a major source of water. Most of the water in the Everglades is fresh, which means it can be purified and ingested by humans without causing problems. The waterways in the Everglades are quite shallow, though, with the wetlands being only nine feet deep at its lowest point and four to five feet deep in other parts. Still, it contains enough water to be used as a source of drinking water for over 8 million people. In a state of 21 million, that is nearly one out of every three people! People enjoy the Everglades in other ways, too. The Everglades National Park offers visitors opportunities to bike, camp, walk, boat, and perform many other fun activities. The Everglades features a diverse and thriving ecosystem, as well as plenty of key features that make it a valuable part of the Florida ecosystem—clearly, it's far more than just a "giant swamp!"

123. What would be the most appropriate title for this passage?
    (A) The History of the Florida Everglades
    (B) Alligators and Crocodiles
    (C) More Than a Swamp: Florida's Most Famous Wetland
    (D) American Wetlands

124. This passage is mostly about
    (A) a huge national park and some of its unique traits.
    (B) the risk humans pose to the Everglades.
    (C) tourism in National Parks.
    (D) a giant swamp in southern Florida.

125. Based on the details of the passage, the Florida Everglades
    (A) is occupied by over 600 types of mammals and reptiles.
    (B) is the largest National Park in the country.
    (C) occupies over 1.5 million acres of land.
    (D) remains unprotected by Florida state law.

126. The author states that
(A) the Everglades is at risk of being drained from too many people drinking from it.
(B) it is illegal to use wetlands as a source of drinking water.
(C) there is not enough water in the Everglades to use for drinking because it is so shallow.
(D) one out of every three people in Florida relies on the Everglades for their drinking water.

127. According to the facts of the passage,
(A) manatees do not live in the Everglades.
(B) the Everglades is home to numerous threatened and endangered species.
(C) alligators are the only reptiles that live in the Everglades.
(D) crocodiles and alligators in the Everglades are bitter enemies.

128. It can be inferred from the passage that
(A) the Everglades has some regions on land and some entirely underwater.
(B) visitors to the Everglades won't see any wildlife because of the tall sawgrass.
(C) the Everglades does not protect the species that live there.
(D) all the animals that live in the Everglades live underwater.

129. Which of the following can be inferred from the passage?
(A) It is safe to swim in the Everglades.
(B) Boating is the only thing to do in the Everglades.
(C) No one has ever been hurt or injured in Everglades National Park.
(D) Tourists visiting the Everglades should follow safety guidelines.

130. The author would most likely agree with which of the following statements?
(A) The Everglades is nothing more than a huge swamp.
(B) The Everglades should be protected.
(C) The only people who should care about the Everglades are those who live in Florida.
(D) The abundance of alligators & crocodiles makes visiting the Everglades too dangerous.

131. As it is used in the passage, the word "massive" most nearly means
(A) deep.
(B) giant.
(C) heavy.
(D) immeasurable.

132. As it is used in the passage, the word "coexist" most nearly means
(A) compete.
(B) exist side-by-side.
(C) grow to the same size.
(D) share resources.

Around the world, records are broken every day. From long-distance egg-tossing to speed-eating hotdogs, people go to great lengths to outperform others, no matter how strange the competition may seem. Why do some people exert so much time and effort to achieve what seem like such trivial goals? According to psychologists, there are three primary motivations people have for striving to beat other people's world records.

Some who chase world records have a desire for power. It's not the feat itself that inspires them, but the idea of knocking someone else out of that position of distinction. They desire the feelings of dominance that being "the best" can create. The competition for many world records is stiff; each year, the Guinness Book of World Records receives about 50,000 applications, and of these, only 5% are accepted. Being able to brag about achieving such a rare distinction can give someone a great feeling of power, which can help the record-setter's sense of confidence and security.

Many others are motivated by a need to achieve. For some, this can mean writing a great book, winning a high-paying job, or solving a global problem. For others, this can mean beating world records. Encouraging this ambition can be good for society. People who are ambitious achievers are often responsible for innovations that improve the quality of life for everyone. It's the ambitious that have cured diseases, built cities, and put humans on the moon. Though world record ambitions may seem unimportant, the drive to achieve speaks to a positive human trait that should be encouraged wherever possible.

Acquiring a sense of belonging is a third reason some people strive for what may seem like such silly or unimportant records. Sure, everyone wants to stand out, but we also want to feel like we belong to a group. Setting or beating a record can help us do both, especially if it's one that many people compete for. If you win, you rise above your opponents, but in striving for the win, you join a group of competitors all with one common goal: to be the best. Michael Phelps' world record for earning the most gold medals at a single Olympics sets him apart from his competitors, but it also makes him a part of their community, one of world-class athletes who all are going for the gold.

Even though some world records—like having the world's longest fingernails—may appear pointless, they can actually benefit both individuals and society. By pushing people to strive to overtake the competition, to set and pursue ambitious goals, and to feel like they belong to a community, world records encourage an excellence that far outweighs their strangeness.

133. This passage is mostly about
   (A) types of record set throughout history.
   (B) why people try to beat other people's accomplishments.
   (C) the history of world records.
   (D) world records that have benefited society.

134. As it is used in the passage, the word "exert" most nearly means
   (A) earn.
   (B) expend.
   (C) have.
   (D) waste.

135. You would probably find this passage in
   (A) a lifestyle magazine.
   (B) a science textbook.
   (C) a psychology journal.
   (D) a sports memoir.

136. According to the passage, people who set out to beat world records are often motivated by
   (A) boredom, freedom, and selfishness.
   (B) achievement, control, and standing out from a crowd.
   (C) innovation, dominance, and success.
   (D) achievement, power, and belonging.

137. It can be inferred from the passage that the desire to break records is
   (A) common.
   (B) misguided.
   (C) rare.
   (D) useless.

138. According to the passage, which of the following is true?
   (A) Winning the most gold medals at a single Olympics is a meaningless record.
   (B) It's uncommon to belong to a group of people who share a common interest.
   (C) Having the world's longest fingernails seems like a pointless record.
   (D) Ambition is a dangerous quality that should be discouraged when noticed.

139. As it is used in the passage, the word "<u>distinction</u>" most nearly means
   (A) apathy.
   (B) height.
   (C) honor.
   (D) separation.

140. According to the passage, two contradictory motivations for chasing world records could be
   (A) achieving success and gaining recognition.
   (B) setting goals for oneself and helping others.
   (C) overcoming one's fears and exerting self-control.
   (D) desiring to belong to a group and wanting to stand apart.

141. According to the passage, an example of a positive effect the human drive to achieve has on the world is
   (A) granting winners bragging rights.
   (B) giving some people control over others.
   (C) advancing scientific knowledge.
   (D) gaining personal wealth.

142. What would be the most appropriate title for this passage?
   (A) Guinness: The Man Behind the Records
   (B) The Pros and Cons of Chasing Records
   (C) The Human Need to Be the Best
   (D) The Strangest World Records Throughout Time

Halley spent her free period retracing her steps—she checked the gym, locker room, chemistry lab, and cafeteria, but could not find her notebook anywhere. She tried not to panic, but she was worried about her notebook getting into the wrong hands! There were no names, but her notes were pretty detailed, and she didn't want anyone to connect what she had written with any of her classmates, who had trusted her to be discreet.

She began walking the same route again—gym, locker room, chemistry lab, and cafeteria—when she saw Ms. Sands coming toward her down the hall. She had something clutched in her hands. Halley gasped. It was her notebook! Ms. Sands' normally smooth brow furrowed when she saw Halley.

"Halley, could you come with me please?" It wasn't so much a request as a polite order. Halley's joy at finding her missing notebook turned into dread—based on Ms. Sand's tone, it was clear her secret was out. She sheepishly followed Ms. Sands into her classroom.

"Halley, I found this on the floor in the hallway—"

"Oh thanks, Ms. Sands, I was looking all over for it!" Halley grabbed for the notebook, but her teacher pulled it out of her reach. She clearly was not ready to give it up yet.

"Do you want to tell me what this is all about?" Ms. Sands asked, clutching the notebook firmly.

"Umm…" Halley debated her options, but knew she wasn't a good liar and that Ms. Sands would see right through her. Her only option was to tell the truth. "Please don't be mad!" she said. "I was just trying to help! They came to me!"

"Who came to you?" Ms. Sands asked. "There's a lot of serious gossip in here, and your name is signed in the front cover." Ms. Sands was losing her patience, but she knew Halley was a good kid and a serious student; there had to be an explanation for this. "Please Halley, just be honest."

Halley began to tell Ms. Sands her story: how word got out about her excellent life-coaching skills, about the meetings she held with her classmates in the mornings before school, about the notes she took regarding their problems and her suggestions for dealing with them.

Ms. Sands nodded her head while Halley was speaking. "I know high school can be challenging," she replied. "And I appreciate you being honest. There's a lot of students who prefer the advice of a peer to that of an adult. But maybe we can find a more straightforward way for you to offer your help to your classmates—how about a weekly advice column for the school newspaper?"

Halley couldn't believe her ears! Moments ago, she was in trouble, and now this?

"I'll have to approve all of your advice, and the students will have to remain anonymous, but I think I can get the principal to allow it. What do you say?"

"Uh…yes. Definitely! Yes!"

With that, Halley decided on the topic of her first column—the value of honesty!

143. This story is mostly about
   (A) a young girl's first writing job.
   (B) a miscommunication between a student and teacher.
   (C) how a secret talent could be used to help others.
   (D) the challenges of being in high school.

144. According to the story, Halley was concerned because her lost notebook
   (A) contained private information shared with her by her classmates.
   (B) had sentimental value.
   (C) was full of gossip she'd overheard.
   (D) had all her math notes for an upcoming test.

145. As it is used in the story, the word "discreet" most nearly means
(A) considerate.
(B) intelligent.
(C) professional.
(D) trusted.

146. The narrator says that Ms. Sands' "normally smooth brow furrowed" to suggest that she
(A) did not like Halley.
(B) had never in a bad mood before.
(C) was suspicious about the contents of the notebook.
(D) was furious to see Halley in the hallway.

147. As it is used in the story, the word "furrowed" as used in the passage, most nearly means
(A) ironed.
(B) reacted.
(C) wavered .
(D) wrinkled.

148. According to the story, Halley considers Ms. Sands to be
(A) brilliant and hard to please.
(B) trustworthy and reasonable.
(C) unfriendly and fearsome.
(D) popular and pretty.

149. According to the story, Ms. Sands asks Halley to write an advice column for the newspaper in order to
(A) punish her for gossiping.
(B) figure out whether Halley is actually giving good advice or not.
(C) help Halley support the student body in a more transparent way.
(D) replace a student who recently quit working on the newspaper.

150. Ms. Sands' most likely "nodded her head while Halley was speaking" because she
(A) wanted Halley to hurry up so she could ask her about joining the newspaper.
(B) was remembering the advice she'd received in high school.
(C) was becoming impatient with Halley's lengthy explanation.
(D) understood why Halley had been giving advice to her classmates.

151. Halley most likely had already "decided on the topic for her first column" because
(A) her meeting with Ms. Sands provided her with the perfect idea.
(B) she likes to get all of her work completed far in advance of deadlines.
(C) she wanted to impress Ms. Sands with her strong work ethic.
(D) she was dreading the writing and just wanted to get it over with.

152. What would be the most appropriate title for this story?
(A) Halley's Big Reveal
(B) The Advice Column
(C) The Notebook Files
(D) Writer's Block

Vocabulary

153. To <u>verify</u> information
   (A) berate
   (B) check
   (C) please
   (D) specialize

154. A <u>captive</u> prisoner
   (A) confined
   (B) delightful
   (C) roaming
   (D) vibrant

155. Actions deserving of <u>contempt</u>
   (A) boldness
   (B) kinship
   (C) hatred
   (D) yielding

156. A <u>loathsome</u> creature
   (A) agreeable
   (B) nosy
   (C) possible
   (D) vile

157. His <u>foul</u> behavior
   (A) appreciated
   (B) nasty
   (C) ostracized
   (D) pointed

158. The train <u>brimming</u> with people
   (A) actualized
   (B) bouncing
   (C) full
   (D) glimmering

159. A troop <u>destroyed</u> the village
   (A) arranged
   (B) demolished
   (C) generated
   (D) wore

160. Neighbors exchange <u>pleasantries</u>
   (A) banter
   (B) corruption
   (C) demands
   (D) portraits

161. A <u>comprehensive</u> investigation
   (A) complete
   (B) foolish
   (C) inedible
   (D) redundant

162. A <u>mysterious</u> disappearance
   (A) alert
   (B) obvious
   (C) peculiar
   (D) revelatory

163. To celebrate a <u>victory</u>
   (A) conduct
   (B) loss
   (C) miss
   (D) triumph

164. <u>Escape</u> to freedom
   (A) abscond
   (B) confine
   (C) hide
   (D) remove

165. <u>Flee</u> from danger
   (A) behave
   (B) escape
   (C) dance
   (D) trap

166. <u>Oust</u> the leader from government
   (A) expel
   (B) help
   (C) irritate
   (D) mediate

167. <u>Accomplish</u> one's tasks
   (A) delete
   (B) fulfill
   (C) generate
   (D) justify

168. The <u>impudent</u> student's outburst
   (A) brazen
   (B) connected
   (C) obedient
   (D) timid

169. A <u>compassionate</u> act of kindness
   (A) cruel
   (B) deranged
   (C) jealous
   (D) warm

170. His <u>fierce</u> tirade
   (A) angry
   (B) beneficial
   (C) delightful
   (D) rational

171. An <u>insensitive</u> comment
   (A) audited
   (B) evolved
   (C) mean
   (D) wise

172. The <u>peak</u> of the mountain
   (A) depth
   (B) honor
   (C) rush
   (D) summit

173. On the <u>precipice</u> of a cliff
   (A) edge
   (B) import
   (C) guard
   (D) opposite

174. To wear a <u>disguise</u>
   (A) audition
   (B) decoration
   (C) mask
   (D) prize

Mathematics

Questions 175-238, 45 Minutes

175. Jack is designing an odometer, a device used to measure speed, for his car. Which of the following units would be appropriate for measuring speed?
(A) inches/second
(B) kilograms/hour
(C) kilometers/second
(D) kilometers/hour

176. The radius of a bicycle's wheel is 10.5 inches. How many inches can the bicycle travel in 1 rotation of the wheel? (Note: use $\frac{22}{7}$ for π)
(A) 33 in.
(B) 66 in.
(C) 330 in.
(D) 660 in.

177. What is the area of the figure shown if WY = 10 and XZ = 12?

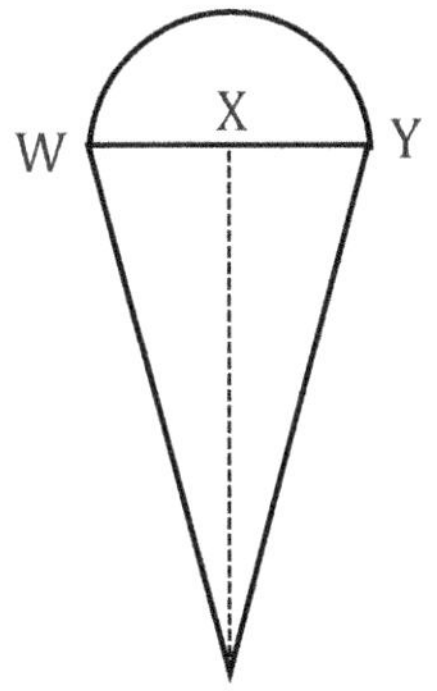
X
W
Y
Z

(A) $60 + 12.5\pi$
(B) $60 + 25\pi$
(C) $120 + 12.5\pi$
(D) $120 + 25\pi$

178. A can in the shape of a cylinder has a base radius of 2 inches and a height of 6 inches. How much soup can it hold? ($V = \pi r^2$h, where r is the radius and h is the height).
(A) 12π in^3
(B) 16π in^3
(C) 24π in^3
(D) 64π in^3

179. Which number is in the hundreds place after simplifying $(6 \times 10^3) + (2 \times 10^2) + (15 \times 10^1)$?
(A) 2
(B) 3
(C) 5
(D) 6

180. Assuming that x is a prime number, 13^2x^2 is the LCM of which of the following?
(A) x and 169
(B) 13^2x^2 and x^3
(C) 13^3, x^3, and 169
(D) 13, 169, and x^2

181. If the prime factorization of 36 is equal to 2^y3^z, what is the value of $y + z$?
(A) 4
(B) 6
(C) 8
(D) 24

182. The area of a parallelogram is 20% less than the area of a square. If the area of the square is 40 square centimeters, and the height of the parallelogram is 4 cm, what is the length of the base of the parallelogram in centimeters?
(A) 2 cm
(B) 6 cm
(C) 8 cm
(D) 12 cm

183. Which of the following statements is false?
(A) A square is a rectangle
(B) A rhombus is a parallelogram
(C) A parallelogram is a rhombus
(D) A rectangle if a quadrilateral

184. Althea has 36 homework problems to solve. She breaks the assignment into smaller parts, and completes the same number of problems each day. What is a possible number of problems she completed each day?
(A) 5
(B) 6
(C) 7
(D) 8

185. Which of the following units would be most appropriate to measure the length of a cat's tail?
(A) cubic feet
(B) inches
(C) meters
(D) yards

186. Which number is in the tens place after simplifying
$(3 \times 10^4) + (9 \times 10^3) + (7 \times 10^2)$?
(A) 0
(B) 3
(C) 7
(D) 9

187. What is the volume of this object?

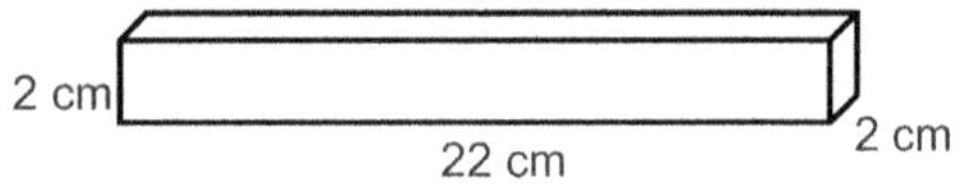
2 cm
22 cm
2 cm

(A) 26 cm^3
(B) 44 cm^3
(C) 88 cm^3
(D) 184 cm^3

188. Which of the following best describes the inequality: $54 - y < 2y + 7$?
(A) Fifty-four minus a number is greater than seven more than twice that number.
(B) A number less than fifty-four is less than seven more than that number.
(C) Fifty-four minus a number is more than twice more than seven times that number.
(D) Fifty-four minus a number is less than seven more than twice that number

189. What is the value of x in the following parallelogram?

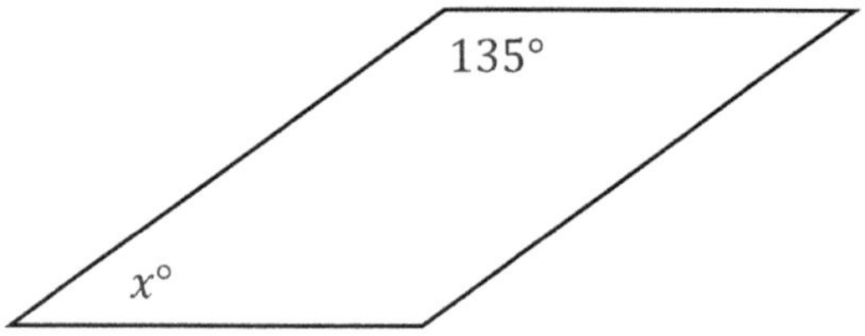
135°
x°

(A) 30°
(B) 45°
(C) 100°
(D) 135°

190. Solve: $\frac{2}{3} + y \geq -2y + 7$.
(A) $y \geq \frac{1}{9}$
(B) $y \leq \frac{2}{9}$
(C) $y \geq 2\frac{1}{9}$
(D) $y \leq \frac{19}{9}$

191. In ΔIJK, what is the measure of ∠LKI?

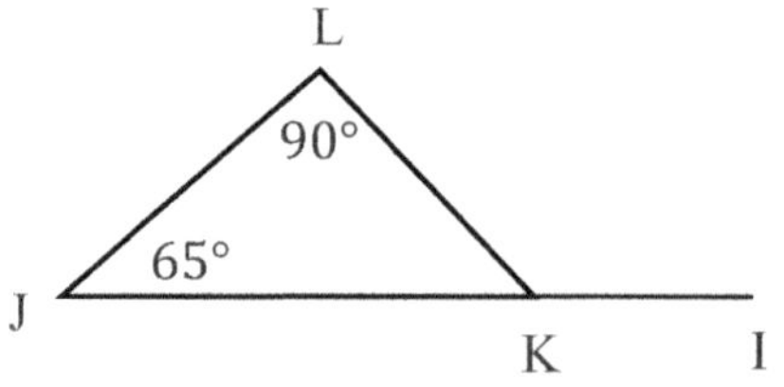
L
90°
65°
J
K
I

(A) 155°
(B) 175°
(C) 176°
(D) 205°

192. What is the LCM of a^3bcd^2ef and $2a^2b^3def$, assuming that a, b, c, d, e, and f are prime numbers?
(A) $abcdef$
(B) $2a^3b^3cd^2ef$
(C) $2a^2b^3cd^2ef$
(D) $2a^3b^3c^2d^2ef$

193. If a line is expressed as $y = -4 + 3x$, what is its slope?
(A) -4
(B) $-\frac{4}{3}$
(C) $-\frac{3}{4}$
(D) 3

194. Which of the following sets of numbers has 11 as the GCF?
(A) 44 and 88
(B) 22, 33, and 55
(C) 33, 44, and 54
(D) 11, 110, and 120

195. What is the difference in area between a square with a perimeter of 12 inches and a rectangle with a height of 4 inches and a width of 9 inches, as shown in the figure?

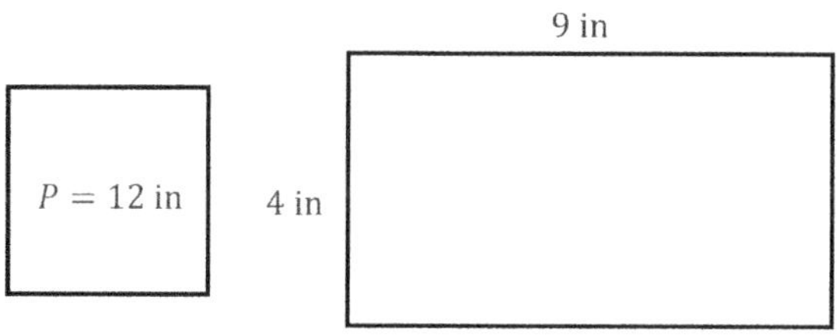
P = 12 in
9 in
4 in

(A) 6 square inches
(B) 25 square inches
(C) 27 square inches
(D) 36 square inches

196. What is equivalent to $(x^3y^2)^4$?
(A) x^6y^8
(B) x^7y^6
(C) x^7y^8
(D) $x^{12}y^8$

197. What is equivalent to $[(a^2b^3c^4) \times (a^3bc^3)]^0$?
(A) 1
(B) $a^5b^3c^7$
(C) $a^5b^4c^7$
(D) $a^6b^3c^{12}$

198. Which of the following fractions is closest in value to 0?
(A) $\frac{1}{2}$
(B) $\frac{2}{3}$
(C) $\frac{3}{4}$
(D) $\frac{4}{5}$

199. Which fraction is largest?
(A) $\frac{3}{4}$
(B) $\frac{3}{3}$
(C) $\frac{4}{4}$
(D) $\frac{4}{3}$

200. If a line is expressed as $y = \frac{1}{3}(x - 7)$, what is its slope?
(A) $-\frac{7}{3}$
(B) $-\frac{1}{3}$
(C) $\frac{1}{3}$
(D) $\frac{7}{3}$

201. Express 0.12 as a fraction.
(A) $\frac{3}{25}$
(B) $\frac{12}{10}$
(C) $\frac{12}{100}$
(D) $\frac{12}{1000}$

202. Express the fraction $\frac{7}{10}$ as a percent.
(A) 7%
(B) 17%
(C) 70%
(D) 107%

Problem Solving

203. Solve: $(-1{,}214) + (-793) =$
(A) $-2{,}007$
(B) -421
(C) 421
(D) 2,007

204. 45 millimeters equals:
(A) .045 centimeters
(B) .45 centimeters
(C) 4.5 centimeters
(D) .45 meters

205. Solve: $\frac{2}{3} \times \frac{5}{6} \times \frac{3}{4} \times \frac{1}{5} \times \frac{3}{8} =$
(A) $\frac{1}{32}$
(B) $\frac{3}{32}$
(C) $\frac{3}{16}$
(D) $\frac{3}{8}$

206. Mrs. Peterson's math class had the following test scores: 78, 95, 92, 78, 94, 85, 92, 95, 63, 92. What was the mode for that test?
(A) 78
(B) 85
(C) 92
(D) 95

207. Jared has four grandsons and eight granddaughters. If he randomly selects one grandchild, what is the probability that it will be a granddaughter?
(A) $\frac{4}{12}$
(B) $\frac{1}{3}$
(C) $\frac{7}{12}$
(D) $\frac{2}{3}$

208. Solve for x: $-0.4x + 1.6 = 6.8$
(A) -13
(B) -1.3
(C) 1.3
(D) 13

209. The length of one side of a triangle is four more than the length of the smallest side and half of the length of the largest side. If the sum of the triangle's sides is 32, what is the length of the smallest side?
(A) 5
(B) 6
(C) 7
(D) 9

210. If $10^x = 100{,}000{,}000$, then $x =$?
(A) 5
(B) 6
(C) 7
(D) 8

211. Which of the following can be approximated to 600?
(A) 38×21
(B) 31×19
(C) 12×39
(D) 23×42

212. A museum sold 80 children's tickets for $3.25 each, and 40 adult tickets for $4.50 each. How much money did they make in total ticket sales?
(A) $180.00
(B) $260.00
(C) $440.00
(D) $930.00

213. What type of triangle is shown?

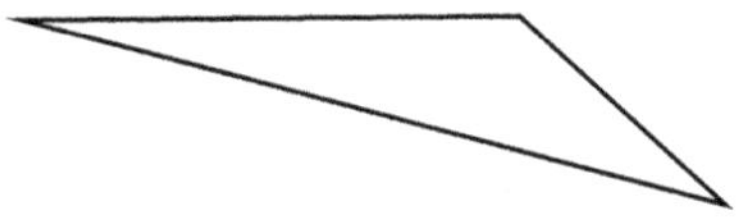

(A) acute
(B) equilateral
(C) obtuse
(D) right

214. What is the value of $2\sqrt{144}$?
(A) 12
(B) 24
(C) 36
(D) 48

215. The following chart shows the amount of money in savings account over 9 months. If this relationship is constant, how much money will be in the account in 1 year?

Use the following chart for questions 215 and 216.

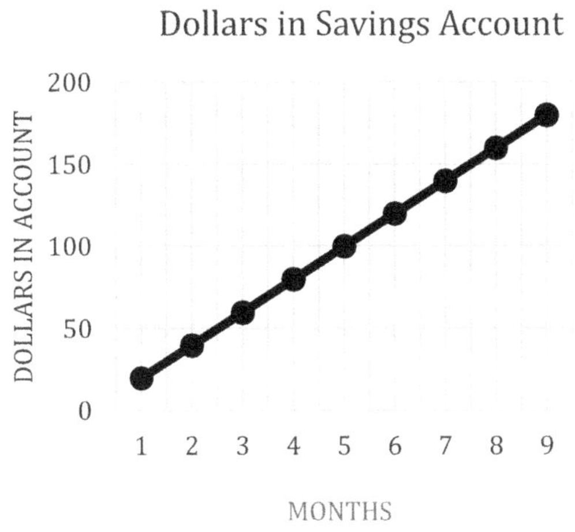
Dollars in Savings Account
DOLLARS IN ACCOUNT
200
150
100
50
0
1 2 3 4 5 6 7 8 9
MONTHS

(A) 200
(B) 220
(C) 240
(D) 260

216. What kind of graph or chart is being used to track the amount of money in the savings account?
(A) pie chart
(B) line graph
(C) column chart
(D) histogram

217. Arianne collects different kinds of feathers on her walks through the woods. In her collection, she has 5 eagle feathers, 15 warbler feathers, and 30 dove feathers. Dove feathers make up what percent of Arianne's feather collection?
(A) 15%
(B) 30%
(C) 50%
(D) 60%

218. Dennis can mow $\frac{3}{4}$ of a yard in one hour. How long will it take Dennis to mow 5 identical yards?
(A) $3\frac{3}{4}$ hours
(B) $4\frac{1}{2}$ hours
(C) $5\frac{3}{4}$ hours
(D) $6\frac{2}{3}$ hours

219. What is 0.123×0.007 rounded to the nearest ten-thousandth?
(A) 0.00086
(B) 0.000861
(C) 0.0009
(D) 0.009

220. Letitia skated for 30 minutes at 30 miles per hour. How far did she go?
(A) 10 miles
(B) 12 miles
(C) 14 miles
(D) 15 miles

221. The following Venn diagram represents how many students enjoy French fries, onion rings, or both. If 24 students were surveyed and 3 indicated that they did not like either French fries or onion rings, how many students enjoy only French fries?

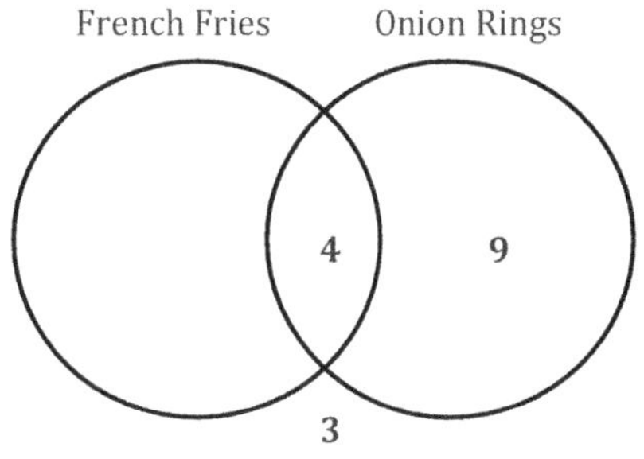
French Fries
Onion Rings
4
9
3

(A) 6
(B) 8
(C) 11
(D) 12

222. What percentage of the figure below is shaded?

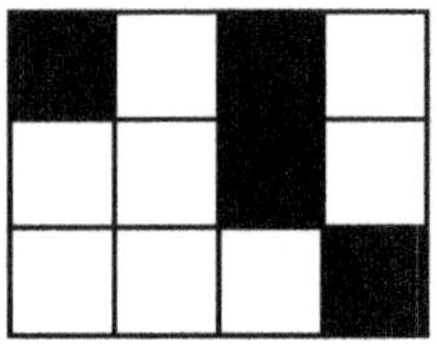

(A) 4
(B) 20
(C) 25
(D) 33

223. What is 3.12 kilometers per hour in meters per minute?
(A) 52 meters per minute
(B) 520 meters per minute
(C) 3120 meters per minute
(D) 312 meters per minute

224. Donovan has a drawer full of games. Four are card games, 3 are board games, and 8 are video games. If he selects a game at random, what is the probability he will choose a board game?
(A) $\frac{1}{5}$
(B) $\frac{3}{11}$
(C) $\frac{3}{8}$
(D) $\frac{8}{15}$

225. A car salesman earns $6,000 per month plus 15% commission on every car he sells. If he sells $20,000 worth of cars one month, how much total money does he earn?
(A) $3,000
(B) $6,900
(C) $9,000
(D) $36,000

226. If the prime factorization of 90 is $2^x \times 3^y \times 5^z$, then what does $x + y + z$ equal?
(A) 2
(B) 4
(C) 5
(D) 6

227. Solve: $2{,}442 \div 6 =$
(A) 46
(B) 47
(C) 407
(D) 470

228. The following data gives the heights, in inches, of a group of 7th-grade students: 71, 62, 64, 58, 60, 66, 59, 63. Which of the following additional heights would change the range of the set?

I. 57
II. 63
III. 67
IV. 72

(A) I only
(B) I and IV
(C) I, II, III, and IV
(D) None of the above

229. The two figures below are similar shapes. What is the length of side *x*?

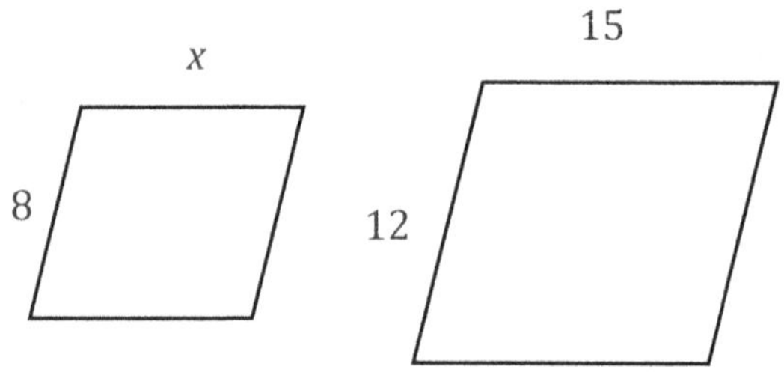
x
8
15
12

(A) 6.4
(B) 10
(C) 12
(D) 22.5

230. Mia and Tom are stuck in traffic going an average of 10 miles per hour. If their home is 22 miles away, how much longer will they be driving for?
(A) 1 hour and 30 minutes
(B) 2 hours
(C) 2 hours and 12 minutes
(D) 2 hours and 20 minutes

231. Which of the following statements are true?

I. A rectangle and a square each has four 90-degree angles.
II. A kite and a rhombus each has four congruent sides.
III. Rectangles, rhombuses, and squares are all parallelograms.

(A) only I is true
(B) I and III are true
(C) I, II, and III are true
(D) none of the statements are true

232. A group of middle school students are surveyed about whether they read for pleasure, play video games, or do both. Of the 200 students surveyed, 30 said that they do neither, 110 said that they read for pleasure, 80 said that they play video games. How many students said that they do both?
(A) 20
(B) 30
(C) 40
(D) 50

233. As a train leaves the station, it has 15 empty seats, 9 seated passengers, and 5 standing passengers. At the next stop, half of the passengers get off, 8 passengers get on, and everyone takes a seat. How many empty seats are there?
(A) 0
(B) 8
(C) 9
(D) 13

234. Solve for p: $2.4 + 0.5p = 1.5p + 5.8$
(A) -3.4
(B) -1.7
(C) 2.4
(D) 3.4

235. Increased by 200%, the number 36 becomes:
(A) 10.8
(B) 72
(C) 108
(D) 720

236. Solve: $6.3 \times 1.8 =$
(A) 1.134
(B) 11.34
(C) 113.4
(D) 1134

237. Which of the following is equivalent to $\sqrt{x^3y^4}$?
(A) x
(B) $x\sqrt{xy}$
(C) $xy\sqrt{x}$
(D) $xy^2\sqrt{x}$

238. Alejandro needs to cut a length of string into two pieces so that the longer piece is five times as long as the shorter piece. If the length of string is 32 inches before he cuts it, how long will the shorter piece be after he cuts it?
(A) $5\frac{1}{3}$
(B) $5\frac{2}{5}$
(C) $6\frac{2}{5}$
(D) $6\frac{3}{5}$

Language Skills

Questions 239-298, 25 Minutes

For questions 239-278, choose the sentence that contains an error in punctuation, capitalization, or usage. If there is no error, select choice (D).

239. (A) Billy grew up swimming in the local pond.
(B) The Smiths lived near Lake Erie.
(C) The great lakes are the sight of many ship wrecks.
(D) No mistake.

240. (A) The planets are so far.
(B) The sun is too warm.
(C) The moon so brightly.
(D) No mistake.

241. (A) Every member of the class were instructed to take notes.
(B) Marianne creates every bracelet from scratch.
(C) Jenny is the only person who can reach the cabinet.
(D) No mistake.

242. (A) Kelly's favorite color is chartreuse.
(B) Aria's family went to the beach every Summer.
(C) The sisters were taking a trip to Iceland in March.
(D) No mistake.

243. (A) Violet shared her ideas with Olaf and I.
(B) She closed the door in his face.
(C) She was the one who won the race.
(D) No mistake.

244. (A) New York City has an extensive subway system.
(B) There are seven Continents in the world.
(C) She left for Rome on the fifth of November.
(D) No mistake.

245. (A) How cold outside?
(B) They played soccer well.
(C) Jennifer left quickly.
(D) No mistake.

246. (A) Every time the mail man came, the dog barks like crazy.
(B) Barry hasn't gone to the dentist in five years.
(C) The concert will take place tomorrow even if it rains.
(D) No mistake.

247. (A) Her grandmother was fluent in Russian.
(B) There is beautiful art in St. Petersburg.
(C) She had grown up in the soviet union.
(D) No mistake.

248. (A) It's almost Poppys birthday.
(B) She sent her sister, who was a teacher, some chalk.
(C) Jessica's landlord's car was parked out front.
(D) No mistake.

249. (A) Her chair was weirdly sticky.
(B) A very dangerous sport indeed.
(C) The chalk was dusty.
(D) No mistake.

250. (A) The politician gains favor with his constituents.
(B) The house on the corner is burning down.
(C) Both Maria and her sister has work after softball practice.
(D) No mistake.

251. (A) She made an excuse; yet she still had to go.
(B) A teacher who taught math was voted teacher of the year.
(C) The students' projects were creative.
(D) No mistake.

252. (A) I recognized the handwriting that was mine.
(B) Jasmine's song was her favorite creation.
(C) We were hoping they'd give me their table.
(D) No mistake.

253. (A) They worked hard, but they needed a vacation.
(B) The governor's bill passed.
(C) Only, if she passed math, could she go to the dance.
(D) No mistake.

254. (A) Jasmine went to the concert and sang along to every song.
(B) Erica wanted to eat lunch, visit her friend, and to play soccer.
(C) The teacher took attendance, introduced the lesson, and explained the assignment.
(D) No mistake.

255. (A) He played piano beautifully.
(B) He shared his expertly opinion.
(C) The banjo was old and dusty.
(D) No mistake.

256. (A) The ghost was scarier than the monster.
(B) The shed is smaller than the house.
(C) The front yard is bigger than the back yard.
(D) No mistake.

257. (A) He pretended that her ideas were his.
(B) She was a girl which loved reading.
(C) His hamster escaped its cage.
(D) No mistake.

258. (A) The story was long but the plot was interesting.
(B) She was strong, yet she couldn't open the door.
(C) All of his ties, which were silk, were lost in the fire.
(D) No mistake.

259. (A) A watermelon's seeds are perfectly edible.
(B) Although she was lost she refused to ask for directions.
(C) He refused to change, yet he wanted to improve.
(D) No mistake.

260. (A) Every person in the class is expected to turn in an assignment tomorrow.
(B) Yesterday I will call the principal and told her what happened.
(C) No one is going to go to the school dance this Saturday.
(D) No mistake.

261. (A) Her favorite guitar company was Fender.
(B) Abel's little sister sage was going to the University of Arizona.
(C) Emerson told his mom, "I can't wait for summer."
(D) No mistake.

262. (A) She spilled her coins all over the floor and had to pick them all up.
(B) Cindy was excited to clean her room, polish her car, and tidy her closet.
(C) Pollen was in the air and all the kitchen countertops.
(D) No mistake.

263. (A) She ain't got no money left in her pockets.
(B) They didn't know how to finish the test.
(C) The teacher wasn't sure how to teach the lesson.
(D) No mistake.

264. (A) She was crowned the winner after her impressive performance.
(B) Michael lost his dog then spent the whole day searching for him.
(C) They could not finish the race because they are running out of time.
(D) No mistake.

265. (A) Neither of the cats are sleeping in the window.
(B) All of her toys are lined up carefully on her bookshelf.
(C) Both of the brothers have failing grades in math.
(D) No mistake.

266. (A) Christine ordered a salad for lunch on Tuesday.
(B) I love fruit: apples, oranges, bananas, and pears.
(C) We toured the Metropolitan Museum of Art on a field trip?
(D) No mistake.

267. (A) The students went on a field trip to the museum of Modern Art.
(B) Jake was eager for his camping trip at Joshua Tree National Park.
(C) Tuesdays were the best day for discounts on tacos.
(D) No mistake.

268. (A) Mr. Brown speaks eloquently.
(B) He plays the trumpet very good.
(C) His daughter is a very bright student.
(D) No mistake.

269. (A) They couldn't get over the terrible loss.
(B) She hated having to complete her chores.
(C) Marcy couldn't never stick the landing.
(D) No mistake.

270. (A) She got sunburned.
(B) Saturday night so exciting.
(C) The teacher took attendance.
(D) No mistake.

271. (A) He was the only Professor left on campus.
(B) Her best friend, Alicia, moved to Arizona.
(C) New York City is home to the Metropolitan Museum of Art.
(D) No mistake.

272. (A) Elise turned in her essay to professor Gomez.
(B) Bethany took a long trip to Paris, France.
(C) The best season for surfing is summer.
(D) No mistake.

273. (A) Their favorite film was mine, too.
(B) Erica shared her lunch with Jake, which was hungry.
(C) Her boss, who always worked late, pressured her to do the same.
(D) No mistake.

274. (A) They were never going to make it on time.
(B) She was so tired of working.
(C) The office was finally closing.
(D) No mistake.

275. (A) The violin was broken.
(B) Each person sang pretty.
(C) Her ankle is sore.
(D) No mistake.

276. (A) Multiple people came forward as witnesses.
(B) The camp for girls are situated outside of town.
(C) The entire town celebrated the team's victory.
(D) No mistake.

277. (A) The stars were not bright enough.
(B) She was hardly ever happy during winter.
(C) She barely never got picked to play.
(D) No mistake.

278. (A) Bethany was nervous to leave her home empty, so a caretaker is hired by her to housesit.
(B) She is concerned that she will be late so she is sprinting to get there faster.
(C) All of the children fell asleep in class and therefore did not finish the lesson.
(D) No mistake.

Spelling

For questions 279-288, choose the sentence that contains an error in spelling. If there is no error, select choice (D).

279. (A) She regretted her grave error in jugment.
(B) The professor canceled class on Monday.
(C) The board was meeting to determine a solution.
(D) No mistake.

280. (A) She wanted to teach them a lesson.
(B) The siblings were always quarreling.
(C) The moon was shinning in the sky.
(D) No mistake.

281. (A) They arrived at a pleasant meadow with a pond of clear water.
(B) The shoes were inexpensive because they were on clearence.
(C) There were six young colts in the meadow besides me.
(D) No mistake.

282. (A) The diamonds were very expensive.
(B) I have never forgotten my mother's advise.
(C) She announced that it was time for them to eat.
(D) No mistake.

283. (A) The president has many acomplishments.
(B) The display was placed at the entrance of the store.
(C) The story took place mainly in a farmhouse.
(D) No mistake.

284. (A) The grandfather was known for his great wisdom.
(B) The mansion was considered quite glamorus.
(C) Every day, the weight grew heavier.
(D) No mistake.

285. (A) It was difficult to guage the distance.
(B) This Friday would be her fortieth birthday.
(C) The show was about a clan of vampires.
(D) No mistake.

286. (A) He hates working in the crowded city.
(B) Her puppy had a lot of energy.
(C) She was expected to do all of her chores.
(D) No mistake.

287. (A) The narrator was the protagonist of the story.
(B) As an editor, she always did a thourough job.
(C) The machine was unfortunately broken.
(D) No mistake.

288. (A) It was difficult to make money in that profession.
(B) She was thinking how strange it was.
(C) The surrondings seemed familiar.
(D) No mistake.

Composition

289. Choose the group of words that best completes this sentence.

Many people find enjoyment in ____________________.

(A) reading a book before bed
(B) to read at bedtime
(C) to be reading before bed
(D) none of these

290. Choose the word that best completes the sentence.

Brian knew he had to be ________ when handling his grandfather's antiques.

(A) careful
(B) casual
(C) careless
(D) cordial

291. Which of the following sentences offers the *least* support for the topic "Why Electronics Can Be Harmful"?

(A) Studies have shown that many people are addicted to their phones.
(B) Staring at screens for long periods of time can lead to eye strain and headaches.
(C) Electronics are a relatively new invention when looking back through all of human history.
(D) Cell phones are covered in germs and bacteria.

292. Which choice most clearly expresses the intended meaning?

(A) Running all morning, tired is what I felt.
(B) After running all morning, I felt tired.
(C) Tired is what I felt after running all morning.
(D) none of these

293. Choose the word that best completes the sentence.

Jeremiah neatly placed his folded clothes on the dresser ____________ his bed.

(A) between
(B) but
(C) beside
(D) beneath

294. Which of these best fits under the topic "Protecting Our Environment"?

(A) Reducing waste and recycling are just two things you can do to help the planet.
(B) Many species of plants and animals live in nature.
(C) Natural resources are useful to humans.
(D) none of these

295. Which of the following themes could be effectively explored in a one-paragraph passage?

(A) How to Build a Computer
(B) Chemistry
(C) How to Make a Bed
(D) None of these

296. Which of the following themes could be effectively explored in a one-paragraph passage?

(A) Dog Walking Safety
(B) World Wars
(C) Geography
(D) none of these

297. Where should the sentence, "However, learning how to be safe on the road is the most important part of driving and should be taken seriously," be placed in the paragraph below?

(1) Getting a driver's license is an exciting milestone for teenagers. (2) All new drivers must complete driver education training before they can get a license. (3) Most states require new drivers to have a licensed driver in the car with them while they are still learning.

(A) Between sentences 1 and 2.
(B) Between sentences 2 and 3.
(C) After sentence 3.
(D) This sentence does not fit in this paragraph.

298. Where should the sentence, "Baking a pie is a fun and easy thing to do," be placed in the paragraph below?

(1) First, you make the crust. (2) Then, you make the filling. (3) Finally, you put the filling inside the crust and bake it in the oven.

(A) Before sentence 1.
(B) Between sentences 1 and 2.
(C) Between sentences 2 and 3.
(D) After sentence 3.

Scoring Practice Test 2

Using your answer sheet and referring to the answer key at the back of the book, calculate the percentage of questions you answered correctly in each section by taking the number of questions you answered correctly in that section and dividing it by the number of questions in that section. Multiply this number by 100 to determine your percentage score. The higher the percentage, the stronger your performance in that section. The lower the percentage, the more time you should spend practicing that section.

Note that the actual test will not evaluate your score based on percentage correct or incorrect. Instead, it will evaluate your performance relative to all other students in your grade who took the test.

Record your results here:

Section	Questions Correct	Total Questions	Percent Questions Correct
Verbal Skills	____	60	____%
Quantitative Skills	____	52	____%
Reading Comprehension	____	62	____%
Mathematics Achievement	____	64	____%
Language	____	60	____%

Remember that, depending on the curriculum at your school, there may be material on this test that you have not yet been taught. If this is the case, and you would like to improve your score beyond what is expected of your grade, consider outside help from an adult—such as a tutor or teacher—who can help you learn more about the topics that are new to you.

Answer Key

The keys are organized by section, and each question has an answer associated with it. Remember: there are detailed answer explanations available online at www.thetutorverse.com/books. Be sure to obtain permission before going online.

Answer Keys

This section provides the answer solutions to the practice questions in each section of the workbook including the diagnostic tests, exercises, and practice tests. **Remember: there are detailed answer explanations available online at** www.thetutorverse.com/books**. Be sure to obtain permission before going online.**

Diagnostic Practice Test

Verbal Skills

1. B	9. D	17. A	25. A	33. A	41. B	49. A	57. B
2. D	10. A	18. A	26. D	34. A	42. A	50. C	58. C
3. A	11. A	19. B	27. A	35. B	43. C	51. A	59. A
4. C	12. D	20. B	28. D	36. C	44. D	52. C	60. D
5. B	13. B	21. C	29. D	37. B	45. C	53. C	
6. B	14. B	22. D	30. D	38. A	46. B	54. B	
7. C	15. B	23. A	31. A	39. C	47. D	55. B	
8. B	16. B	24. C	32. B	40. B	48. D	56. D	

Reading

61. B	69. D	77. D	85. C	93. B	101. D	109. C	117. B
62. C	70. A	78. C	86. A	94. A	102. C	110. C	118. A
63. D	71. C	79. B	87. B	95. A	103. D	111. A	119. C
64. A	72. B	80. C	88. A	96. B	104. C	112. D	120. D
65. C	73. A	81. A	89. B	97. A	105. A	113. C	121. B
66. B	74. D	82. C	90. D	98. B	106. D	114. B	122. B
67. B	75. B	83. D	91. D	99. C	107. B	115. C	
68. A	76. A	84. D	92. C	100. A	108. D	116. D	

Language Skills

123. A	131. B	139. A	147. C	155. A	163. D	171. B	179. D
124. A	132. D	140. B	148. A	156. A	164. A	172. A	180. C
125. A	133. C	141. B	149. C	157. A	165. B	173. B	181. C
126. B	134. D	142. A	150. C	158. C	166. B	174. B	182. D
127. A	135. A	143. D	151. A	159. B	167. C	175. C	
128. C	136. D	144. C	152. B	160. A	168. A	176. B	
129. A	137. B	145. D	153. B	161. C	169. B	177. B	
130. D	138. C	146. B	154. B	162. D	170. C	178. C	

Exercises

Verbal Skills

Verbal Classifications

1. A	9. D	17. A	25. A	33. D	41. A	49. D	57. A
2. B	10. D	18. A	26. C	34. A	42. C	50. C	58. A
3. A	11. A	19. A	27. D	35. C	43. A	51. C	59. B
4. C	12. B	20. B	28. A	36. D	44. A	52. D	60. B
5. B	13. B	21. B	29. A	37. B	45. C	53. B	61. C
6. A	14. D	22. B	30. A	38. B	46. D	54. B	62. C
7. B	15. B	23. B	31. C	39. B	47. C	55. A	63. C
8. D	16. B	24. C	32. B	40. D	48. A	56. B	64. C

65. A	68. A	71. D	74. C	77. C	80. C
66. D	69. B	72. B	75. C	78. C	81. A
67. A	70. D	73. B	76. D	79. B	82. D

Synonyms

1. B	11. B	21. B	31. C	41. B	51. A	61. C	71. A
2. A	12. B	22. C	32. D	42. A	52. D	62. C	72. A
3. C	13. D	23. B	33. A	43. B	53. B	63. C	73. B
4. C	14. C	24. C	34. C	44. B	54. C	64. D	74. B
5. D	15. C	25. D	35. C	45. A	55. C	65. B	75. D
6. B	16. D	26. B	36. A	46. A	56. D	66. A	76. C
7. A	17. D	27. A	37. C	47. C	57. B	67. D	77. C
8. B	18. A	28. B	38. B	48. B	58. B	68. B	
9. A	19. B	29. B	39. C	49. D	59. C	69. D	
10. A	20. D	30. D	40. D	50. B	60. A	70. C	

Antonyms

1. C	7. C	13. B	19. D	25. D	31. B	37. C	43. B
2. D	8. D	14. B	20. D	26. D	32. A	38. A	44. C
3. C	9. D	15. A	21. C	27. C	33. B	39. C	45. B
4. C	10. B	16. A	22. A	28. C	34. B	40. B	46. C
5. B	11. B	17. D	23. D	29. A	35. A	41. C	47. A
6. A	12. C	18. C	24. C	30. B	36. B	42. D	

Verbal Analogies

1. C	8. C	15. B	22. B	29. C	36. C	43. D	50. A
2. B	9. A	16. B	23. C	30. D	37. B	44. D	51. D
3. B	10. D	17. B	24. A	31. A	38. A	45. A	52. B
4. C	11. C	18. B	25. A	32. B	39. C	46. C	
5. B	12. B	19. C	26. B	33. B	40. B	47. D	
6. A	13. C	20. C	27. B	34. B	41. B	48. C	
7. B	14. C	21. C	28. B	35. B	42. D	49. A	

Logic

1. A	8. A	15. C	22. A	29. B	36. B	43. A	50. B
2. A	9. A	16. C	23. A	30. C	37. B	44. A	51. A
3. A	10. A	17. C	24. B	31. C	38. C	45. B	52. C
4. B	11. B	18. B	25. B	32. C	39. A	46. B	
5. A	12. B	19. B	26. C	33. C	40. B	47. B	
6. A	13. A	20. C	27. B	34. C	41. C	48. C	
7. B	14. B	21. A	28. B	35. C	42. A	49. A	

Reading Comprehension

Expository

Passage #1	*Passage #2*	*Passage #3*	*Passage #4*	*Passage #5*	*Passage #6*
1. D	1. D	1. D	1. D	1. D	1. A
2. D	2. A	2. D	2. C	2. C	2. B
3. A	3. C	3. C	3. B	3. D	3. D
4. C	4. C	4. B	4. A	4. C	4. C
5. C	5. D	5. C	5. D	5. D	5. D
6. D	6. B	6. C	6. A	6. C	6. A
7. C	7. A	7. B	7. A	7. A	7. B
8. D	8. A	8. A	8. C	8. C	8. D
9. A	9. B	9. C	9. B	9. C	9. C
10. B	10. A	10. B	10. C	10. B	10. B

Passage #7	Passage #8	Passage #9	Passage #10	Passage #11	Passage #12
1. D	1. C	1. B	1. A	1. C	1. B
2. D	2. B	2. C	2. D	2. A	2. C
3. A	3. A	3. C	3. D	3. C	3. C
4. D	4. D	4. D	4. C	4. A	4. B
5. B	5. A	5. B	5. A	5. B	5. D
6. A	6. B	6. D	6. B	6. A	6. A
7. A	7. C	7. D	7. A	7. D	7. B
8. C	8. A	8. A	8. D	8. B	8. A
9. D	9. D	9. C	9. A	9. B	9. B
10. B	10. C	10. A	10. C	10. A	10. C

Narrative

Passage #1	Passage #2	Passage #3	Passage #4	Passage #5
1. C	1. A	1. D	1. C	1. A
2. B	2. D	2. C	2. B	2. C
3. D	3. B	3. C	3. D	3. A
4. D	4. A	4. B	4. C	4. D
5. B	5. C	5. B	5. A	5. C
6. A	6. D	6. A	6. B	6. D
7. D	7. B	7. A	7. D	7. A
8. C	8. A	8. A	8. B	8. C
9. A	9. C	9. B	9. C	9. B
10. D	10. B	10. C	10. A	10. A

Persuasive

Passage #1	Passage #2	Passage #3	Passage #4
1. D	1. B	1. B	1. D
2. C	2. C	2. D	2. C
3. B	3. D	3. C	3. C
4. D	4. D	4. D	4. A
5. A	5. B	5. B	5. B
6. D	6. A	6. A	6. C
7. B	7. A	7. B	7. A
8. A	8. C	8. D	8. B
9. C	9. D	9. C	9. B
10. C	10. C	10. C	10. D

Vocabulary

1. D	16. A	31. B	46. A	61. A	76. C	91. C	106. C
2. C	17. C	32. A	47. B	62. C	77. B	92. C	107. C
3. D	18. B	33. D	48. D	63. D	78. D	93. D	108. D
4. A	19. C	34. A	49. C	64. C	79. D	94. C	109. D
5. B	20. A	35. D	50. B	65. D	80. C	95. B	110. C
6. C	21. C	36. B	51. B	66. D	81. D	96. D	
7. B	22. B	37. A	52. A	67. C	82. D	97. B	
8. A	23. C	38. D	53. D	68. D	83. D	98. C	
9. C	24. C	39. A	54. D	69. D	84. A	99. C	
10. C	25. B	40. B	55. B	70. C	85. B	100. B	
11. A	26. A	41. B	56. B	71. B	86. A	101. D	
12. C	27. C	42. D	57. B	72. D	87. B	102. A	
13. D	28. B	43. C	58. D	73. B	88. A	103. A	
14. C	29. A	44. C	59. A	74. A	89. D	104. B	
15. D	30. A	45. C	60. C	75. A	90. C	105. C	

Language Skills

Punctuation and Capitalization

1. D	14. C	27. A	40. B	53. B	66. A	79. C	92. A
2. B	15. C	28. B	41. A	54. C	67. A	80. B	93. A
3. C	16. C	29. B	42. B	55. A	68. C	81. C	94. B
4. B	17. A	30. A	43. D	56. D	69. B	82. C	95. C
5. D	18. C	31. C	44. B	57. C	70. C	83. C	96. B
6. D	19. D	32. A	45. C	58. A	71. C	84. C	97. B
7. B	20. C	33. A	46. A	59. A	72. C	85. C	98. B
8. B	21. B	34. C	47. B	60. C	73. C	86. A	99. B
9. C	22. A	35. D	48. C	61. D	74. C	87. B	100. C
10. B	23. A	36. B	49. A	62. D	75. A	88. B	
11. A	24. B	37. A	50. A	63. D	76. B	89. B	
12. A	25. D	38. B	51. B	64. A	77. A	90. A	
13. A	26. B	39. A	52. D	65. B	78. A	91. A	

Usage

1. A	16. D	31. B	46. B	61. D	76. B	91. A	106. A
2. D	17. D	32. A	47. A	62. B	77. B	92. B	107. B
3. B	18. A	33. A	48. B	63. B	78. A	93. D	108. D
4. B	19. B	34. A	49. B	64. B	79. A	94. C	109. B
5. C	20. B	35. A	50. B	65. C	80. B	95. B	110. C
6. A	21. B	36. B	51. C	66. C	81. A	96. B	111. D
7. C	22. C	37. A	52. C	67. A	82. A	97. B	112. A
8. C	23. A	38. A	53. A	68. A	83. C	98. D	113. A
9. B	24. A	39. C	54. C	69. C	84. C	99. A	114. C
10. B	25. C	40. B	55. C	70. B	85. A	100. A	115. B
11. A	26. A	41. D	56. D	71. A	86. B	101. B	116. A
12. D	27. A	42. C	57. A	72. A	87. B	102. D	117. B
13. B	28. C	43. C	58. D	73. C	88. B	103. C	
14. C	29. C	44. A	59. C	74. C	89. A	104. B	
15. C	30. B	45. C	60. A	75. C	90. A	105. C	

Spelling

1. B	8. D	15. A	22. C	29. A	36. B	43. B	50. D
2. C	9. B	16. B	23. A	30. C	37. B	44. C	51. B
3. B	10. B	17. A	24. C	31. B	38. C	45. A	52. D
4. A	11. C	18. C	25. B	32. A	39. B	46. C	
5. B	12. C	19. A	26. B	33. B	40. D	47. B	
6. B	13. C	20. A	27. A	34. C	41. A	48. B	
7. A	14. A	21. D	28. C	35. C	42. B	49. A	

Composition

1. C	8. A	15. A	22. A	29. B	36. A	43. C	50. C
2. D	9. B	16. C	23. A	30. C	37. B	44. C	51. D
3. B	10. D	17. C	24. D	31. B	38. A	45. D	52. C
4. D	11. C	18. B	25. A	32. C	39. D	46. A	
5. B	12. C	19. B	26. B	33. C	40. D	47. D	
6. B	13. B	20. C	27. A	34. A	41. A	48. B	
7. A	14. C	21. D	28. C	35. B	42. A	49. C	

Practice Test 1

Verbal Skills

1. D	9. D	17. B	25. C	33. B	41. D	49. A	57. C
2. C	10. D	18. D	26. C	34. D	42. C	50. C	58. A
3. C	11. C	19. C	27. B	35. B	43. C	51. A	59. A
4. A	12. A	20. C	28. C	36. B	44. C	52. A	60. D
5. D	13. D	21. B	29. D	37. B	45. B	53. B	
6. A	14. B	22. A	30. D	38. D	46. C	54. C	
7. B	15. C	23. C	31. D	39. A	47. D	55. B	
8. B	16. C	24. B	32. A	40. B	48. C	56. D	

Quantitative Skills

61. B	68. B	75. D	82. C	89. A	96. B	103. A	110. B
62. C	69. D	76. B	83. C	90. B	97. A	104. A	111. D
63. B	70. C	77. C	84. C	91. A	98. B	105. D	112. D
64. C	71. A	78. C	85. D	92. B	99. C	106. C	
65. D	72. D	79. B	86. A	93. D	100. B	107. D	
66. A	73. B	80. D	87. C	94. B	101. A	108. B	
67. D	74. C	81. A	88. B	95. A	102. C	109. D	

Reading

113. C	121. C	129. B	137. C	145. D	153. A	161. B	169. C
114. C	122. A	130. B	138. C	146. C	154. B	162. C	170. B
115. D	123. C	131. B	139. B	147. D	155. D	163. D	171. C
116. A	124. A	132. B	140. B	148. A	156. C	164. B	172. D
117. D	125. D	133. D	141. A	149. C	157. B	165. D	173. C
118. D	126. B	134. B	142. D	150. A	158. C	166. C	174. C
119. B	127. A	135. B	143. B	151. D	159. B	167. D	
120. A	128. C	136. B	144. B	152. A	160. D	168. C	

Mathematics

175. C	183. C	191. C	199. C	207. A	215. C	223. C	231. C
176. C	184. C	192. D	200. C	208. C	216. A	224. D	232. C
177. A	185. A	193. D	201. A	209. C	217. C	225. C	233. C
178. B	186. B	194. D	202. D	210. A	218. A	226. C	234. C
179. A	187. B	195. C	203. A	211. C	219. B	227. C	235. B
180. C	188. B	196. B	204. C	212. B	220. A	228. C	236. C
181. C	189. B	197. B	205. A	213. B	221. A	229. C	237. C
182. C	190. D	198. B	206. C	214. C	222. B	230. D	238. B

Language Skills

239. A	247. C	255. C	263. A	271. B	279. B	287. D	295. D
240. A	248. C	256. B	264. D	272. B	280. C	288. C	296. D
241. A	249. C	257. D	265. D	273. A	281. B	289. A	297. C
242. C	250. C	258. B	266. D	274. B	282. C	290. B	298. C
243. B	251. C	259. B	267. B	275. B	283. C	291. B	
244. C	252. A	260. A	268. C	276. C	284. B	292. B	
245. C	253. B	261. C	269. A	277. C	285. C	293. A	
246. B	254. C	262. A	270. C	278. C	286. B	294. B	

Practice Test 2

Verbal Skills

1. C	9. D	17. C	25. C	33. B	41. C	49. C	57. A
2. B	10. A	18. C	26. A	34. D	42. C	50. B	58. C
3. A	11. D	19. A	27. C	35. C	43. C	51. C	59. B
4. A	12. B	20. B	28. A	36. D	44. A	52. A	60. C
5. D	13. A	21. A	29. A	37. D	45. D	53. C	
6. D	14. C	22. B	30. A	38. B	46. B	54. B	
7. B	15. A	23. A	31. A	39. D	47. C	55. D	
8. D	16. D	24. D	32. A	40. B	48. B	56. B	

Quantitative Skills

61. B	68. B	75. C	82. C	89. C	96. B	103. A	110. C
62. A	69. C	76. B	83. B	90. D	97. B	104. B	111. D
63. C	70. A	77. A	84. D	91. D	98. C	105. C	112. B
64. C	71. B	78. A	85. D	92. B	99. C	106. B	
65. A	72. B	79. C	86. D	93. A	100. D	107. D	
66. B	73. D	80. B	87. C	94. A	101. A	108. D	
67. D	74. C	81. A	88. B	95. C	102. B	109. D	

Reading

113. C	121. D	129. D	137. A	145. A	153. B	161. A	169. D
114. C	122. A	130. B	138. C	146. C	154. A	162. C	170. A
115. D	123. C	131. B	139. C	147. D	155. C	163. D	171. C
116. B	124. A	132. B	140. D	148. B	156. D	164. A	172. D
117. C	125. C	133. B	141. C	149. C	157. B	165. B	173. A
118. B	126. D	134. B	142. C	150. D	158. C	166. A	174. C
119. A	127. B	135. C	143. C	151. A	159. B	167. B	
120. B	128. A	136. D	144. A	152. B	160. A	168. A	

Mathematics

175. D	183. C	191. A	199. D	207. D	215. C	223. A	231. B
176. B	184. B	192. B	200. C	208. A	216. B	224. A	232. A
177. A	185. B	193. D	201. A	209. A	217. D	225. C	233. C
178. C	186. A	194. B	202. C	210. D	218. D	226. B	234. A
179. B	187. C	195. C	203. A	211. B	219. C	227. C	235. C
180. D	188. D	196. D	204. C	212. C	220. D	228. B	236. B
181. A	189. B	197. A	205. A	213. C	221. B	229. B	237. D
182. C	190. C	198. A	206. C	214. B	222. D	230. C	238. A

Language Skills

239. C	247. C	255. B	263. A	271. A	279. A	287. B	295. C
240. C	248. A	256. D	264. C	272. A	280. C	288. C	296. A
241. A	249. B	257. B	265. A	273. B	281. B	289. A	297. A
242. B	250. C	258. A	266. C	274. D	282. B	290. A	298. A
243. A	251. A	259. B	267. A	275. B	283. A	291. C	
244. B	252. C	260. B	268. B	276. B	284. B	292. B	
245. A	253. C	261. B	269. C	277. C	285. A	293. C	
246. A	254. B	262. C	270. B	278. A	286. D	294. A	

Made in the USA
Coppell, TX
27 August 2024

36504932R00122